It's All a Kind of
Magic

PUBLISHED WITH
SUPPORT FROM

FIGURE FOUNDATION

It's All a Kind of
Magic

The Young Ken Kesey

RICK DODGSON

THE UNIVERSITY OF WISCONSIN PRESS

The University of Wisconsin Press
1930 Monroe Street, 3rd Floor
Madison, Wisconsin 53711-2059
uwpress.wisc.edu

3 Henrietta Street
London WC2E 8LU, England
eurospanbookstore.com

Printed in the United States of America

Library of Congress Cataloging-in-Publication Data

Dodgson, Rick.
It's all a kind of magic : the young Ken Kesey / Rick Dodgson.
    p.   cm.
Includes bibliographical references and index.
ISBN 978-0-299-29510-3 (cloth : alk. paper)
ISBN 978-0-299-29513-4 (e-book)
1. Kesey, Ken. 2. Authors, American—20th century—Biography. I. Title.
PS3561.E667Z66   2013
813′.54—dc23[B]
2013010411

For

Mum, Dad, Estelle, Alex, Amalia, and Willow

Contents

Illustrations

Preface

I first met Ken Kesey in the summer of 1999. I had just started graduate school at Ohio University—in Athens, Ohio—and I was casting about for something sixties-related to write about for my PhD dissertation. I had initially considered writing about some of the intentional communities that had sprung up around Athens in the late 1960s, but then I discovered Kesey's website, IntrepidTrips.com. Having already read Kesey's *One Flew Over the Cuckoo's Nest* and Tom Wolfe's *Electric Kool-Aid Acid Test*, I was well aware of Kesey's role in the history of the 1960s. I was surprised to find that nothing substantial had been written about his adventures since Wolfe's book came out in 1968. A considerable body of work devoted to scrutinizing Kesey's writings had emerged in the 1970s, but there was no sign of a serious biography or proper history devoted to this supposed "father of the counterculture." This is what historians like to call a "gap in the literature." I wrote Kesey an e-mail to introduce myself—just a stab in the dark, really—but to my amazement, he responded. We corresponded briefly; me desperate to impress, him willing to write back quick one-liners without ever really answering my questions. After a few weeks of this e-mail cat and mouse, he finally agreed to meet, inviting me to come and visit his farm in Pleasant Hill, Oregon. He had still not agreed to be the subject of my dissertation, and I had become convinced that the only way to get him to seriously consider my request was if I asked him in person, face to face.

With that thought in mind, my family and I—Alex, my wife, and Amalia, our two-and-a-half-year-old daughter—set off in our van to drive across the country to meet the man. I could have flown on my own, but the family road trip seemed far more appropriate, and a whole lot more fun. We arrived in late June to find Kesey busy with his preparations for a trip to England. He and the surviving Pranksters, many of whom also lived in Oregon, had received money from a British TV company to ship themselves and their bus—a second-generation Further—over to the UK as part of a series celebrating the Summer of Love. I was nervous to meet Kesey, but he was welcoming and approachable. He took me out to the garage to show me the new bus—the original Further lay rotting in some woodland on the other side of the house—and then he led me into an archive room in the garage that was full of old journals, papers, photos, and reels of vintage film and audio tape. The room had been constructed to be fireproof, but I remember that the heavy metal door was propped open, defeating its whole purpose. Kesey pulled out a heavy-looking note-book from a cardboard box, explaining that this was his personal diary from the mid to late 1950s, when he was a speech and communications major at the University of Oregon (U of O), located just a few miles away in Eugene. Inside the book, Kesey's untidy teenage handwriting filled page after page, detailing his everyday activities and his every thought. Wow! The budding historian within me knew that I was looking at an incredible historical resource: an unfiltered, personal account of the past, an insight into the developing mind of an important historical actor. This journal was the sort of Holy Grail artifact that all historians dream of discovering. Kesey did not seem to care too much. He tossed the book back into the box, and suggested we go to meet Ken Babbs, his right-hand Prankster.

Babbs lived a few miles away in a place called Dexter, in a house he had built himself on a nice piece of land next to a running stream. Sitting in Babbs's kitchen, I finally got up the courage to ask the big questions. First, I wanted to know whether Kesey was writing an autobiography or work-ing with a biographer or historian already. If he had said "yes," I knew that I would have to find something else to write about for my dissertation, but he simply shook his head, indicating "no." So far, so good. Second, I wanted to know whether he would be willing to help me if I decided to make him the subject of my own writing. I knew that this was important, because without Kesey's cooperation, I doubted that anyone else was going to co-operate either, and my dissertation would be a nonstarter. When asked to describe my project, I explained that I hoped to write about the history of Kesey and the Merry Pranksters as part of my graduate studies in history.

Asked if I was writing a book, I explained that if I pursued a career in academia, as I hoped to do, then the possibility existed for my dissertation to be published as a book. But at this time, such a possibility remained a distant ambition. Kesey and Babbs looked at each other briefly, shrugged, and nodded in assent, in a very matter-of-fact fashion. This was not the most expressive or enthusiastic sign of support, but it was far better than a "no," and there was more to come.

Kesey and Babbs took me to the IntrepidTrips office, a small storefront close to the post office in Pleasant Hill. Here, they had assembled some computers and some film and audio editing equipment. With the assistance of some of their grown-up kids, they had started producing videos out of all the footage they had shot of their famous cross-country bus trip in 1964. Kesey showed me some footage of Neal Cassady—the real life Dean Moriarty from Jack Kerouac's *On the Road*—who had been the driver on that trip. The footage was shaky and grainy, but it clearly showed Cassady, shirtless and excited, driving the original Further bus up the New Jersey turnpike, with New York looming in the distance. Another wow moment! While Kesey expounded on Cassady, describing him as an avatar—a deity in human form—I could not take my eyes off the computer screen, witnessing for the first time the famous Cassady in action. The audio captured him in the middle of one of his endless pun-filled raps, commenting on everything around him and whatever came to mind: the traffic, shifting gears, past adventures, ideas for a movie script, literary references, and extemporaneous philosophical musings. Amazing! Kesey told me that they planned to release a whole series of videos and CDs culled from their film and audio archives, everything from the Bus Trip to the Acid Tests and beyond.

Later that night, I returned to Kesey's farm to witness a rehearsal for a play that Kesey had written—*The Search for Merlin*—that he and his Merry Prankster friends planned to perform on their UK trip. Among the players were some "new" Pranksters, such as Phil Dietz and John Swan, and many of the originals: Mike "Malfunction" Hagen, Carolyn "Mountain Girl" Adams, Ken Babbs, Roy Sebern, "Anonymous," and George "Hardly Visible" Walker. I could not make much sense of the performance, which was far from polished, but I was delighted to witness the Merry Pranksters, these famous countercultural icons, all together in the same room, laughing and fooling around together, just like back in the day. Kesey was still clearly the leader of the group, and the director of their production, but the atmosphere was relaxed and playful. Back in the farmhouse, Faye Kesey, Kesey's wife, had prepared a meal for everybody. While we ate, Kesey and the others peppered me with a few questions about England— my country of origin—in preparation for their trip. I don't remember saying anything particularly useful, but I was able to tell them all about the spectacular Minack Theatre in Cornwall, an outdoor amphitheater perched on the cliffs above the ocean, where they were booked to give a performance on August 1 to coincide with a rare solar eclipse.

Alex, Amalia, and I spent the night in our van, parked by the bus garage on Kesey's farm. I was so excited that I could barely sleep. I was thrilled to meet Kesey and the Pranksters, and elated by the prospect of writing about their adventures. The following day, I tried to broach the subject of an interview with Kesey, but he was reticent. Faye had already warned me that if I had questions, I should probably ask them along the way, rather than expect Kesey to sit down and talk. Instead, while Kesey went off to cut the grass around his house, he invited me to spend time in his archives, looking at the journals and papers that he had shown me the previous day. He did not need to ask me twice. I was anxious to speak to him more formally, but I knew that the real historical treasure existed in those archives. I spent the rest of the day in there, reading through journals that documented most of Kesey's life, including I-Ching journals where he recorded his daily readings. The best journal by far was the one from the 1950s, written before the distractions of adulthood, fame, and family kept Kesey from devoting as much time to his diary. There was much more besides Kesey's journals: copies of letters that he had written to Larry McMurtry while he was on the run in Mexico in 1966; a suitcase full of hundreds of photos; random files of newspaper clippings; one of Mountain Girl's journals from the mid-sixties; a few old posters and fliers—including an original Acid Test flyer from 1966—and all sorts of videos and cassettes, including some recorded during the Grateful Dead's trip to Egypt in 1978, when the group played in front of the pyramids. A box of old reel-to-reel tapes contained even older recordings. One marked "Kerouac New York Party" hinted at the incredible amount of history that was kept in this room. It was overwhelming, really.

The next day, at the urging of both Kesey and Babbs, I went to visit the special collections library at the University of Oregon. In 1973 Kesey and

Babbs deposited all their old papers there, creating a collection called the Ken Kesey Papers 1960–1973. This was another incredible archive of great material, some of which actually dated from the mid-1950s, despite the name of the collection. The papers included at least ten folders of correspondence from the early 1960s, much of it between Kesey and Babbs, but there were also business letters, fan mail, and letters to and from family. Faye Kesey had spent time in the collection, attempting to put dates on Kesey's letters, and working with an archivist to provide contextual information for scholars working with the papers. The collection also included short stories and essays, mostly unpublished, that Kesey had written at college; a collection of more than twenty tape recordings made by Kesey and friends in the early 1960s; the original manuscripts for *Cuckoo's Nest* and *Sometimes a Great Notion*; sketches that Kesey had drawn of people on the hospital ward when he was writing *Cuckoo's Nest*; a manuscript for *Zoo*, an unpublished novel Kesey wrote at Stanford before he started work on *Cuckoo's Nest*; an outline and sample chapter for *One Lane*, an unfinished and unpublished project that Kesey started working on before the 1964 bus trip; and a whole bunch of other notebooks, drawings, and random papers.

For the second time in a couple of days, I found myself staring at an incredible collection of primary historical resources. Kesey gave me written permission to obtain photocopies of some of these materials, and so I identified a few choice pieces and gave the archivist a list. This was an expensive process, so I could only afford to order a small selection, but it was more than enough to whet my appetite for more. I returned the next day, and the next, and the next, furiously making notes on my laptop, but mostly just working through the collection to see what was there. It was clear to me that these resources—along with the materials at Kesey's farm—were enough to form the foundation of my dissertation. I was beside myself with glee. It was also clear that if I wanted to get the most out of these collections I was going to have to come back the following year.

Babbs had invited me and the family to attend his July 4 party, which was the next time I encountered Kesey and the other Pranksters in person. Also in attendance were dozens of friends and family, including Sunshine Kesey, Kesey's daughter with Mountain Girl; Chuck Kesey, Kesey's younger brother; and a number of Babbs's kids. A stage was set up next to the house to feature music and poetry through the afternoon. Picnic tables groaned under the weight of all the food and drink brought by guests. Children of various ages ran around the property, hiding behind trees, playing tag or ball. At one point Kesey organized a game of balloon stomp, something they used to play on Perry Lane, his old Stanford haunt. Participants each had a balloon attached to their ankles, which they had to try and protect, all the while trying to stomp on everybody else's balloon. It was one hell of a scene. The highlight of the event was when Kesey and Chuck fired off a small but exceedingly loud brass cannon. The kids loved it.

This was a party, so I did not want to bother Kesey, Babbs, or anyone else with questions about my project, but I did snatch a five-minute conversation with Kesey in Babbs's kitchen. He asked me how things were going, to which I gave an enthusiastic response. I asked him whether I could visit the farm again to do some more work in his personal archives. He was fine with the idea, and told me to just turn up at the farm and get on with it. I think he preferred that idea to me bothering him with questions or demands on his time. He was particularly busy with plans for the UK trip, which was less than a month away. I asked if I could photocopy materials from his archives, and he happily agreed, even offering me the use of the photocopy in the IntrepidTrips office, telling me where the key was hidden in case nobody was around. I made a point of asking him if there was anything he did *not* want me to photocopy, to which he replied that I could photocopy whatever I wanted. The following day I returned to the farm and settled into the archive to identify things to photocopy. This is what historians do on their research trips: they photocopy as much material as they can so that they can then work with the papers in the comfort of their home offices. Rather than use the IntrepidTrips photocopy machine, I took items from the archive to the local Kinkos where the machines were better and faster. I cannot recall exactly what I photocopied in all, but I do remember copying Kesey's journal from the 1950s in its entirety. I was scheduled to leave a couple of days later. I spent another day in Kesey's personal archives, and before I left, I asked him whether I could come back the following year to do more. He agreed without hesitation.

Over the course of the next twelve months, I started to collect all sorts of Kesey related material: books, magazines, newspapers, videos, CDs, photographs, and more. One of my more unusual research tools was eBay.

While I could rarely afford to bid on all the Kesey items, the site allowed me to identify the location of numerous forgotten interviews or articles in newspapers or various underground sixties publications. I also built a website—Pranksterweb.org—hoping to further my research by getting in touch with people outside of Kesey's family or inner circle. Through the website I was able to contact lots of people, including attendees at the Trips Festival, which took place in San Francisco in early 1966; Hammond Guthrie and Jim Cushing, both Acid Test attendees; Lynn Rogers, a woman who encountered Kesey and friends down in Mexico over the summer of 1966; and Stewart Brand, a participant in some of the early Acid Tests and later publisher of the Whole Earth Catalogs.

The following summer, 2000, I flew out to Oregon alone, leaving Alex and Amalia to look after our newborn, Willow. Kesey and Babbs continued to be cooperative, even though I'm not sure that they remembered who I was at first. Kesey agreed to sign a form to allow me to conduct a Freedom of Information Act search to see if I could unearth his FBI records (which no longer exist, I discovered). Babbs declined a similar request. Kesey was particularly enthusiastic about my use of the Internet in my work, seeing it as a way to approach this history from an interesting perspective. Babbs was kind enough to place a link to my Pranksterweb research site on the front page of the IntrepidTrips website. Endorsing my project in this way was very important. It added legitimacy to my work and helped open doors that might otherwise have remained closed. I asked Kesey if he would be willing to write a letter of introduction for me, for the same purpose. He suggested that I write it myself, and if he liked it, he would sign it. I came up with a couple of versions, one formal, the other more humorous. He chose to sign the latter. It read as follows: "If you are reading this, then the gaze of Rick Dodgson has fallen upon you. For the past two summers Rick has made the trip out to Oregon to delve and probe into the Prankster archives in the misguided belief that they will allow him to make sense of the universe (and form the basis of his history dissertation). Despite this, as far as I can tell, he is not a complete idiot. I have given him free reign [*sic*] to rummage in my dusty drawers and I am helping him out as much as I am able in other ways. I would ask that you please do the same."

I spent two weeks out in Oregon on this particular trip, working mostly in Kesey's personal archive and at the U of O. There I continued taking notes on the Kesey papers, but I also spent a good deal of my time straining my eyes on a microfilm machine, digging out old newspaper articles about the young Kesey, and discovering a treasure trove of his early journalistic efforts in the *Daily Emerald*, the U of O student newspaper. Babbs was kind enough to invite me again to his July 4 party, at which I was able to set up my first couple of interviews. I started with Mountain Girl, who was incredibly gracious and forgiving of my nervousness. I also interviewed Anonymous, who was equally charming and helpful, and a couple of Kesey's former professors at the U of O, Robert Clark and Horace C. Robinson. My one disappointment on this trip was that Kesey refused to sign a release form allowing me to quote from his papers. He said he would have to see my work first.

The following summer, 2001, I arranged a four-week internship at the U of O, working on the Ken Kesey collection. As it turned out, they asked me to do very little. I organized the folders somewhat, helped locate Kesey's *Cuckoo's Nest* sketches for their inclusion in a new edition of the book, and wrote a very short biography of Kesey for the library's use, but other than that I spent day after day taking notes for my own research. While working through the papers, I also listened to the collection of audio cassettes that made up part of the holdings. These tapes varied widely in quality and usefulness. Some were virtually incomprehensible, others simply full of music and inaudible conversation. Among the best was one of Kesey telling stories about his early days at Stanford. Another captured him recording his thoughts as the bulldozers moved in to demolish his house on Perry Lane in the summer of 1963. Listening to these recordings was time consuming, laborious work, but the occasional perfect quote or new piece of information made the effort worthwhile. Venturing only occasionally outside of the library, I spent a day or two out at Kesey's place completing my research in his personal archives, scanning some photos on a personal scanner that I had brought with me. By this time—my third visit—he remembered who I was and actually consented to a sit-down interview. To keep things interesting, we looked at some photos from his collection, using them to spark memories and stories. This approach worked, but only to a degree, as Kesey would begin talking about one photo, then get distracted by the next, never quite finishing one story until he was on to another. I regret not doing a better interview, but it was the best I could do under the circumstances.

When it came time for me to head home, I ventured out to the farm one last time to say my goodbyes. Kesey had always been somewhat personally distant over the course of our meetings, but on this occasion he was warm and friendly. He asked about my family, and we talked a little about Faye's health, which had been problematic. I had no idea he was sick himself. He told me that I should stay at the house next time I came out, rather than stay in a motel. He even gave me a quick man-hug as I went to leave. This was in early July 2001. In early November I found myself in New York, attending a conference at Hofstra University. Naturally, the news media were still full of stories concerning the terrible events of September 11 and its aftermath, but as I sat watching TV in my hotel room, I noticed a brief mention on the ticker tape scrolling across the bottom of the screen that Kesey had been hospitalized with liver problems. On Saturday, November 10, I made my way into Manhattan to view what was left of the World Trade Center, at that point still a huge pile of rubble. While I stood looking at the mess, and wondering what madness had befallen us, I received a phone call telling me that Kesey had died. I would never claim to have been close to Kesey—I knew him through his papers, not personally—but I found myself shedding a tear when I got home and reported on his death on my website. I'm not sure whether I was crying over his passing, or because of the terrible events of that previous month. Either way, these were depressing days.

Over the course of the next couple of years, I continued my research up and down the West Coast. I went back to Oregon again a couple of times, mostly to interview surviving Pranksters. I also spent lots of time in California speaking to characters from Kesey's past: good people from the Perry Lane days, the La Honda period, the bus trip, the Acid Tests, and beyond. It was quite a journey, now that I think of it. I made some great finds, including the FBI agent who arrested the fugitive Kesey in October 1966, and the long lost "Who Cares Girl" from the Watts Acid Test. I spoke with Tom Wolfe by phone, and e-mailed with Owsley "Bear" Stanley, the "Acid King" of Haight-Ashbury. I did yoga in Venice Beach with Denise Kaufman, former Acid Test Prankster turned celebrated yogi; and had lunch with Hog Farmer Wavy Gravy in Berkeley (he insisted on the pork). It was not all fun. At least two people cried during their interviews. A few people did not want to talk to me, and a couple did so somewhat reluctantly. Many of the actors in this book are still with us. This history is still alive for them, and it is a difficult history for some. Not everything is merry about this story. Everyone I met, though, was gracious and helpful. I would like to thank them for sharing their lives and thoughts with me. Faye kindly allowed me to quote from all of Kesey's unpublished papers in my dissertation. She has chosen not to extend the same permissions to this publication. Ken Babbs has also decided not to offer permission to quote from his letters and papers in this book. He tells me that he is now writing his own account of his time with Kesey and the Pranksters and that he wants to retain these sources for his own use. George Walker has likewise not given his permission to quote from our interview, for similar reasons. I look forward to reading their efforts.

I never stopped researching, but I finally finished writing in the spring of 2006, much to the relief of my advisor and my family. Newly graduated, I taught at the University of Tennessee at Martin for a year, and then I landed a job at Lakeland College in Wisconsin in 2007. There I remain, happily teaching and residing in Sheboygan, the acclaimed Surf Capitol of the Midwest.

Acknowledgments

I would like to thank Katherine Jellison for her guidance during the writing of this project. I am also beholden to Joan Hoff for her early encouragement, to Alonzo Hamby for his unwavering support, and to Alex Liosatos, my grammatically perfect wife for helping finalize the manuscript. Thanks must also go to Gwen Walker and Sheila McMahon at the University of Wisconsin Press, Sue Breckenridge for the copyediting, and Liz McKenzie for all her valuable advice. I owe a great debt to Kesey, his family, and his close friends, for I could not have written this book without their assistance. I am also grateful to James Fox and his staff at the University of Oregon Library, Special Collections, for their assistance during my research in the collection of Ken Kesey Papers 1960–1973. I spent lots of time working in various library archives in San Francisco, Menlo Park, Palo Alto, Stanford University, San Francisco State University, and the University of California, Berkeley, where I would like thank everybody who helped me in my efforts. Thanks also to the officials at the San Mateo courthouse who led me to the court documents related to Kesey's legal troubles in the mid-1960s.

I am especially grateful to all those who kindly agreed to be interviewed for this project. I spoke to a number of people from Kesey's Perry Lane days, including Vic Lovell, Chloe Scott, Ann Lambrecht (Steve "Zonker" Lambrecht's sister), Jim Wolpman, Lola Walker, Welvin Stroud, Roy Sebern, Paul DeCarli, and Dorothy and Jim Fadiman. Roy Sebern was particularly helpful, walking me around Perry Lane, and showing me around Kesey's old property at La Honda, currently owned by Terry Adams and Eva Knodt. Ed McClanahan came to Athens, Ohio, and read at an event held to memorialize Kesey. In San Francisco I interviewed photographer Jeff Blankfort, FBI Agent George Galloway, Prankster "manager" Julius Karpen, and Ramon Sender, one of the organizers of the Trips Festival. In the same city, Paul Krassner told me stories about his time with Kesey. I also met with Joe Lysowski, who was with Kesey in London in 1969. In Berkeley I visited with Wavy Gravy, and through him I talked to Prankster Paul Foster, then residing in a home in Redding, northern California. Down in Santa Cruz, I spoke to Peter Demma (Sally Demma's brother), Leon Tabury (a close friend of Neal Cassady), Jami Cassady (Neal's daughter), and Anne Murphy (Neal Cassady's girlfriend during his Prankster days). I spent a fascinating evening in San Jose talking to John Cassady (Neal's son) and Carolyn Cassady (Neal's wife). I also spent an uncomfortable hour talking to Caitlin Cassamo, daughter of Kathy Cassamo (a.k.a. Stark Naked), who was still upset about the way her mother had been treated on the 1964 bus trip.

In Los Angeles I interviewed Denise Kaufman and Judy Harrington from the Acid Test period, as well as the Reverend Paul Sawyer, Prankster Lee Quarnstrom, and one of Kesey's old lawyers, Brian Rohan. In Oregon I spoke with Faye Kesey, Geneva Kesey (Kesey's mother), and most of the surviving Pranksters, including Ken Babbs, George Walker, Mike Hagen, Anonymous, Gretchen Douglas, Carolyn Adams, and Ron Bevirt. Ron Bevirt kindly put me in touch with Owsley "Bear" Stanley, the famous LSD chemist, who corresponded with me via e-mail (where he lived up to his reputation as a contrarian, eventually advising me to choose a different subject to write about). I also e-mailed with Lisa Law, spoke with Tom Wolfe by phone, and chatted with the Grateful Dead's Mickey Hart on his tour bus. This list is far from complete, so let me just apologize to anyone I have missed and thank them for agreeing to speak to me.

Finally, thanks must also go to my family, Alex, Lilee, and Willow, for their love and support, and to my friends Bill Kamil, Kirk Tyvela, Kim Little, Scott Beekman, Brent Geary, Steve Mowrey, Kris Poland, Andrew Lampela, Warren Taylor, Jimmy Kisor, and Donald Cribbet for their insights and contributions along the way.

Chronology

1926   February 8. Neal Cassady born in Utah.

1935   September 17. Ken Elton Kesey born in La Junta, Colorado.

1943   Kesey family moves to Oregon.

1956   May 20. Ken Kesey marries Faye Haxby.

1957   Kesey graduates from the University of Oregon, Eugene.

1958   Ken Babbs graduates from Miami University, Ohio.

Fall. Ken Kesey and Ken Babbs begin studying at Stanford University.

1959   Kesey and Faye move to Perry Lane.

1960   Kesey enrolls in drug experiments at local VA hospital.

Summer. Kesey works at VA hospital. Starts writing *One Flew Over the Cuckoo's Nest*.

1961   Summer. Kesey and Faye back in Oregon. Kesey carries out research for *Sometimes a Great Notion* in Florence, Oregon.

1962   January. *One Flew Over the Cuckoo's Nest* published by Viking.

July. Babbs, Kesey, and John Babbs visit World's Fair in Seattle.

July 16. Babbs ships out for Vietnam. Kesey begins writing *Sometimes a Great Notion*.

1963   July. Perry Lane demolished. Faye and Kesey move to La Honda.

Fall. *One Flew Over the Cuckoo's Nest* debuts on Broadway with Kirk Douglas. President John F. Kennedy shot in Dallas, Texas.

1964   May 18. Babbs out of the military. Kesey buys school bus.

June–August. Bus trip to New York World's Fair.

1965   April 23. Police raid La Honda.

June 21. Charlatans play at the Red Dog Saloon, Virginia City, Nevada.

July. Bob Dylan gets booed at the Newport Folk Festival.

August 7. Hell's Angels party at La Honda.

August 11. Riots in Watts, Los Angeles.

September 5. Michael Fallon uses the term "hippie" in article in *San Francisco Examiner*.

October 15–16. Vietnam Day Committee rally in Berkeley.

October 16. A Tribute to Dr. Strange at the Longshoreman's Hall, San Francisco.

November 27. First Acid Test at the Spread, Soquel.

December 4. San Jose Acid Test.

December 11. Muir Beach Acid Test.

December 18. Big Beat Acid Test.

1966   January 3. The Psychedelic Shop opens at 1535 Haight Street, San Francisco.

January 8. Fillmore Acid Test.

January 18. Kesey and Mountain Girl busted in San Francisco.

January 20–22. Trips festival at Longshoreman's Hall, San Francisco.

January 29. Sound City Acid Test. Kesey flees to Mexico.

February 5. Northridge Acid Test, Los Angeles.

February 11. Watts Acid Test, Los Angeles.

March 19. Pico Acid Test, Los Angeles.

April 7. Sandoz stops providing LSD to researchers.

Spring–summer. Kesey and the Merry Pranksters in Mexico.

September. Kesey returns to United States.

October 1/2. Whatever It Is? San Francisco State Acid Test.

October 6. LSD possession illegal in California. Love Pageant Rally.

October 21. Kesey recaptured by the FBI in San Francisco.

October 31. The Acid Test Graduation at the Calliope Company Warehouse, San Francisco.

1967   January 14. The Human Be-in, or the Gathering of the Tribes, Golden Gate Park, San Francisco.

June 16–18. Monterey Pop Festival. Summer of Love.

June 23. Kesey goes to jail.

November 11. Kesey gets out of jail, goes back to Oregon.

1968   February 4. Neal Cassady dies in Mexico.

July. Tom Wolfe's *Electric Kool-Aid Acid Test* published.

1969   Kesey in London, working at Apple Records.

August 15–17. Woodstock Festival, New York.

1984   January 23. Jed Kesey dies.

1992   Kesey diagnosed with diabetes.

1997   Kesey has a stroke.

2001   November 10. Kesey dies after an operation on his liver.

Cast of Characters

In alphabetical order (*Prankster nicknames*):

Alpert, Dick (later Ram Dass). Stanford. Leading figure in psychedelic circles with Timothy Leary. Friend to Vic Lovell, his initial connection to Perry Lane and Kesey.

Anderson, Lee. Resident of Perry Lane. Musician, drummer.

Babbs, Anita (née Esberg). Married to Ken Babbs, 1959–65.

Babbs, John (*Sometimes Missing*). Born in Ohio. Younger brother to Ken Babbs. Aboard for the 1964 trip but not much else.

Babbs, Ken (*Intrepid Traveler*). Born in Ohio. Met Kesey at Stanford in 1958. Served in the Marines, 1959–64. Kesey's best friend. Core Prankster, around for almost everything.

Berry, Wendell. Kentucky. Writer. Part of the Stanford and Perry Lane writing crowd. Lifelong friend to Kesey.

Bevirt, Ronald (*Hassler*). Born in Illinois. U.S. Army, Fort Ord, with Gurney Norman. First met Kesey at Perry Lane in 1963. Took photos of the 1964 bus trip. One of the main players in the Merry Pranksters. Co-owner with Peter Demma of Hip Pocket Bookstore in Santa Cruz.

Bondoc, Gigi. Lived in the Keseys' Perry Lane house, while Kesey was in Oregon in 1962. Married to Ron Bondoc.

Bondoc, Ron. Lived in the Keseys' Perry Lane house, while Kesey was in Oregon in 1962. Married to Gigi Bondoc.

Boise, Ron. La Honda. The Spread. Artist. Creator of the Thunder Machine sculptures. Drove Kesey to Mexico in 1966. Died in 1966.

Brand, Stewart. Stanford. San Francisco State University. Developed America Needs Indians multimedia exhibition that was included in some early Acid Tests. Famously sold buttons calling for photographs of Earth from space. Organized Trips festival and Whatever It Is? event. Later published Whole Earth Catalog and founding member of the Electronic Frontier Foundation.

Browning, Page (*Des Prado, ZeaLot*). Palo Alto. La Honda. Core Prankster, around for almost everything. Died 1984.

Burton, Jane (*Generally Famished*). Major character on Perry Lane. Aboard for the 1964 bus trip. Taught at San Jose State University.

Cassady, Neal (*Sir Speed Limit, Fastestmanalive*). Born in Colorado. Inspirational figure for the Beats and the Merry Pranksters. Cassady was the real-life Dean Moriarty in Jack Kerouac's *On the Road*. Driver on the 1964 bus trip, around for almost everything. Died in Mexico, 1968.

Cassady, Carolyn. Neal Cassady's wife. Author of *Off the Road: My Years with Cassady, Kerouac and Ginsberg* (1990).

De Carli, Paul. Resident of Perry Lane.

Demma, Peter. Perry Lane. Co-owner with Ron Bevirt of Hip Pocket Bookstore in Santa Cruz. Brother to Sally Demma.

Demma, Sally. Perry Lane. Sister to Peter Demma. Died 1963.

Garcia, Jerry (*Captain Trips*). Guitarist and vocalist, Grateful Dead. Died 1995.

Hagen, Mike (*Mal Function*). University of Oregon, part of the Greek community, through which he knew Kesey. Cameraman on 1964 bus trip. Core Prankster, around for almost everything.

Kesey, Chuck (*Brother Chuck*). Ken's brother. Aboard for the 1964 trip but not much else.

Kesey, Faye (née Haxby). Married to Ken Kesey. Along for the whole ride. Mother to Shannon, Zane, and Jed Kesey.

Kesey, Fred. Father to Ken and Chuck Kesey. Married to Geneva. Died 1969.

Kesey, Geneva. Mother to Ken and Chuck Kesey. Married to Fred.

Kesey, Ken (*Chief, Swashbuckler*). Born in Colorado, raised in Springfield, Oregon. *Sine quibus non.*

Kesey, Sue. Married to Chuck Kesey.

Kreutzmann, Bill. Drummer, Grateful Dead.

Lambrecht, Ann. Married to Paul Robertson, through whom she knew Kesey. Sister to Steve Lambrecht.

Lambrecht, Steve (*Zonker*). Brother to Ann Lambrecht, through whom he knew Kesey. Last man aboard on 1964 bus trip. Core Prankster, around for almost everything. Died 2001.

Lehmann-Haupt, Carl. New York. Kesey's neighbor on Perry Lane. Tried to help get Kesey's early work published. Brother to Sandy Lehmann-Haupt.

Lesh, Phil. Bass player, Grateful Dead.

Lish, Gordon. San Francisco. Journalist and friend to Kesey. Published *Genesis West* literary magazine.

Lovell, Vic. Born in California. Major character on Perry Lane. Stanford psychology graduate. Introduced Kesey to drug experiments at Menlo Park VA hospital. Kesey dedicated *One Flew Over the Cuckoo's Nest* to Lovell in return.

McClanahan, Ed. Kentucky. Writer. Part of the Stanford and Perry Lane writing crowd. Lifelong friend to Kesey. Married to Kit.

McKernan, Ron "Pigpen." Keyboards and vocalist, Grateful Dead. Died 1973.

McMurtry, Larry. Texas. Writer. Part of the Stanford and Perry Lane writing crowd. Lifelong friend to Kesey.

Norman, Gurney. Kentucky. Writer. Part of the Stanford and Perry Lane writing crowd. Lifelong friend to Kesey. U.S. Army, Fort Ord, with Ron Bevirt.

Scott, Chloe. English. Major character on Perry Lane. Dancer. On the 1964 bus trip briefly. Performed at the Trips festival and Whatever It Is? Festival.

Sebern, Roy. Perry Lane resident. Artist. Painted and named Furthur. Did not go on the 1964 bus trip. San Francisco State University. Core Prankster. Acid Test light show artist.

Stone, Robert. New York. Writer. Part of the Stanford and Perry Lane writing crowd. Lifelong friend to Kesey.

Walker, George (*Hardly Visible*). University of Oregon, part of the Greek community through which he knew Kesey. Also attended Stanford and Berkeley. Cameraman on 1964 bus trip. Core Prankster, around for almost everything.

Walker, Lola (*Rita Zita*). University of Oregon. Part of the Perry Lane circle. Married to George Walker briefly. Aboard for the return leg of the 1964 bus trip but not much else thereafter.

Weir, Bob. Guitarist and vocalist, Grateful Dead.

White, Robin. Writer. Early Perry Lane resident and Stanford student. Introduced the Keseys to Penny Lane.

Wolpman, Jim. Major character on Perry Lane. Law student. Lifelong Kesey friend. Now a judge.

It's All a Kind of
Magic

Introduction

In a small meadow behind a fading red barn lies the final resting place of a singular American individual. The grave has a headstone that resembles the man it marks. It is a thick sturdy slab of granite, planted and resolute in the Oregon soil, smooth about the face but rough around the edges. "KEN ELTON KESEY," the chiseled words proclaim. "SEPT. 17, 1935. NOV. 10, 2001." Only the epitaph, "SPARKS FLY UPWARD," hints at the remarkable life lived between those bookend dates.

Ken Kesey was a child of the Great Depression, born to a dairy family who settled in Oregon during World War II. The young Kesey liked to read comic books and do magic tricks to entertain his brother and the rest of his family. As a high school senior he was named "Most Talented" for his prodigious output on the stage, on the football field, and particularly on the wrestling mat, where his ferocity had earned him the nickname the "Hooded Terror." At the University of Oregon he was the definition of a Big Man on Campus: a fraternity man, a letterman on the wrestling squad, a leader of the student body, a columnist in the school newspaper, and a regular in theatrical productions. When a creative writing scholarship took him to Stanford in 1958, he quickly became the "stud-duck" around the seminar table in Wallace Stegner's famed creative writing program. The list of his Stanford peers deserves a special entry in the Who's Who of twentieth-century American literature: Larry McMurtry, Robert Stone, Wendell Berry, Ed McClanahan, and Gurney Norman. Kesey beat them all to the punch. His first novel, *One Flew Over the Cuckoo's Nest* (1962), perfectly captured the antiauthoritarian pulse of the times and was

3

acclaimed by critics and readers alike. Its production as a play on Broadway, starring Hollywood superstar Kirk Douglas in the lead role, made the book into a best seller. His second book, *Sometimes a Great Notion* (1964), was not greeted so kindly by the critics, but it is still regarded as one of the best books in twentieth-century American literature for the quality of its prose and the scale of its ambition. Literary legend Malcolm Cowley told Kesey that he was a "genius," and in 1962 Beat icon Jack Kerouac declared him to be a "great man and a great new American novelist." Kesey was not yet thirty.

As if that were not enough, Kesey then staked a second claim on history far beyond the world of letters. This next chapter of Kesey's life lies outside the scope of this book—which explores Kesey's life from his birth in 1935 to the writing of *Sometimes a Great Notion*—but it is worth noting here what came next. In 1964 he and his friends—who called themselves the Merry Pranksters—bought a bus for a road trip, filmed their drug-fueled odyssey, threw a few parties to view their movie, and somehow found themselves in the vanguard of a psychedelic cultural revolution that reshaped the world. Kesey's life from that point on was not without its controversies. He was arrested twice for possession of marijuana—bad enough—but worse when he jumped bail on those charges in early 1966 and lived for the summer as a fugitive in Mexico. Upon his return in the fall, he was chased down by the FBI on the streets of San Francisco, hauled before the court numerous times, humiliated, and ultimately sentenced to six months in a county jail for all his troubles. By the fall of 1967 he was back in Oregon, out on parole after serving three months of his sentence and willfully withdrawing from public sight. The second half of Kesey's life was much quieter than the first, focused mostly on family and community, but he had already made his mark. His obituary in the *New York Times* concluded that by the time he died Kesey's very name had come to suggest "an idea of something larger, a time, a possibility, an actual shift in the ways of being."[1] Not bad for a dairy kid from Springfield, Oregon.

Kesey's grave lies on the eighty-acre farm that he called home for the last thirty-odd years of his life. Here he settled after he got out of jail in the fall of 1967, living in a big old converted barn with his wife, Faye, and their three children, Shannon, Zane, and Jed. Kesey and Faye were junior high school sweethearts, and they had been married for almost forty-five years by the time he died in November 2001, just two months after 9/11.

Faye Kesey shared in her husband's every wild adventure, and even though her name will not appear much in the details of the story told here, she too deserves her place in the history books. Every astronaut needs a reliable ground crew, and more often than not it was Faye who provided the stable foundation for all of Kesey's flights of fancy. This fact was not lost on Kesey. He dedicated his last major work to Faye, describing her as "a deep keel in the raving waves, a polestar in the dark, a shipmate."[2]

Clues to Kesey's eventful life are scattered everywhere around the farm. Behind the grave is a large, expansive meadow, host over the years to dairy cows, peacocks, llamas, and the occasional festive gathering of humans. Out front is a cool, serene pond, where Kesey once almost drowned pretending to kill the water monster that his children insisted inhabited its murky depths. To the far right of the grave are some tumbledown outbuildings, one of which houses a writing room, the last in a long line of nocturnal hideaways for Kesey and his restless imagination. Lying right next to Kesey's final resting place is another grave, proof that his colorful life was not without its tragedies. The grave is home to Jed, his youngest son, who died in 1984, at age twenty, in a road accident that also claimed the life of Jed's friend Lorenzo West. In the distance, on top of Mount Pisgah, is a monument to Jed and Lorenzo. Every Easter, Kesey and his family hiked up to the peak to mark Jed's passing.[3]

The converted barn lies about seventy feet away from the graves. In the garage by the front door, a white Cadillac Eldorado sits waiting for someone to recharge its battery. To its right is an enclosed garden, home to the fruits of Faye's green thumbs. On the side of the barn facing the road, high under the eaves, is painted a large white star on a blue circular background. The star offers a useful landmark for those who come in search of Kesey, but it is mostly an expression of his patriotism and a symbol of his rebelliousness. Nowadays, you have to burn the flag to get anybody's attention but back in the early sixties when Kesey and his friends developed a habit of decorating themselves in the colors and patterns of the stars and stripes, such irreverence marked them as outsiders, if not worse.

Inside the house, the brightly painted floors and bathrooms tell of psychedelic tastes and sensibilities preserved well past their due date. The walls whisper of laughter and late night raps, and the air seems to vibrate with the echoes of music and countless midnight "sessions." The open living room still looks big enough to wrestle in, a favorite Kesey family pursuit—

the rug is actually a wrestling mat. Photographs and pictures of kin and friends cover the walls, and bookshelves sag with the wisdom of old colleagues and older inspirations. The dinner table, nestled in one corner by some French windows, bears the scars of numerous communal meals, more products of Faye's silent industry.

The table looks out onto the pond and some woodland beyond. Fifty yards or so into the trees, across a makeshift wooden bridge tangled with blackberry brambles, stands an old 1939 International Harvester school bus. Kesey reckoned this to be his greatest artistic creation, but it is now a mossy shadow of its former colorful self, rusting and rotting back into the earth, evidence that "nothing lasts," a statement still visible in the peeling paint above its corroded door. The bus odometer is stuck at 64,359 miles, but distance alone cannot measure its full journey or capture its historical significance. On a hand-painted sign above the windshield, one can still just about make out the bus's name and legendary destination: "Further,"[4] the original psychedelic bus!

Kesey's adventures with the Merry Pranksters on Further secured them all an unexpected place in the history books, but it was Tom Wolfe who made them all into countercultural legends. Wolfe was a rising star in journalism when he arrived in San Francisco in late 1966. He was chasing a lead about "Kesey the fugitive," but he chanced upon something much better: an escapade featuring a famous author, powerful psychedelic drugs, and scrapes with the law, all set against the flowering of a new hippie counterculture in beautiful San Francisco. Wolfe showed up just as Kesey's adventure was winding down, but he managed to capture the story brilliantly in *The Electric Kool-Aid Acid Test* (1968). The book was a huge best seller and firmly established Wolfe's career. Though it does not pretend to be a history book—no citations at all—the scale of its success has virtually made it into a definitive text. When we remember Kesey, it is Wolfe's version of Kesey that most of us imagine: a swashbuckling cultural rebel whose pharmaceutical proclivities, existential lifestyle, and acidified visions led the "Freak" charge of the 1960s. Similarly, when we think of the Merry Pranksters, it is Wolfe's account that has fixed in our minds their image as a group of young psychedelic warriors, careening around the West Coast in Further, dispensing LSD and rebellion in equal measures, somehow seeding the whole hippie revolution that came in their wake.

So how much of that is true? Good question. Wolfe is a fine journalist who diligently checked his facts as best he could with Kesey before the publication of *Kool-Aid*, so the sequence of events is largely accurate, as is Wolfe's description of individuals and their actions. On the other hand, Wolfe employed a consciously hyperbolic writing style in an effort to convey the energetic zeal of his subjects and their times. While this made for an exciting read, the style lent itself to some exaggeration, particularly when it credited Kesey with virtually a *causal* role in the emergence of the counterculture, casting him and his friends as its "one electric source."[5]

Kesey and the Pranksters certainly played their part in the evolution of the counterculture, but it makes no sense to call them its "source" or to imagine that it would not have happened without them. Their most significant public acts—the Acid Tests—were staged in and around California over the winter months of 1965–66, and they were certainly an important moment in the flowering of the hippie counterculture at that critical time, but they were not its creator. The Acid Tests were artistic happenings that featured the Pranksters' bus trip movie, music from their friends the Grateful Dead, and lots of weird lights and sounds. People certainly took LSD at the Acid Tests, but these events were not vehicles for its mass distribution. The number of people who were initiated into the world of acid—that is, took LSD for the first time—at the Acid Tests courtesy of Kesey and the Pranksters is probably fairly small, a few hundred at most. This is a low number compared to the millions of people who were introduced to the drug courtesy of the late Stanley "Bear" Owsley and other underground LSD chemists of the day. While Kesey and his friends might have shared their drugs with friends and associates in the early West Coast psychedelic scene—that was the communal nature of it—they were never the "Pied Pipers of Acid" of popular imagination. The Acid Tests are important because of their artistic form and because of their timing, but they played only a small role in the circulation or spread of LSD. Wolfe's book probably turned on far more people to psychedelic culture than the Acid Tests, but how does one compare the impact of the deed with the impact of its telling? Kesey is an important historical figure, but he would not be remembered as the "Father of the Hippies"—a title that never sat well with the man himself—were it not for *The Electric Kool-Aid Acid Test*.[6] Still, Kesey remains a hero to many who have followed in his psychedelic footsteps. Any Dead-head, Phish-head, or

Pot-head worth their salt can recall the mythic adventures of Kesey and the Merry Pranksters aboard their psychedelic bus. Kesey was not above playing the heroic role he had been cast, but he also felt constrained by the myth that Wolfe had bestowed upon him.

While Kesey did not create the wave of cultural change that broke upon America in the mid-1960s, he was prescient enough to sense it coming and smart enough to realize that he was in a privileged position—thanks to the success of *Cuckoo's Nest*—to catch it early and carve his name on its face (that is, to *do* something with this unusual opportunity). His two novels had established Kesey's literary credentials, but taking that wave— to continue my surfing analogy—was the moment when he wrote himself into the history books: right there, in the decision to turn and push himself over the lip into an uncertain future. To his credit, he tried to do something positive with the opportunity that had come his way. Some might disagree with that assessment—there were certainly casualties along the way—but Kesey never set out to hurt or manipulate anybody, never tried to instigate violence or conflict, never put profit before art or ideals. Also to his credit (and probably Faye's) is the fact that while Kesey could sometimes be egotistical, he never lost his basic humanity, never started to imagine himself "all knowing," never set himself up as a guru or treated his friends like followers (even if they sometimes acted like it). Did Kesey really know what he was doing at this moment? Not really, at least not with any clarity. His decision to step away from writing in 1965 and enter a more public artistic arena was a brave move that suggests intent, but Kesey was following his instincts, not a great master plan. His motives were initially largely self-serving—ego, for the sake of art, for fame and fortune—but once he realized that larger issues were at stake, his motives also became more idealistic and utopian.

If he had known what was in store for him, he might have decided otherwise. In standing up on that wave for all to see, Kesey also found himself standing up against the powers that be. As soon as the authorities— the police—noticed him, they went after him, and they swatted him down. His ride was over before it was done. Busted twice—once in April 1965 and again in January 1966—the authorities used the prohibition on marijuana to effectively shut Kesey down. This was not insignificant. The year 1966 was critical in the evolution of San Francisco's counterculture. It was the year when everything started to come together: the people, the music, the style, the drugs, the events, the philosophy, the whole Haight-Ashbury scene. Since the publication of *Cuckoo's Nest* in 1962, Kesey had developed a certain standing among like-minded scenesters on the San Francisco peninsula. This was an age when writers were still important cultural figures. People like Norman Mailer and Joseph Heller were literary celebrities, their names and works familiar in popular culture as well as in academia. Kesey's literary success granted him status and influence, but the busts robbed him of the ability to do more. Had he been around for more of 1966, Kesey might have taken a leadership role in the burgeoning San Francisco Freak scene, but by the time he got back from hiding out in Mexico late in the year, his moment had gone. The recently named "hippie" scene had expanded and developed in his absence, leaving him behind and largely unknown by most of the new kids hanging around Haight-Ashbury. He was much older than most of these teenage newcomers, just another balding thirty-year-old who was not to be trusted. As if to confirm these doubts, soon after his capture, Kesey publically disavowed LSD in an obvious effort to avoid a long sentence.

Kesey could have pushed back, could have made his case a cause célèbre, could have made his legal martyrdom a big story, could have risen in the national consciousness to rival Timothy Leary as a spokesman for the counterculture, but he declined. Why? Partly because he did not feel particularly connected to the whole Haight-Ashbury hippie crowd—he felt that they had turned on him during his struggles with the law—but mostly because he was a family man, with a wife, three kids, and a large extended family waiting for him back in Oregon. No wonder he chose to serve his time and go home. By comparison, look what happened to Leary. He was given a thirty-year jail sentence for possession of a tiny amount of marijuana. Then he broke out of jail with the assistance of the Weathermen, a radical group, before fleeing the country to live in exile in Algeria and Afghanistan, before he was chased down and captured. Kesey was never going to make those choices. He had faced the beast, the "Combine," and felt its power, and that was enough for him.

The wave that Kesey rode in the sixties turned out to be a massive force for cultural change, one that washes over American society still. It has been more than fifty years since the decade dawned, and yet it still divides us, drawing a line across American society whether people know it or not. When conservatives speak of the culture war, it is the counterculture that they have in their sights. The conservative movement of the last forty years has been, in part, a generational backlash against the sixties and everything that the hippies stood for. But this movement is essentially a rear guard action attempting to recover lost ground with few prospects of success. While Nixon's "Silent Majority" turned out to have a pretty loud, powerful voice in the public arena, in the private sphere—in everyday life—it has largely fallen on deaf, young ears. If truth be told, the culture war is over and the hippies won. In twenty-first-century America, there is a yoga studio on every Main Street, rock music is the new classical, and the medical and recreational use of marijuana is more widespread than ever. More important, the progressive values and ideals of the counterculture—love, peace, compassion, understanding, environmentalism, the embrace of diversity, nonviolence, and more open-minded attitudes about religion and drugs, sex and sexuality, race, and gender—have become absorbed and accepted into mainstream American society, fundamentally changing its morals, its manners, and its ethics. Traditional ways of thinking survive and thrive in some places more than others, but their grip on our imagination has been significantly loosened, their view of the world significantly undermined, and their claims to truth significantly weakened. Important battles are still being fought—gay marriage, the War on Drugs—but one can never imagine American society going back to what it was before the 1960s. As others have noted, the process has been accelerated by commerce. The music of the counterculture, its fashions, its symbols, its style, were all quickly appropriated by the world of advertising and business, turned into consumable goods, and sold freely in the American marketplace.[7] Though this process may have weakened and diluted the antimaterialistic values of the counterculture, the mass consumption of these ideas helped move them from the fringe of American society to the center. Hippie values may not be the norm in every household or every region of the country, but the fact that they exist as viable alternatives to traditional ways of thinking is an indication of their ultimate victory.

Kesey's name is so identified with the sixties that it is easy to forget that he was a product of the forties and fifties. This was an unusual period in U.S. history. On the surface, post–World War II America deserves its reputation as a conservative period of recovery and rebirth. The G.I. Bill offered returning veterans the chance of an education and a move up the social ladder. The thriving economy fueled the growth of suburbs, and filled them with Baby Boomer families aspiring to live a happy *Leave It to Beaver* lifestyle. A grandfatherly Republican President Eisenhower and a Congressional turn away from New Deal politics only seemed to confirm the conservative nature of the period. Yet the fifties was also a decade fraught with tension and uncertainty. An unprecedented nuclear arms race with the Soviet Union cast a dark, unsettling shadow over the country. The concept of Mutual Assured Destruction was supposed to deter the likelihood of nuclear war, but it left little margin for error, and therefore little room for comfort. Wisconsin Senator Joseph McCarthy's relentless pursuit of communist spies in American society was popular with his Republican party and beyond, but it was rabid in its approach and radical in the way it trampled on political freedom and stifled free speech. It can hardly be called a conservative movement. In the South, the Brown vs. Board of Education Supreme Court ruling (1954) gave rise to both the modern civil rights movement and a white backlash that promised "massive resistance" to any efforts to undermine Jim Crow. The Kinsey Reports on male (1948) and female (1953) sexuality were regarded as controversial at the time of their publication, but again they suggest that beneath the surface—or at least behind the bedroom door—sexual attitudes in the 1950s were far less conservative than was generally acknowledged in public.

Similarly, while mainstream American culture in the 1950s was fairly conventional and vanilla in its sensibilities; on the more experimental fringes, rebels and artists were already sowing the seeds of a counterculture. Surfers on the West Coast and in Hawaii were developing a unique beach culture that was received by their elders as an incomprehensible affront to that bedrock of American values: the Protestant work ethic. Motorcycle clubs and urban gangs also seemed to pose a challenge to traditional values and conventional lifestyles. Senator Estes Kefauver (TN) was so concerned about these sorts of youthful aberrations that he staged Congressional hearings on juvenile delinquency in April 1955. Much hand-wringing ensued. In art, avant garde painters such as Arshile Gorky and Jackson Pollock were creating a new movement in abstract expressionism that shook up the art world, and eventually put New York City at its western center. Beat writers such as Jack Kerouac, Allen Ginsberg, and William Burroughs were exploring the underbelly of American society and finding new ways to express their discoveries. They enjoyed only a limited audience in the 1950s but their ideas, their attitudes, and their lifestyles would be highly influential in the decade to follow. Last but not least, the emergence of rock and roll posed a serious challenge to traditional values and standards in the 1950s, particularly those related to race and sexuality. When Elvis Presley appeared on the *Ed Sullivan Show* in September 1956, he performed in front of an audience of 60 million people, more than 80 percent of the television viewing public. While the parents might have squirmed and their children screamed at Elvis's every sexy gyration, both young and old alike could probably sense that change was coming.

Kesey was actually a little too old to be into rock and roll, a teenybopper phenomenon. He was twenty-one, married, and a junior at college by the time Elvis first appeared on the *Ed Sullivan Show* (there is no mention of the event in Kesey's journal). Kesey cared more for movies than he did music, but whatever musical tastes he had as a young man were shaped by his family and his location. Oregon was hardly at the heart of the rock and roll revolution, and Kesey's family was folksy and traditional in their musical inclinations, just as in their values. Kesey grew up at the heart of a close-knit extended family that had survived the Great Depression and World War II. His elders emerged from two decades of trauma with an undiminished faith in the American Dream and a belief that with hard work, their children would have it better than they had. Those family values shaped Kesey's character and his outlook on life, and must be understood if we are going to understand the man.

This book begins with an examination of Kesey's childhood in Colorado and Oregon. In those years, we will see a young man driven to succeed, testing the limits of his talents on the stage, on the wrestling mat, and in the classroom. In the first chapter we see him raised with traditional American values, informed by the Cold War, by the Texas cowboy side of his father, and by the frontier, logging-mill-spirit of Springfield, Oregon, his hometown. We see him as a teenager developing a magic act that he used to perform at home, at school, and for groups of farmers who worked with his father. By the time he got to college, Kesey was an entertainer of some note. He was a regular in college theatrical productions, and he earned a steady income with his magic act (which by then included hypnotism and ventriloquism). At one point Kesey even had his own segment on regional TV, but his real ambition was to make it in Hollywood, either as an actor on the silver screen, or as a screenwriter behind it. In chapter 2, we see him taking his talents to Hollywood, testing himself outside of his natural Oregonian environment during his summer breaks at college. Kesey failed to make a dent in Los Angeles as an actor, and by the end of his time at the University of Oregon we see him focusing on his writing.

In the fall of 1958, Kesey accepted a scholarship to attend Wallace Stegner's Creative Writing Seminar at Stanford University in Palo Alto, California. Chapter 3 traces Kesey's early career at Stanford. We find him in his early twenties and at the top of his game, mixing it up around the writing seminar table in the Jones Room, learning to be a writer by competing with his peers. Kesey and Faye moved into a bohemian section of Palo Alto called Perry Lane, a street full of graduate students, artists, and philosophers. Here Kesey met a group of friends who sharpened his intellect and shaped the rest of his life. One of them, Vic Lovell, a psychology graduate student and Perry Lane resident, told Kesey about an interesting way to earn money by volunteering for some drug experiments then being conducted at the local Menlo Park Veterans Administration (VA) hospital. This was 1960 and the pharmaceuticals being tested had a collective name: psychedelic—meaning "mind-expanding"—drugs. Kesey signed up for the experiments, unaware that the experience would change the course of his life. Chapter 4 describes this transformative moment in some detail, but it also sets Kesey's experience in the larger history of psychedelic drugs, stretching back to ancient times, through the Cold War 1950s, and into the 1960s when Timothy Leary, a former Harvard professor, became their most famous public advocate. Chapter 5 describes Kesey's life in the wake of the drug experiments, when an interest in these seemingly magical substances led him and his friends on a journey of exploration and play. Kesey took a night-shift job in the mental wards of the VA hospital, where he started writing *One Flew Over the Cuckoo's Nest*, inspired both by the cracked individuals in the ward and the psychedelic substances sparking his synapses. The end of the chapter finds Kesey temporarily back in Oregon researching his next book—*Sometimes a Great Notion*—oblivious to the fact that the publication of *Cuckoo's Nest* the following year, 1962, was going to make him one of the most famous writers in the United States.

Chapter 6 describes Kesey's last years on Perry Lane and the start of the writing of *Sometimes a Great Notion*. Kesey's greatest triumph in this period was taking his family to New York to see Hollywood superstar Kirk Douglas play the lead role in a Broadway adaptation of *One Flew Over the Cuckoo's Nest*. On the trip back from New York, Kesey and his friends learn of John F. Kennedy's assassination in Dallas on November 22, 1963, a tragedy that shook their youthful innocence. Also in this chapter we meet Neal Cassady, the real life Dean Moriarty from Jack Kerouac's seminal Beat novel, *On the Road* (1957), and a selection of other interesting characters, some of whom would later play a role in the Merry Pranksters. Kesey's growing celebrity is contrasted with the experiences of one of his best friends from Stanford, Ken Babbs, who served as a Marine helicopter pilot in Vietnam during this period. In mid-1963, a handful of the houses on Perry Lane—including those rented by Kesey and Vic Lovell—were demolished to make way for a new development. This effectively brought Perry Lane's bohemian scene to an end and forced Kesey and his family to relocate. Our final chapter finds Kesey established in a new home in La Honda, up in the redwood hills that separate Palo Alto from the Pacific Ocean. Here, as 1963 turned into 1964, we find him completing *Sometimes a Great Notion*—a gargantuan task—and taking stock of his situation and his times. As he contemplates his own recent turbulent past, he senses that change is in the air, and he starts to believe that he and his generation are on the verge of something "fantastic."

1

Sparks Fly Upward

THE OLD FRONTIER

Fred Kesey had been born and raised in Texas and Oklahoma. Geneva
Smith, his wife, grew up in Arkansas. In the 1930s they found themselves
on the move, following the same trail as thousands of other dustbowl
Okies and busted Texas farmers desperate to escape the ravages of the
scorching climate and the Great Depression. Just like the Joad family in
John Steinbeck's *The Grapes of Wrath*, the Keseys packed up their lives
and headed west in search of new opportunities over distant horizons. But
Fred Kesey was no Steinbeck, no "lefty," and no big critic of American
capitalism. He was restless and ambitious for sure, but he was not any sort
of radical. His faith in the American dream was simple and uncompli-
cated; he believed that his future was his to make or break, tough times
or not.

Fred and Geneva Kesey stayed a while in California, but eventually settled in Colorado in a little town called La Junta, close to where Geneva's
parents had also recently put down. La Junta was not much of a place, but
it was better than the road. The Keseys made a pretty good life for themselves in this sleepy little place, in large part because Fred found work at a
local creamery. By no stretch of the imagination were the Keseys rich, but
by the desperate standards of the day neither were they poor. They lived
in an old white house, weathered cream, that stood on top of a sagebrush
hill. The view out front was not much to crow about—a yard at the bottom of the hill filled with discarded farming machinery—but out back
was a beautiful pasture, home to wildflowers and even wilder horses.[1]

On September 17, 1935, Geneva gave birth to Ken Elton, their firstborn. Three years later she had another boy, named Joe, though most people called him Chuck. As a young infant, barefoot and sporting a head of bright white hair, Ken would spend hours in the sun-cracked dirt garden, playing with the water hose and tending a little weed patch. Mostly he was just waiting for the moment when his father would come home from the creamery for lunch. Those lunchtimes were the highlights of Ken's day. Sometimes, as his father lay on the floor resting in his white over-alls, the young Kesey would consider putting tacks in the road to stop him from going back to work. He never quite dared to carry out the prank. Geneva had her hands full looking after the house and the two boys, but the place echoed with her laughter and the made-up songs and old-timey standards she sang to entertain them. Ken would pick wildflowers off the hill to give to his mama: small bouquets of buttercups, long-stem daisies, and big poppy-like flowers that were as frail as they were beautiful. Some-times he would take his dog and wander in the prairie behind his house, imagining that the sound of thunder he could hear in the distance was really the rumble of wild horse hooves chasing across the great expanse of land that lay before him.

Life in Colorado was not necessarily easy, but Ken's childhood was happy and secure, rich in experience if not in wealth. Chuck worshiped his older brother. The two would build forts out of tumbleweed, create hideouts with their friends, and play with the toy airplanes that their grandpa used to make for them out of tobacco tins. One of their favorite pursuits was catching and racing insects. The track was a chalk circle in the garage of their house, and the race consisted of releasing the bugs out of a thumb-tack box in the middle of the circle and seeing who made it to the edge first. Sow bugs were an early favorite, but they were so slow and dim-witted that they could take up to an hour to finish the race. The two boys tried goading them on with the hot beam of a magnifying glass, but that did not seem to make them go any quicker. After experimenting with daddy long-legs, tumblebugs, lightning bugs, grasshoppers (with their wings removed to stop them from getting away), and crickets, they settled on cockroaches as the best racing stallions of the insect world. Each boy collected, named, and branded with a dab of fingernail polish a whole stable of roaches, keeping them in an old washtub and feeding them with coffee grounds. Competition was fierce even though there were no prizes beyond the glory of victory. Much to Chuck's delight, one of his cockroaches was a consistent winner, regularly beating his brother's favorite racer. Ken reacted to this affront to his elder-sibling status by sneaking out into the garage one night and pulling off one of the legs of his champion roach. Chuck never did work out why his prizewinner suddenly started taking a more circuitous route to the finish line, but justice was eventually served when he caught a shrew and entered it in a race against his brother's favorite cockroach (there was nothing in the rules to say that mammals were excluded from racing). They put the shrew and the roach together under the box in the middle of the circle, and counted down to the start of the race. When they flipped over the box, there sat the shrew, blinking in the sunlight and licking his little lips. Kesey's racer was nowhere to be seen. Ken squashed the shrew in a fit of despair, so Chuck retaliated by filling the washtub with stove-oil, killing all their cockroaches and bringing to an end their season of bug racing.[2]

The young Ken Kesey was not above getting into a little trouble. His mother once caught him making out with a neighbor girl in the old chicken house that the boys used as a den. He was not yet seven. Another time he stowed away in the back of his grandparents' old beat-up car and was only discovered as they neared their home, clear on the other side of La Junta. His most spectacular act of juvenile delinquency occurred after his family had temporarily relocated to California. Attempting to smoke out a hive of bees, Kesey succeeded in accidentally setting ablaze seven hundred acres of land. It would not be his last inflammatory act in the state of California, but it would certainly be one of the most unforgettable events of his young life, rivaled only in his memory by the time his grandparents gave him a half dollar. Such are the disproportions of youth.

The war came, and difficult decisions had to be made. Despite Geneva's objections, Fred signed up for the Navy in 1942, even though he was well past draft age. It was a tough call for this family man, but he was not about to let his two younger brothers—already stationed somewhere in the Pacific—be the only Keseys fighting the good fight against the fascists. His decision spelled the end of their time in La Junta. In the summer of 1943, Fred came home on leave from boot camp and announced that the family was moving to Oregon to join Grandma and Grandpa Smith. These two old-school pioneers had moved up there the previous year, leaving behind the boxcar they had briefly called home outside of La Junta.

They had settled on a farm in a little place called Coburg in the heart of the Willamette valley, about five miles north of Eugene. Coburg was not a metropolis—no parking lots, no parking meters, not even a traffic light at the time—but it fit the Smiths' needs perfectly. Grandma Smith sent back glowing reports to the family they had left behind in Colorado. "Beautiful scenery all the way," she wrote. "As regards irrigation, it looks to us like heaven above is just *loaded* with rain."[3] "Beautiful scenery" and "rain," words that find their way into most descriptions of Oregon.

It was decided that Geneva and the boys would live in Coburg with Grandpa and Grandma Smith while Fred shipped off to war. Fred's brothers had made the same decision, sending their families to stay on the Smiths' farm until they got back from their service. The Kesey family set out in August 1943, traveling across arid deserts and high mountain passes. Ken was not happy to leave Colorado, but his father reassured him that if the Willamette Valley was not to their liking, they could just keep going all the way to the Pacific Ocean. Ken was not sure he believed in oceans. He had heard about them but never seen one for himself. "Sure, there mighta been big oceans at one time," he told his kid brother on the long journey, "but by now they are mostly drying up. Like that Salt Lake place we passed. It's called heat evaporation. There ain't enough rain on the planet to keep an ocean filled in heat like this."[4] On the third night, they crossed over the Cascade Mountains and wound their way down into the Willamette Valley and then up to Coburg. It was past midnight before they arrived at the farm. Grandma Smith made the boys feel welcome by offering them buttermilk flavored with some delicious wild blackberries, the mere taste of which was enough to make Ken reconsider his doubts about the family move to Oregon. The following morning, while gorging on more fresh blackberries from the bushes at the edge of the lawn, he decided that "maybe Grandma and them pioneers was right about this land after all."[5]

The Smiths' place was beautiful. It had a stream that was deep enough for the kids to learn to swim in, and lots of wide open space to run about in. It was mostly a dairy farm, but there was also a vegetable patch where Grandma cultivated tomatoes, string beans, and various greens. Grandpa raised sweet corn in a separate patch, and a small orchard provided a sweet harvest of apples, pears, and plums in the fall. The cow pasture ran alongside the Willamette River. The hazel and black walnut trees that grew on the riverbanks acted as a natural fence, keeping the cows from wandering into the water.

Over time, it became Ken's job to stroll down to the pasture in the morning and call the herd in for milking. It was the perfect job for the young boy; he could holler at the top of his lungs and let his mind wander far and wide. He would also help out in the milking sheds, separating out the cream from the milk before he put it into special little cans. Then he would wheel out the two or three larger cans of whole milk to the side of the road, ready to be picked up by the local creamery's milk truck. This would all be accomplished before school; another round of milking would take place when he returned in the afternoon. In the summer, Ken, Chuck, and other local kids would earn six cents a pound picking beans on the bean farms scattered around the river's edge. As they got older there was more to be gathered between those beanpoles than just beans. "That's where you learned about sex and illicit magazines and stuff," Kesey fondly recalled. "Lots and lots of kids had their first encounter with sex in those bean rolls."[6]

Ken's chores kept him busy, but this was the life he became accustomed to. It could be hard work, but it had its rewards, especially when he got to hang around with his elders. Once, while he was helping his grandfather shovel manure among a bunch of sneezing cows, the mischievous old man positioned Ken right behind a cow so that when it sneezed, a ball of manure shot out of its rear end and flew past the kid's ear like a cannonball. Everyone fell about laughing. Ken's lifelong love of pranks clearly had a long heritage. He and his brother were always playing practical jokes on each other. Once, Kesey found a golf ball hidden in his bedroom curtains. Chuck had positioned it so that when his brother pulled the curtains, the ball would fall and hopefully hit him on the head. Chuck and Ken were quite a pair.

In quieter moments, Grandma Smith would sit the boys around the table lamp, hold her hands up in the light, and count off an old favorite nursery rhyme on her fingers: "William, William Trimble toes, he's a good fisherman, catch his hands put 'em in the pans, some lay eggs, some not, wire, briar, limber lock, three geese in the flock, one flew east, one flew west, one flew over the cuckoo's nest; O-U-T spells 'out,' you dirty dish rag you go out!" Two decades later, mining the memories of his childhood for inspiration, Kesey would use a line from this poem as the title of his most famous book.

After Fred Kesey's training was completed, it was time for him to enter active service with the navy. Before he left, he took his family to see the Pacific Ocean for the first time. They crossed the Coast Range and parked in a turnout overlooking the vast expanse of water. "Sure is big, ain't it?" Ken's father wondered aloud. "Yep," Grandpa Smith agreed. "And that's just the top of it."[7] A few days later, Fred Kesey left for the Mare Island Naval Shipyard at Vallejo, California. Standing in front of the house in Coburg, he bid farewell to his kids, saluting them proudly. Ken returned the gesture, and through his tears he could see that his father—his hero regardless of any war—was crying too.

FAMILY VALUES

Fred's participation in the war was mercifully short and uneventful. Like thousands of other returning veterans, he quickly set about rebuilding the life he had left behind. In 1946 he moved Geneva and the kids to Springfield, about eight miles south of Coburg, into a little house at 120 West Q Street, on the main road into Eugene. This would be Ken Kesey's home for the next ten years. His bedroom overlooked the backyard, where he and Chuck had built a cage to house raccoons or whatever other creatures they had been able to capture. The room was a typical kid's room, full of toys and memory-laden junk. A cedar chest sat at the end of the bed, storage space for games and, later, magic tricks and ventriloquist dolls. Photographs of family and friends shared shelves with books, comics, and a little sports trophy. By the time Ken was in his teens, lots of his own artwork graced the walls of his room, all testimony to his interests and abilities as an artist. A few of them had distinctly Western themes, such as the portrait of Buffalo Bill, or the painting of an Indian paddling a canoe. There was a self-portrait in a wrestling stance, while another depicted two men fighting in the rigging of a tall ship. There was also a surrealistic image of a hand reaching through fire to grasp at some money. A lone hanging bulb illuminated the pictures and their surroundings, its shade long since destroyed in a pillow fight between the boys. Ken's bed stood next to the window. Late at night, he would lie there with his two front teeth resting on the windowsill, saying his prayers and staring at the stars. This was such a regular ritual that eventually he gnawed the paint away on that sill and left tooth marks on the wood beneath its surface. In the distance, he could make out the blinking radio tower of the local radio station, KEED, and beyond that the Coburg hills. A few times a week, just before midnight, a logging train would make its way through the hills and wind its way into Springfield, passing within a block of the Kesey home. He thought, "Someday I'll go someplace on that train," perhaps trying to imagine what travels the future held.[8]

Fred Kesey worked at the Darigold Creamery in Springfield. He started as a foreman, but before long he was managing the place. The creamery was a cooperative—the Eugene Farmer's Co-op—meaning that it was owned and operated by local farmers. They shared in costs and profits and elected a board of directors from among themselves to oversee operations. At its peak, around 1,250 farms from all over the region belonged to this co-op, some of them so small that they would often send in a single can of cream to be churned into butter. The Kesey kids often helped out in the creamery.[9] Ken once got into big trouble after he mixed together all the ice-cream "reruns"—stuff that had not sold or that had melted during shipping—and concocted a twenty-case run of bright red ice cream. He sent it out to various stores under the label "BLOOD ROYAL" and waited in good faith for the compliments he felt would surely come his way. His father only learned of his son's unusual initiative after a number of bemused grocery store owners started to return the foul creation to the creamery in bulk. Undeterred, Ken and his brother Chuck next tried to figure out a process to distill whey—a liquid byproduct of the cheese-making process—and make it into liquor rather than sell it for two cents per gallon to local farmers. In the early sixties they even tried to work out a way to make a marketable psilocybin mushroom wine that they planned to call "Milk of the Gods."[10] Fred Kesey was not a big fan of this last idea— "If you two try to manufacture this stuff," he told them after having tried psilocybin for himself, "I'll crawl all the way to Washington on my bloody hands and *knees* to get it outlawed!"[11]—still, their creative entrepreneurial spirit was obviously something that they had picked up from him.

A good illustration of this aspect of Fred's character can be seen in his response to the Cold War nuclear arms race of the 1950s. While most Americans quietly struggled to accommodate themselves to the realities of "living under the bomb," he saw it as an opportunity to get rich. New Year's Day 1956 found Fred, Ken, and two others hiking through three-foot-deep snow in the Ochoco Mountains of Oregon (located about three hours east of Springfield) prospecting for uranium. The adventure almost ended in disaster. After just a few hours of hiking, they were all exhausted—they had foolishly left their snowshoes in their truck—and they were completely lost, unable to find the cabin that they hoped would offer some shelter for the night. They ended up sleeping inside a tipped-over tool shed, huddled side by side in their sleeping bags, covering their faces to avoid the snow blowing in through the rat holes gnawed in the walls of their sanctuary. They hiked out the following day, Geiger counter in hand, investigating likely looking piles of rocks as they went and picking up a few samples that seemed to offer at least a trace of hope. Subsequent trips were as fruitless as the first, but the lesson for the Kesey sons was in the endeavor and the ambition, not the outcome.[12]

Fred was a self-made man. He never graduated high school, yet he achieved the sort of material success—a comfortable middle-class existence with enough money to send his children to college—demanded of him by his culture and his times. But that was not enough for this "big, rebellious cowboy who never did fit in," as his eldest son once recalled of him.[13] Fred was the sort of man who needed a challenge, new fire in his belly to spur him on to the next frontier, to the next opportunity. He clearly lived a very different life than his son, yet he never questioned Ken's right to make the choices he made, concerned though he may have been about some of their consequences. Fred Kesey's politics were conservative, but there was nothing conformist about his carpe diem approach to life and nothing surprising about the way his son adopted much the same outlook. Fred was a powerful influence on his son in many ways. He was the head of the extended Kesey family, the king whom young Ken adored and sought to emulate. The young boy also admired his mother, Geneva, though she sometimes had to work hard to keep him in check. "He had a mind of his own," she recalled.[14] At age eleven, Kesey wrote an affectionate poem for her titled "Mother, Mine" that seemed to acknowledge his mischievous ways: "She corrected all my wrongs, and paid for all my duds," he wrote. "She bought me all my play things and fed me all my spuds. She tucked me in the covers and brought me up just right. She wore out 15 razor straps to make me see the light."[15]

Ken Kesey learned the values that shaped his life from his family, and also from the place where he grew up. Springfield was an old logging and milling town, blue-collar to the core, its people proud of the frontier traditions that still informed their view of the world. The Kesey family personified those traditions, having forged their own particular Oregon Trail in recent memory. Theirs was a relatively conservative worldview that treasured family and community, fostered ambition and determination, and admired personal courage and integrity. They maintained the core belief that an individual had the right to shape his or her destiny if that person possessed sufficient will and strength of character to succeed. Despite the untraditional course that the younger Kesey followed in his life, he never relinquished those core values. In fact, he believed that he was trying to live them out to their logical, libertarian, all-American conclusion. He was well aware of the absurdity of being held up as an icon of some sort of anti-American counterculture when he actually saw himself as a defender of the American way. "I've always been far more conservative than Barry Goldwater can imagine," he told an interviewer on the *CBS Sunday Morning Show* in 1990. "I still believe in all that stuff . . . I haven't ever developed any kind of cynicism about the American Dream."[16]

It is no surprise that the young Ken Kesey was particularly attracted to the individualistic American creed. It was a lesson he learned and embraced early in his life. In a poem titled "The Earth Is Your Canvas and You Are the Artist," written in 1943 for a school class, the young Kesey firmly insists that it was up to the individual to create the life of his or her choosing.[17] While these sorts of traditional American values remained the norm in mainstream culture, the postwar period of the 1950s witnessed a healthy academic debate over America's social character. Intellectuals fretted over the virtues and/or vices of being an "inner-directed," traditionally individualistic American or an "outer-directed" member of mass society, as modern America seemed to demand.[18] When William Faulkner visited the University of Oregon (U of O) campus in April 1955, he came out firmly on the side of tradition. "I believe that the individual always wants to be an individual," he lectured the audience. "There are any number of people in America who believe in their individuality and who, like I, believe in Man. I protest against reducing man to a mass. Man has got to be himself."[19] Kesey was in the audience, and one can easily imagine him nodding in agreement. In an interview from 1963, he quoted a friend to try to clarify his personal perspective. "[Ken] Babbs once said it perfectly," Kesey explained. "A man should have the right to be as big as he feels it's in him to be."[20] This individualistic creed would later feature prominently in Kesey's second book, *Sometimes a Great Notion*, the plot of which was a meditation on the place of individualism in modern America: the "inner-directed" Stamper clan clashed with the "outer-directed" notions of the local logging union. Kesey even incorporated Babbs's line in the text, describing frontier-era Oregon as a place where "THERE IS ELBOW ROOM FOR A MAN TO BE AS BIG AND IMPORTANT AS HE FEELS IT IN HIM TO BE."[21]

Kesey's personal politics and his actions in the sixties were an expression of his individualistic ideal. "Look," he told his friend Gordon Lish in 1963, "I don't intend to let anybody make me live in *less* world than I'm capable of living in. . . . I get weary of people who use pessimism to avoid being responsible for all the problems in our culture. A man who says we're on the road to disaster is seldom trying to wrench the wheel away from the driver. I prefer the troublemaker. He tells them he doesn't like the way they're running the show; that he thinks he could do better, that the fact is he's going to *try*."[22] Kesey was convinced that the social revolution that he and others like him sought in the sixties was, at its root, a personal process and not something that could be realized through mass politics or a group movement. "We've got to keep it on a one-to-one basis," he explained to a journalist later in the decade. "That's why I'm opposed to an organized movement."[23] Kesey's individualistic brand of politics set him apart from the more communitarian ideals of many of his sixties peers, but his thoughts were fully in keeping with his background and his character. "I have a strong line of that old redneck American running through me," he once told TV personality Bob Costas, "along with a revolutionary crazed hippie dope smoking personality."[24] As a student at the U of O, Kesey stood out from the crowd, but he was no radical. "He had a compelling aura about him very different from everyone else, this leadership quality," remembered John Herman, one of Kesey's Beta fraternity brothers. "But he wasn't a proponent of any life style that was unusual. . . . It was all about sorority girls and going down to the river to drink beer, it was a wonderful time . . . very much a party atmosphere."[25]

It's All a Kind of Magic

Ken Kesey was a natural performer, possessed of ability, charisma, and bountiful self-confidence. He loved being the center of attention, and his father was fond of saying that he "could draw a crowd in a desert."[26] This urge to perform was apparent from an early age, and Fred Kesey did what he could to foster Ken's development. One of his responsibilities as manager of the Darigold Creamery was to travel around the state to attend what used to be called producer's meetings. It was his job to read a report to the assembled co-op members, detailing profits and losses, and keeping people up to date with the operations of the creamery. In the days before television, these gatherings at old Grange Halls and church meeting rooms tended to be opportunities for all involved to let their hair down a little. Fred took Ken and Chuck with him on these trips and let them put on a small magic show to entertain the farmers and their kids. Ken enjoyed the spotlight. "We didn't know what we were getting into," he recalled, "but we were perfectly happy to perform anywhere with any kind of audience. Boy those farm kids just ate it up."[27]

Kesey's introduction to magic had been something of an accident. An avid reader of comic books as a boy, he had clipped a coupon out of a Batman comic and sent off for some superhero decals to stick on his bedroom window. When the package arrived, the decals came with a free book of magic tricks. It was nothing special—more like a pamphlet than a book—but it was enough to get him hooked. He started with simple coin and card tricks, the sleight of hand basics. He moved on to larger illusions after sending away for a catalog of stage magic. This was the source of most of the tricks that he and Chuck performed at the producer's meetings. From there, he took up ventriloquism and, eventually, hypnotism. This last skill was not without its concerns. "He hypnotized his brother once," his mother, Geneva, recalled, "[then] got a little scared because he was afraid Chuck wasn't coming back."[28]

The stage tricks could get quite elaborate. One favorite at the producer's meetings involved Kesey picking out a red-headed boy from the audience as part of a supposed demonstration about how to pasteurize milk. While he and Chuck took an ice pick and pretended to drill a hole in the victim's skull, Kesey would explain that to pasteurize milk you had to put it into a container and heat it up. Reminding everybody that redheads were supposed to be more hotheaded than other people, Kesey would take some milk and pretend he was pouring it into the freshly drilled hole in the kid's head. Naturally, he made sure to spill a little in the process so that some of it ran through the poor boy's hair and down his face, much to the amusement of the audience. Kesey would tell the crowd that the freshly pasteurized milk would travel through the body and emerge out of the human-pasteurizer's elbow. He would then pump the kid's arm up and down and, just as he had predicted, a stream of milk would magically pour forth, eliciting wild applause.

Besides the farmers' shows with Chuck, Kesey performed a solo magic act at various Springfield High School functions. An enthusiastic newspaper review from April 27, 1951, recounted his part in that year's annual talent show. "Francis McGinnis sang 'To Think You've Chosen Me,'" noted the reporter, "and following this solo were slight [*sic*] of hand tricks by Ken Kesey. Ken's bold assurance led him to bake a cake in Mr. Sabin's hat while he languished on the sidelines at the faate [*sic*] of his crowning glory. However Ken's culinary talents soon produced a delicious angel food cake. Soft drinks to the audience were also provided by Kesey."[29]

Kesey's High School yearbooks made much of his abilities and accomplishments. His junior yearbook (1952) pictured him on the football team and the wrestling squad, as a member of the National Thespian Society, and as a member of "Varsity S," in charge of "keeping order at school sponsored activities and generally upholding the school's reputation."[30] One telling inscription by Kesey to classmate Frances McGinnis indicates that he did not necessarily take his duties that seriously. In bright red pencil he scribbled, "Fran, I sure will miss your tight sweaters and sexy glances from english. Ken Kesey." Next to the inscription, ever the magician, Kesey sketched a rabbit coming out of a top hat.[31] His senior yearbook listed him as a "social promoter" and as a member of the Senior Council and the Debate Club. Pictures showed him wrestling, playing football for the varsity team, performing in various plays, and posing as the anointed king of the "Frosty Fantasies" annual winter party. One photo showed Kesey performing a magic trick for a female classmate under the simple caption "Most Talented."[32]

Kesey's career as a showman continued unabated at the University of Oregon in Eugene, where he enrolled in the fall of 1953 as a speech and communications major. His stage work subsidized his studies. "My first two years," he later claimed, "I almost put myself through college with magic shows around town."[33] His fees varied anywhere from ten to twenty-five dollars per performance, quite a sum of money back in those days (by comparison, Kesey's wrestling scholarship paid fifty dollars per semester).

Kesey performed for anyone who wanted to hire him—from parties for children to gigs for farmer's meetings—but he also entertained quite often at various places around the U of O campus: at various fraternity/sorority houses, at homecoming festivities, and at the annual U of O variety show. In his first year on campus Kesey recruited a few of his dorm mates into his routine. While Kesey told lewd jokes with his ventriloquist dummy, Dink, his roommate, Boyd Harris, played bongos, and another dorm resident named Conrad would do a fire-eating act. At the end of the show Kesey would tell the audience that he had hypnotized Boyd and made him impervious to pain. To prove his powers—or perhaps Boyd's tolerance—Kesey would then have an audience member stub out a hot cigarette in Boyd's unflinching palm.[34] Kesey actually got pretty good at hypnotizing people—he bought a book on the subject—amazing his Beta brothers when he hypnotized one of the Kappa sorority girls.

Such was Kesey's enthusiasm for the spotlight that a fraternity man from Phi Delta Theta described him as "a one-man entertainment committee." "I remember the first time I met him," recalled Brian Booth, still a resident of Oregon and a lifelong friend of Kesey's. "I was going through rush and he was a Beta. . . . He had a ventriloquist's dummy, he was doing card tricks and magic . . . When it came out later that he was a writer, people were shocked that this athlete, this character, was such a fine writer."[35] The 1955 *Oregona* (the University of Oregon's yearbook) contains two revealing photographs of a white-suited, twenty-year-old Kesey performing his act. One photograph captures him standing at center stage holding his ventriloquist dummy. Kesey's eyes are closed, but his mouth is wide open, hooting and hollering with free abandon. The cowboy puppet in his arms seems to wear a look of amusement and mild surprise at the force of Kesey's exclamation. The second photograph shows Kesey in the midst of a trick: "liven[ing] up the intermission during the Senior Ball," so the caption tells us, "with his live wire humor and amazing feats of magic."[36] This was no longer just a child impressing a group of adults with his "bold assurance." The photo depicts a talented man with an obvious appetite for theatrics.

Kesey's early experiences with magic played an important role in his development as a performer and a storyteller. Each of the tricks had a story to go along with it, and it would usually fall to Kesey to come up with the narrative and the appropriate lines for him and his brother. In the same way, the storyline was essential to the performance of the ventrilo-quist act that he first developed in high school. "You've got a character," he explained years later. "He sits on your knee. You put words in his mouth."[37] It was another way to tell a story through performance. He tried to incorporate the skills he learned as a magician into his writing, recognizing that there is an element of trickery in a good story. "Magic is essentially focusing the person's attention on where you want it to go," he once told an interviewer. "You learn a lot of tricks about how to get people interested and how to keep their attention there while you are pulling the trick over here." He cited Hemingway's *Farewell to Arms* as a prime example of "literary magic": "You get to the end of the book and as you are reading along in the book you are thinking, 'I don't know why this guy, Hemingway, is so good? It didn't look that good to me.' But as you get to the end of the book, and she is dying, suddenly you find yourself weeping and you realize that he had planted this in you all along from the beginning. He lets you identify with these people without going into their emotions. He lets you have the emotions. He lets you have your own emotions and opinions instead of forcing you to have the emotions of the characters. When I first read that I thought, 'I can do that, I can write stuff and make people feel just the same way I could do stuff and make people see when I was a magician.'"[38]

In later years, Kesey often referred back to his time as a magician as the root of his writing career, but he would also emphasize that the writing should not be seen as separate from its presentation. "[Writing] has been elevated to the point that people think it is the 'thing,'" he told one interviewer. "It isn't. Shakespeare doesn't come alive until it's on stage. It's about performance."[39]

Kesey achieved critical acclaim through his literary abilities, but his artistic ambitions went beyond the boundaries of the written word. Though he returned again and again to writing throughout his life, the constraint of what he saw as an increasingly outdated and limited form of communication was always a source of frustration. Asked in 1993 whether he preferred performance to writing, he answered in the affirmative. "I've been dating Emily Brontë," he said, "and the old dame just ain't putting out like she used to."[40] Kesey saw himself as a twentieth-century shaman, using whatever tricks he could lay his hands on to entertain and maybe even enlighten his audience. "To me, it's all the same stuff," he told a reporter from the *Los Angeles Times*. "The magic shows, the writing, the acid trips, the readings. It's what I've always been trying to do; the focus of my attention has always been magic."[41]

All the World's a Stage

Kesey was involved in many theatrical productions during his school and college years. He took his craft seriously, joining the National Thespian Society, an organization "Devoted to the Advancement of Dramatic Arts in the Secondary Schools." One of his earliest parts was as the judge in a high school production of the hit Broadway comedy *Dear Ruth*. A local newspaper gave Kesey and his on-stage wife high marks for their performance: "The parts most likely to be recalled with a chuckle of pleasure in later years were that of Judge and Mrs. Wilkins," the reporter wrote. "Ken Kesey and Pat Ardinger had the audience 'literally rolling in the aisles' with their quips and matrimonial arguments."[42] In 1952–53, Kesey performed in another high school play called *Submerged*. He also took the student director's chair for the senior class production of *Cheaper by the Dozen*, a comedy set in New Jersey during the 1920s. In the school production of *Showboat*, he played the part of Uncle Tom, sang in the boys' chorus, and even found time to help out with the makeup.

Kesey often combined his enthusiasm for sports with his urge to perform. At one pep rally, he treated a gym full of students to a skit that was supposed to pass the "spirit of football" on to the forthcoming basketball season. As classmate Gary Eddy read a mock testament over the "dead football spirit," Kesey burst forth as the king's messenger, telling the assembled masses, "If the football spirit was good enough for football, then it should be good enough for basketball."[43] After another student, dressed as a medicine man, performed a ceremony to restore the spirit to life, Kesey then proceeded to lead the student body in a yell, "the Big M."

Kesey continued to pursue the spotlight in a college theatrical career that regularly found him treading the boards of the university stage. As a freshman in the spring of 1954, he landed a small, nonsinging role in *One Touch of Venus*, a musical comedy that had made it on Broadway and been turned into a film starring Ava Gardner. By January of the following year, Kesey had moved himself up the credits, playing a number of speaking roles in *Captive at Large: A Play of Here and Now*. This was an obscure work that the program described as a "free-form play [that] touches on many subjects, from the state of the theatre to academic freedom." The university newspaper, *Oregon Daily Emerald*, gave it a positive review, praising Kesey for making "a good showing" in his various roles.[44]

It is worth noting that this production was very different from any that Kesey had appeared in previously. Its staging was intentionally unusual and interactive, consciously setting out to break down the barriers between audience and performance, just as Kesey and the Pranksters would attempt with some of their activities a decade later. The opening monologue of *Captive at Large* informed the crowd that the "play is yours as well," exhorting them to participate in the evening's creative endeavors. Lines were sometimes delivered directly to particular individuals in the crowd, and the action took place all around the auditorium. Some actors made their entrances from the seated ranks of the audience and even from the lobby of the theater. The subject of the play was also far more left field than was typical for a college production of the day. It boasted a plot that was full of the sort of antiestablishment social commentary that would eventually find free expression in both of Kesey's major novels, particularly *One Flew Over the Cuckoo's Nest*. Playwright David Mark portrayed contemporary American society as authoritative and manipulative; a place where people's freedoms were limited and where they were continually subjected to the will of an authority figure called the Superintendent. The "captive" referred to in the play's title is a man who resists the constraints placed upon him by society and insists upon his right to be a "free man." The authorities fear that such ideas could undermine the stability of their regime, so they hunt him down and put him on trial. It was heady stuff, and the individualistic ideology that it promoted must have appealed to Kesey's own rebellious sensibilities.

In addition to his theater work, Kesey starred in his own weekly fifteen-minute children's show on local television through 1954 and the early months of 1955. Essentially an extension of his stage act, the show combined magic tricks with jokes and the occasional poem. He and his ventriloquist dummy had first appeared on TV a couple of years earlier, advertising his father's creamery business during the *Cisco Kid* program (a popular kids' Western show). With so many other college activities, Kesey did not have much time to devote to the TV show, often throwing together a script just the day before a live broadcast. He occasionally tried to push the station manager for more airtime or a better spot—one of his ideas was to do a college sports show featuring interviews with the best athletes—but to no avail. If he had put a little more effort into his preparation, things might have been different, but his performances were usually average or sometimes worse.

Kesey's greater concern in the spring of 1955 was his fraternity's appearance in the Duck Preview Vodvil variety show. This was an annual competitive event, part of the University of Oregon's efforts to attract visiting high school seniors to their fold. This year, the Betas performed a skit written by Kesey called "Come Back, Little Sh-Boom." Their routine was good enough to put them into the final, where Kesey was named "best actor" for his part in their performance. He also won the loudest laughter from the audience when he made his entrance on a rope descending from the roof of the building.[45]

An Odd Duck?

Kesey rushed and pledged for the Betas in his first semester at the University of Oregon. In his sophomore year (1954–55) he moved into the Beta house, a big old house located next to the millrace (an artificial branch of the Willamette River that ran behind the fraternity property).[46] Every year, the Betas would host a spring term dance on the banks of the millrace, bringing in a brightly decorated portable dance floor for their guests. Kesey loved being a Beta, one of the "Boys from the Millrace." Housemates were constantly in and out of one another's rooms, horsing around, swapping sports stories and girl gossip, and plotting their next move against rival fraternities. The camaraderie, the brotherhood, the high jinks; it suited Kesey perfectly. He did not even seem to mind the hazing, a widely accepted practice within fraternities at the time. In the Beta house, junior members would get physically attacked—"tubbing," they called it—for numerous infractions, from being disrespectful to their fraternity brothers, for failing to fulfill their domestic duties around the house, or for simply forgetting the words and actions to any of the Betas' special songs. Kesey once got tubbed for refusing to tub one of his junior brothers, and he once got hosed down for falling behind on his house duties, but he took it in stride. It was the price of admission to the club, and by the standards of the day, he did not see the violence as excessive.

As a member of the Order of the "O" in his junior year, Kesey would have been responsible for maintaining campus regulations and traditions. Woe betide any student who walked on the wrong piece of grass, who wore the wrong sort of beanie, or who dared to walk across the Oregon Seal set in the sidewalk outside the Student Union building. Typical punishments included getting smacked by a paddle-wielding member of the Order of the "O," being branded with a red mark on the forehead, or getting dunked in the millrace or Fenton Hall pool. Oregon State University students caught on campus fared even worse. According to one account, they "sometimes had an 'O' cut into their hair and were forced to wash the windows of the student union or polish the Oregon Seal." Violence and intimidation actually became so common that during homecoming in 1954, two hundred female students launched a demonstration to protest the activities of the Order of the "O." The men responded by later hosing down fifty women outside the Sigma Chi house.[47]

Kesey reveled in the rituals and the boisterous traditions associated with Greek life, particularly during his sophomore year, when he lived in the Beta house (he couldn't afford it in his junior year, and he was married by the time he was a senior). He enthusiastically attended chapter meetings, participated in pledging new members during "Hell Week," and played quarterback on the Betas' intramural football team. He serenaded sorority houses, yelled in the annual Noise Parade, and, as we've seen, he wrote, acted and directed in many of the Betas' theatrical efforts on campus. When the Betas joined a big rally on campus in late 1954, Kesey was right at the heart of the event, chanting "no class today" along with his fraternity brothers and going into classrooms to pull students out. It was not all just mindless fun. People in the Beta house also studied hard, or worked on a variety of creative projects on behalf of the fraternity or the college. Now and again long-winded discussions would take place regarding current affairs, popular culture, or philosophical matters. Kesey and a few of his housemates once argued religion late into the night, for example. Kesey treated the exercise as an intellectual jousting match, taking on the philosophical opinions of others one by one, all the while maintaining a Socratic vagueness about his own opinion, a typical Kesey thing to do.

Opinions around the house would have probably been mostly conservative. Almost all fraternity men in the 1950s tended toward careers in business or the professions, and they were generally more economically, politically, and socially conservative than other students.[48] As institutions, fraternities played an important role in maintaining and promoting the conservatism of the 1950s, and even into the 1960s when there were plenty of countervailing forces on campuses across the nation. No less a man than FBI director J. Edgar Hoover praised fraternity men for their efforts in the fight against communism and radicals. And in 1968, when the Students for a Democratic Society (SDS) organized a huge strike at Columbia University in New York, the fraternities on campus—including the local chapter of Beta Theta Pi—led the student opposition to the strike and organized counterdemonstrations. Kesey was not really that interested in politics, but his political opinions at this time would have been fairly conservative, largely inherited from his father, a self-made, successful businessman. Kesey was far more libertarian than his father on social or religious issues, but they would likely have both been pro-capitalism, pro-American, anti-communist, anti-union (see Kesey's *Sometimes a Great Notion*), and anti-authoritarian (in a populist-individualist-anti-big-government kind of way). These views would probably have been the conventional wisdom among most of Kesey's fraternity brothers as well.

And yet, despite their conservative politics and attention to tradition, fraternities also had their rebellious side. Behind closed doors, and especially once the sun went down, much of the juvenile trouble making that occurred on college campuses was courtesy of fraternity men who were "conservative, anti-intellectual, rule-abiding Big Men on campus by day and hard drinking, profane, violent men by night,"[49] as one study concluded. The drinking, the hazing, the pranking, and the sometimes violent rivalries with other frat houses were all par for the fraternity course, regardless of the rules set by college administrators or student judiciary committees. A lot of the time, the trouble began with a practical joke, a feature of college life in the 1950s. During Kesey's sophomore year, for example, an un-named "Prankster" set off the fire alarms in the basement of the University of Oregon student union building during homecoming, causing hundreds to evacuate before the situation was resolved.[50]

The most notorious prank of the 1950s was the "panty raid," where fraternity (and nonfraternity) men would invade a sorority house or women's dormitory and make off with women's underwear as trophies. The first reported panty raid took place at the University of Missouri in 1952, with hundreds of men participating in the attack. Though the incident was

widely condemned by college administrators and in the press, the activity
caught on, with copycat raids occurring in the months and years to follow at Michigan, Duke, Miami, Nebraska, and elsewhere. One happened
at the University of Oregon in 1955, Kesey's junior year. On November 27,
1955, about two hundred jeering and cheering men stormed Carson Hall,
Sherry Ross Hall, and Hendricks Hall, all women's dormitories. Some
women taunted the men in the crowd from the upper floors of their
dormitories, dropping bags full of water on their heads. A few hurled
their panties out of their windows, to the delight of the baying mob below.
Dean of Men Ray Hawk arrived at the scene in a city police car. He mingled with the crowd, shouting, "Go home boys, you've had your fun."
Locked doors and windows kept the men out of Carson and Hendricks,
but eight men got into Sherry Ross via a fire escape. Three were caught
and threatened with expulsion. The incident was not without its humor.
The *Oregon Daily Emerald* reported that "a lone trumpeter in a nearby
men's dorm spurred [the raiders] on by alternately sounding the infantry
'Charge,' and 'Mighty Oregon.'"[51]

Kesey had nothing to do with any of these events, but he had his fun
at other times. Once he and some Beta brothers surreptitiously liberated
a canoe from a rival fraternity. In the dead of night they carted it uptown
and left it on the second-floor balcony of the student union for everyone
to witness the following morning. Another time, Kesey printed up some
signs advertising an "All-Campus Hump" and recruited some fellow Betas
to help him put them up all around campus. He also once hatched a plan
to kidnap a homecoming queen. He set off across campus determined to
turn on the charm and lure her from her room for a supposed photo
shoot, but he chickened out along the way. One of his most notorious
pranks made the papers, got his fraternity into serious trouble, and almost
resulted in criminal prosecution. Water fights were a common occurrence
on the U of O campus, particularly when the temperature started to warm
toward the end of the spring semester. In May 1955, on a lark, Kesey made
a sling capable of lobbing water-filled balloons a considerable distance
at considerable force. Somehow, the Beta brothers fixed the contraption
to the back of a 1930 automobile, and Kesey and seven others proceeded
to drive around the campus, terrorizing and amusing everybody they encountered. Not so funny was the moment when they fired a balloon at
the Alpha Phi sorority house on Hilyard Street. The projectile flew across

the road, smashed through a front window, and scattered shards of glass around the room. Nineteen-year-old sorority member Carolyn Heckman suffered minor scratches as a result. It could easily have been far worse if she had been closer to the window. Carolyn told the police that she was surprised by the incident. So were Kesey and his buddies, one of whom told a reporter, "We didn't even think it would work."[52] The police told the men to dismantle their weapon and pay for the broken window. By way of an apology, the Betas also had to care for the Alpha Phis' yard for the next year.

Kesey's fraternity membership was significant to him. It did not define his identity—his personality was too big and his interests too wide for that—but it was an important part of who he was at college and subsequently. Many of his closest male Prankster friends were fraternity guys and alumni from the University of Oregon, including Mike Hagen (Beta Theta Pi) and George Walker (Phi Delta Theta). Kesey's enthusiasm for his fraternity might strike one as odd given his standing as a countercultural rebel and their reputation as preppy bastions of conservatism. But that is to misunderstand the man and his times. Kesey would have had no qualms embracing the Greek life, and no problems fitting in with his fraternity brothers.

Fraternities and sororities were an important part of campus life in the 1950s. They were often at the heart of the social life on campus, and they usually maintained strong links to college athletics and student government. To a certain extent, if you wanted to be popular or a powerful player on a college campus, the easiest route for a man was to join a fraternity. And for those women looking for a husband with good standing and economic prospects, one way to encounter likely candidates was to join a sorority and mix with fraternity men. But the women had to be careful. According to Nicholas L. Syrett's study of white college fraternities, pre–World War II models of masculine decorum were fading fast.[53] By the fifties, the more women a fraternity man had sex with, the more prestige and respect he got from his fraternity brothers. Promiscuity would have been frowned upon in earlier, more "gentlemanly" times, but in the 1950s it was increasingly a mark of a man's masculinity. This put women in an impossible position, faced with men looking to get laid, but also looking for a virgin to marry. Kesey and Faye were already a couple by the time Kesey joined his fraternity, but this did not stop him from pursuing or occasionally seeing other girls. The difference between him and his Beta brothers was that Kesey did not try to hide his behavior from Faye, something that amazed his peers. A later friend, Larry McMurtry, recalled that "Kesey didn't see jealousy of any sort as a problem. How could it be a problem?"[54] This arrangement—mutual freedom to see other people outside of their relationship—seems to have been something that Kesey and Faye worked out early in their time together, and it is an arrangement that they maintained throughout their marriage. They were certainly not "swingers," but the open nature of their relationship would have positioned Kesey and Faye outside the social and cultural norms of the 1950s.

Kesey set himself apart from his Beta brothers in other ways. For a start, he did not drink, a major social faux pas in a world in which "the men who could drink the most," notes Nicholas Syrett, "were the most accomplished and the most masculine."[55] Alcohol greased the Greek social wheels at the University of Oregon, just as elsewhere. Whether champagne during pledge week, beer at the numerous frat house parties, or hipflasks fueling the talent show skits, alcohol was everywhere. Kesey accepted the rare sip of beer, but he only got drunk twice during his time at college, and one of those nights was his bachelor party.

The fact that Kesey was accepted into the Betas in spite of his strange (non)drinking habits should tell us something about his raw likability, but also something about his standing at the time. As one of the best wrestlers on the University of Oregon squad, Kesey possessed impeccable athletic credentials. On this point alone he would have been welcomed into the Betas, drinker or not. And as one of the most successful jocks on campus, no one would have doubted Kesey's masculinity. His interest in theater may have raised a few eyebrows among the more hypermasculine of his wrestling and fraternity buddies, but probably not as much as one might think. When Kesey attended college in the mid-1950s, television was still in its infancy—his family had a set, but Faye's did not—and so the practice of families and friends making their own entertainment still persisted in popular culture. Performing skits and singing songs also had a long tradition in Greek life, and so Kesey's skills and experience would have been welcomed by the Betas, not seen as "sissy."

Kesey's first couple of years at college had been a resounding personal success. By the end of his second year his grades were not much to shout about, but that was mostly because he had thrown himself into an astonishing number of extracurricular activities. He was a fraternity man and an accomplished performer, and he held an important position in student affairs (he was chairman of the Exchange Assembly, a crosscampus organization). He was a celebrated athlete, and despite being something of an odd duck in some aspects of his libertarian take on life, Kesey was popular both with the ladies and with his fraternity brothers. He was also a leader among his peers—there was talk at one time of his running for student body president—and possessed of a gregarious character to which others were drawn. Even his professors recognized this personal magnetism. "Kesey was a great personality and powerful presence," recalled George Wickes, one of Kesey's English professors. "Quite charismatic. Magnetic. He always had people around him. He always attracted people that way."[56] Speech professor Robert Clark, then Dean of Liberal Arts, taught Kesey in an "Introduction to Rhetoric" course. Clark was particularly impressed with Kesey's abilities, recalling that although the young student was inclined to stray from the given assignment, he always performed "brilliantly" in the classroom. On one memorable occasion, the whole class burst into a round of spontaneous applause after one of Kesey's presentations, something Clark had never seen happen before.[57] After experiences like this, it must have been with some confidence that Kesey decided to test his abilities on a bigger stage—Hollywood. As it turned out, that confidence had to withstand a trying couple of months.

Ken Kesey performing a magic trick for the senior ball at the University of Oregon in 1955. As teenagers, Kesey and his younger brother, Chuck, used to travel around with their father to dairy cooperative producers' meetings, where they would perform a magic act for all the other farm kids.

(Image courtesy Special Collections and University Archives, University of Oregon Libraries)

Ken Kesey and dummy performing a ventriloquist act in the annual variety show at the University of Oregon in 1955. Kesey subsidized his college expenses by performing at various venues and fraternity houses in Eugene. His father claimed that Ken could "attract a crowd in a desert."

(Image courtesy Special Collections and University Archives, University of Oregon Libraries)

Ken Kesey dressed as a fortune teller in his freshman year (1954) for an annual student carnival at the University of Oregon. Kesey's theatrical flair predated his turn to literature toward the end of his college career. In later years Kesey often referred back to his time as a magician as the root of his writing career, recognizing that there is an element of trickery in telling a good story.
(Image courtesy Special Collections and University Archives, University of Oregon Libraries)

Ken Kesey's main athletic pursuit was wrestling. He was second in the state in his division as a high school wrestler, a feat that helped him gain admittance to the University of Oregon, where he established himself as one of their best grapplers. Here, standing in the middle of the back row, he poses with the wrestling team in his freshman year, 1954.

(Image courtesy Special Collections and University Archives, University of Oregon Libraries)

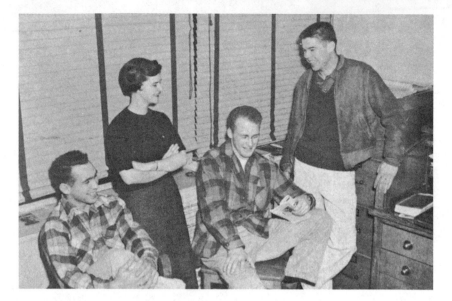

In his sophomore year at the University of Oregon, Kesey wrote a weekly column called "Gulliver's Trifles" for the university newspaper, the *Daily Emerald*. Here he sits in the *Emerald* office with fellow columnists Bud Hinkson and Bobbye Harris, and cartoonist Bob Fudge. This position was Kesey's first serious literary endeavor.

(Image courtesy Special Collections and University Archives, University of Oregon Libraries)

Kesey appeared in a number of stage productions at the University of Oregon, including *One Touch of Venus* in 1954, *Captive at Large* in 1955, and *Macbeth*, shown here, in 1956. Kesey appears as Ross, one of the noblemen on the right. He thought he deserved the lead, but the director, Horace C. Robinson, thought otherwise.

(Image courtesy Special Collections and University Archives, University of Oregon Libraries)

Kesey wrestling in his junior year at the University of Oregon. In a four-year career with the Oregon Ducks, Kesey was easily their top wrestler in the 177-pound division. He won all but six of his thirty-three starts in Oregon's trademark green-and-yellow kit, placing third in the Pacific Coast Intercollegiate (PCI) wrestling championship in his sophomore year. Kesey went undefeated in his senior year, only losing in the final of the PCI championship, dislocating his shoulder in the process. The injury kept him out of the Vietnam War.

(Image courtesy Special Collections and University Archives, University of Oregon Libraries)

Kesey was a proud member or the Beta Theta Pi fraternity at the University of Oregon. He often wrote, directed, and starred in the Betas' efforts at the annual Duck Preview Vodvil variety show. In 1957 the Betas performed a musical adaptation of the biblical story of creation, with Kesey as the narrator, backed by a male-voice chorus. Kesey appears at right, in blackface and white wig, reading from the bible.

(Image courtesy Special Collections and University Archives, University of Oregon Libraries)

Kesey and Faye moved into no. 9 Perry Lane, close to the Stanford University campus, in 1959. Perry Lane was in an unincorporated section of Menlo Park, on land that still belonged to the university. The small timber-frame cabins on the Lane were built by the U.S. Army to house soldiers during World War I. By the 1950s the Lane had become the bohemian center of Palo Alto, home to graduate students, artists, writers, and dancers.

(Photo by Hank Kranzler; image courtesy Hank Kranzler estate)

2

From Hollywood to the
Written Word

In June 1955 Kesey set out for the bright lights of Los Angeles.[1] It was
an obvious though still courageous move for anyone who wanted to break
into the movie business. Amateur stage productions and magic shows at
kids' birthday parties were all well and good, but for someone as ambitious as Kesey they were nothing compared to the chance of appearing on
the big screen. He was a regular at the movie theater, usually catching a
couple of shows a week, sometimes sneaking into drive-ins in the trunk
of Chuck's car if cash was tight. In his freshman year he saw *Phantom of
the Rue Morgue*, *Johnny Guitar*, *The Long Wait*, *Suspense*, *Knock on Wood*,
Flight to Tangiers, and lots more besides. Kesey admired Lawrence Olivier
in *Hamlet* and Rock Hudson in *Magnificent Obsession*, and lesser-known
players such as Lon Chaney. But if there was one actor Kesey wished to
emulate, it would have been Marlon Brando. Brando's brooding, rebellious, hypermasculine lead role in *The Wild One* set him apart from his
Hollywood peers in the 1950s, and like so many young men of his generation, Kesey wanted to be just like him.[2]

Kesey had talent to spare, and he knew it. His bluster could sometimes
be overwhelming, but he was charming and likable enough that people
forgave his youthful hubris. In Oregon, Kesey was already a Big Man on
Campus, but he lusted after more, seeking fame and fortune just as avidly
as his father sought uranium in the Ochoco Mountains. The young Kesey
was tirelessly ambitious. He sent poetry and short stories out to publishers, wrote to people like Red Skelton and Robert Newton for advice, and

occasionally dreamt up crazy schemes to get his name in the papers, such as starving himself while sitting atop a flagpole. All of which ultimately came to naught. Going to Hollywood was the next step, but it was a big step for this nineteen-year-old Oregonian, an adventure into the unknown. Even though he and Faye had relatives living in California to ease their move to the state, Kesey struggled to adapt to his new surroundings. Here was a country boy in one of the biggest cities in the world, far removed from his semirural existence back in Oregon. You can take the man out of the country, as they say, but you can't take the country out of the man. To Kesey's credit, and probably to the detriment of his chances, he stubbornly refused to be anybody except himself. But he still had to contend with the phoniness of everybody else. After being there just a few days, he met an actor who looked and acted as if he were twenty-five, even though he was actually forty. Kesey thought this typical of Hollywood as a whole: soulless, shallow, self-obsessed, and fake. It was an attitude about the place that he would never fully renounce. "There's been a one-step removal from our [human] connection to life," Kesey said years later. "I'll tell you where you can see it: Go to LA."[3]

Hollywood in the 1950s was a strange place and that's for sure. The late forties had seen the place shaken by an anticommunist witch hunt. House Un-American Activities Committee (HUAC) hearings in 1947 had called numerous actors, producers, screenwriters, and movie industry professionals to testify about their supposed links to the Communist Party of America. Ten individuals, the "Hollywood Ten," refused to cooperate with the hearings, and they were jailed and fired as a result. The major studios, scared that their profits would be hit by the bad publicity surrounding the hearings, made little effort to stand up for their own. Caught in the harsh glare of Cold War hysteria, the studios responded by embarking upon their own campaign to root out communism in the movie industry. A secret blacklist was the result. Hundreds lost their careers. By the time Kesey arrived in Hollywood in the summer of 1955 the "Hollywood Ten" hearings were long past, but the effects of the blacklist were still being felt. Had anyone chosen to ask, Kesey would have been wise to reveal his own anticommunist leanings, but at this lowly stage in his career, no one really cared.

Beyond its troubles with Cold War politics, Hollywood also had to cope with a new challenger in the world of popular entertainment: television.

The new medium had enjoyed a remarkably quick rise in the hearts of Americans since World War II. At war's end in 1945, only 6,500 sets existed in the United States, most of them in bars in major metropolitan areas like New York and Chicago. By 1948 that figure was above a million, by 1950 over 11 million, and by the time NBC became America's first nationwide broadcaster in 1951, they were serving approximately 15 million television sets, the vast majority now in American homes. By 1960 that number was close to 70 million television sets in roughly nine out of ten households across the nation.[4] As the percentage of Americans owning televisions rose year by year, so too did the number of TV stations broadcasting into their living rooms. In 1952, for example, there were only 108 TV stations across the land. By just the following year there were 334, more than three times as many, and that number continued to grow throughout the decade.[5] The effect on the movie industry was dramatic. It started to lose many of its best writers, actors, and directors to television. It also lost much of its audience. Between 1945 and 1950, the number of people going to the local movie theater on a weekly basis dropped from 60 million to 40 million.[6] By the end of the decade the number was roughly half what it had been at the start. As a result, Hollywood made far fewer movies per year than it had the previous decade, and the major studios—those that survived—began making shows for television or renting out their studio facilities to new television production companies.

Kesey, our young hopeful, found an industry in flux, but not necessarily in decline. The movie studios responded to their changing fortunes by catering to a new and lucrative audience: teenagers. Drive-in movie theaters flourished in the 1950s, perfect locations to view the science fiction or epic classics of the era (and escape from the prying eyes of your parents). Kesey, Faye, Chuck, and their friends spent many a Friday or Saturday night at the local drive-in, the same as millions of other fifties teenagers across the land. Movies featuring rock and roll, the new form of music that was sweeping the nation, attracted huge young audiences in the second half of the decade. Kesey particularly enjoyed *Blackboard Jungle*—he saw it at least twice—but he was never that big on rock and roll (one of his favorites from this period was the traditional ballad "Sylvie," sung by Harry Belafonte). Also enormously popular were movies featuring Marilyn Monroe, James Dean, and Marlon Brando.

Marilyn Monroe was in the process of divorcing Joe DiMaggio by the time Kesey arrived in Tinseltown in the summer of 1955. Kesey saw her in *The Seven Year Itch* shortly after he got there. He loved it. James Dean, the "first American teenager," was still alive at this time. *East of Eden* had come out in April, further enhancing Dean's reputation, but he died in September in a car wreck, a month before the release of his best movie, *Rebel without a Cause.* Kesey was certainly a fan of Dean's. He thought that the young actor was fabulous in *Rebel without a Cause,* and he was as shocked as everybody else at the news of his death (Kesey was only four years younger than Dean). Interestingly, though Kesey mourned Dean's passing, he also admired the young actor for living "fast," for pushing his life to the limits. Kesey thought that living an adventurous or reckless life was a way to make one's existence somehow more meaningful. To a certain extent, that "live fast, die young" philosophy has always been romanticized in American culture—cowboys, gangsters, frontiersmen, warriors—but it would not have won mainstream approval in the 1950s when the phrase entered the lexicon.[7] Fred and Geneva Kesey, and others of their generation who had lived through the Great Depression and World War II, would have found the sentiment offensive and associated it with juvenile delinquency and hedonistic ne'er-do-wells like the Beat writers and their followers. Jack Kerouac's classic *On the Road* (1957) is the decade's clearest expression of this existential philosophy. In one of its most famous passages, Kerouac's character, Sal Paradise, speaks in praise of the fast-living Dean Moriarty (Neal Cassady) and others like him: "[T]he only people for me are the mad ones," proclaimed Sal, "the ones who are mad to live, mad to talk, mad to be saved, desirous of everything at the same time, the ones that never yawn or say a commonplace thing, but burn, burn, burn like fabulous yellow roman candles exploding like spiders across the stars."[8]

Kesey respected James Dean, but Marlon Brando was his favorite. Brando was still riding high on the success of two recently released now-classic movies, *The Wild One* (1953) and *On the Waterfront* (1954). Kesey had watched both of these films back in Oregon. A big fan, he correctly predicted that Brando would win an Oscar for his performance in *Waterfront.* Brando was important to Kesey, and not just as an actor to admire. The celebrated Brando had first made his critical mark on theater at the age of just nineteen, when he was voted Broadway's Most Promising

Actor in 1944. It took him only three years to fulfill that promise, achieving stardom with his performance in Tennessee Williams's play *A Streetcar Named Desire* (1947) in his early twenties. Moving to the movies in the early 1950s, Brando quickly became one of Hollywood's hottest stars, nominated for an Academy Award for Best Actor for four years straight, 1951, 1952, 1953, and 1954. Brando represented a model of cool, youthful success that Kesey was determined to emulate.

Kesey's connections to the upper levels of Hollywood were nonexistent. Though he had a few names and friends to contact, such as one Dr. Lumsden, Kesey had no guaranteed work or even auditions lined up. He had neither permanent accommodation arranged, nor any real idea of how to break into the system. This was not going to be easy. For the first time in Kesey's life, he was not the biggest fish in the pond. He was fortunate to find an agent—a Mrs. Jean Haliburton from Texas—who was willing to work with him, and she sent him away with instructions to work on a three-minute scene in preparation for auditions at the studios. Within a week or so, he had an audition at Paramount, but no immediate offers of work came out of it. Don't call us, we'll call you.

Kesey stayed with friends at first—the Kirkpatrick family—but he soon found an apartment in the Irish/Italian neighborhood of Angelino Heights, one of the oldest neighborhoods in LA, not too far from where today's LA Dodgers' baseball stadium is located. Kesey made friends with the people in his apartment block, including sixty-four-year old Mrs. Mason, who would give Kesey tea and muffins when he stopped by to visit. Mrs. Mason was a spiritualist. Much to Kesey's amusement, when he tried out a couple of his old magic mind tricks on her he almost had her convinced that he was clairvoyant. Kesey also made friends with a couple of Mexican sisters living next door (he discovered a peephole into their apartment). Sometimes Kesey would just walk the sunbaked streets of the neighborhood, peeking in the open windows of apartments, listening to all the strange accents and observing the hot, sweaty occupants sitting in their underwear watching television. Living in a mixed-ethnicity neighborhood would have been very new to Kesey. Springfield was about as ethnically vanilla as it was possible to get, so growing up his interaction with anybody from a different background would have been very limited.

While he waited for more auditions, Kesey read, wrote a lot, tanned himself in the hot July sun, and tried various lotions and potions to stop his hair falling out. The few opportunities that came his way in the first weeks of July turned out to be nothing of the sort. When he went to read for a part as a prizefighter, he was told they wanted a Latin American for the role. On another occasion, someone called to tell him that he had an audition that afternoon at the Goldwyn studios for a part as a football player. But before Kesey left the house, another call told him that the part had been cut. Despite these disappointments, Kesey remained confident in his abilities, though this was probably a self-protective necessity in these frustrating circumstances. Daily calls to his agent produced nothing but promises of a return call the next day, and as July dragged to a close, an impatient Kesey began planning a comedy routine to perform in an amateur TV talent show as a way to promote himself.

The first week of August brought some progress and a little excitement for Kesey. While visiting some of the major studios with a couple of friends, Kesey met Debra Paget, John Derek, and Cecil B. DeMille on the set of *The Ten Commandments*. DeMille was one of the biggest directors in Hollywood at this time, famous for his epic, lavish productions. His spectacular circus movie *The Greatest Show on Earth* had won best picture at the Oscars in 1952. *The Ten Commandments* was his last film, but it was one of his most extravagant and one of his most successful, earning more money in its year of release, 1956, than any other movie. It featured Yul Brynner as pharaoh Ramses II, and Charlton Heston as Moses miraculously parting the Red Sea (with some three hundred thousand gallons of water). On another set, Kesey mingled with Mitzi Gaynor, Doris Day, and Jimmy Stewart on a shoot for *The Man Who Knew Too Much*. Kesey also spied that movie's famous director, Alfred Hitchcock, on the other side of the lot, but he never got a chance to talk to him.

Kesey was mixing with Hollywood royalty, but he was still very much a pauper visiting from outside the castle walls. An actor he had met on the set of the *Ten Commandments*, known as Cap, took an interest in Kesey and invited him to his apartment after the shoot for a "talk." Kesey's freshman roommate, Boyd Harris, witnessed the incident. "[U]p drives a guy in a red Thunderbird convertible," Harris remembered. "The driver said, 'Ken. Ken. Ken. Come here,'" and then offered to help Kesey break into the movies.[9] Both Harris and Kesey suspected that Cap had something else in mind besides talking, but Kesey hopped into the convertible anyway, hoping that he might have finally found a useful contact. Once at the apartment, Cap tried to seduce Kesey, but Kesey faked an earache and left without taking a turn on the older man's casting couch. Unwilling to give up the lead completely, Kesey returned the next day to offer his friendship as long as Cap promised not to make any more advances.

Kesey's encounter with Cap was his first introduction to the sleazy underbelly of the movie industry, where sex was the common currency, where roles had a carnal price, and where naked ambition was the norm. Despite its glitzy exterior, taking one's chances in Hollywood was still very much the "trip through a sewer in glass-bottomed boat" that Wilson Mizner had declared it back in the 1920s. Director Darryl F. Zanuck was known as the "king of the casting couch," but there were plenty of pretenders to the throne.[10] Women bore the brunt of the abusive casting practice, where the line between consent and exploitation was woefully thin. But some women played the game to their own advantage and won, perpetuating the whole sorry charade in the process. The practice was widespread and a matter of open discussion and ridicule. During a laborious day filming *The Ten Commandments*, one desperate actress was supposed to have exclaimed, "Who do you have to fuck to get *out* of this picture?"[11] Kesey was not alone in facing homosexual advances from male industry insiders. Superstar talent agent Henry Willson (who represented Rock Hudson, Robert Wagner, and Natalie Wood) was a notoriously manipulative figure who was not above luring his male clients onto his couch for sexual favors.[12] Some accounts even have him blackmailing his own clients by threatening to reveal their homosexual trysts to the press.[13] Kesey was lucky to have Mrs. Halliburton for an agent, even though she never really found him any work.

Hollywood had suffered (earned?) a reputation as a place full of sin and fornication since the 1920s when a series of well-publicized sex scandals exposed its sordid secrets to the world. The arrest and trial of Fatty Arbuckle for rape and manslaughter in 1921–22 was one of the best-known scandals of the period, but it was by no means the only one. The 1950s proved to be no different. As the decade began, Swedish actress Ingrid Bergman, a married woman, had an affair and a baby with Roberto Rossellini, who was also married, the director of her latest film. When the affair became public, Bergman was denounced on the floor of the U.S. Senate as an "instrument of evil" and an "apostle of degradation" by conservative Democratic senator Edwin Johnson of Colorado. The disgrace forced Bergman to retreat back to Europe. An even bigger scandal erupted in mid-decade when the daughter of Hollywood superstar Lana Turner was accused of murdering Turner's mobster boyfriend. The case went all the way to trial and won international attention when Lana Turner dramatically took to the stand to defend her daughter's actions. She claimed that her daughter was just trying to protect her mother from a violent assault. Turner's performance as a witness helped win her daughter an acquittal. It also boosted her own flagging career and helped sell tickets to her big comeback movie, *Peyton Place* (1958). Only in Hollywood!

Short of such publicity, Kesey was still desperate for any sort of break. Much as he wanted to work in the movies, he would have been quite happy to settle for television (where he actually had quite a bit of experience). The beginning of August 1955 found Kesey honing his act in preparation for an appearance on a TV talent show. After so many setbacks, he relished the opportunity to show his stuff in a setting that he thought might finally get him noticed (even though the contest was held in the garage of a car lot). He performed twice, once at ten on Saturday morning and then again after midnight. Nothing he tried seemed to get the audience going. At one point he walked over to the camera and cleaned the lens with a cloth, succeeding in shaking up the cameraman but not the audience, which remained as impassive as ever. Though his friends told him that he looked good on TV, the sound was bad and the audience reception cold. It was a big disappointment. A despondent Kesey packed up his stuff and took off, heading south down the coast road searching for solace in the cool air of the night.[14]

By the time he returned to LA a few days later, his lack of success and the approaching summer's end had tempered the high expectations that had originally fueled his stay. Though he continued to do the occasional writing—finishing a short story he called "Boom-Boom at the Beach"— he now spent most of his time relaxing with friends and thinking of home. There were no more daily calls to Mrs. Haliburton and no more talent shows. Kesey and Boyd Harris went on a couple of adventures to Mexico, where they spent most of their time watching bullfights, chasing girls, and dabbling in the seedier side of life. On the first of these trips, Kesey bought some pornography from a store that happened to be offering twenty-five dollars for well-written pornographic stories that it would mimeograph and sell to its more literary customers. Ever one to spot an opportunity to utilize his talents, Kesey wrote a story about "the venereal adventures of one Dan Iron,"[15] described by Harris as "this terrible nasty sleazy thing that ends in orgasmic death."[16] Unimpressed, the store owner offered the young author five dollars for the story, but Kesey turned him down, choosing instead to scatter his erotic efforts to the wind as he and Harris set off on the long drive home. Accompanying Kesey and Harris on the ride north ride was a parrot that Kesey had bought in Tijuana. They smuggled the animal across the U.S. border in the back of the car, but the parrot died within days of leaving its home country, mimicking Kesey's summer dreams of stardom. Kesey buried it surreptitiously in Forest Lawn Cemetery in the Hollywood Hills.

CAMPUS WONDER BOY

By the end of the summer, Kesey was back in Oregon, happy to resume his high-profile campus existence. Hollywood's doors had remained closed to him, but the audacity of his youthful efforts to break them down only emboldened his confidence on his home turf. At the University of Oregon at least, his star was already bright enough that work came his way un-invited. Before the fall quarter had even started, Bud Hinkson, president of the student association, asked Kesey to write and direct a skit for the university's orientation assembly. Kesey threw something together quickly, and the performance went well on the day, but the larger significance might be that Kesey got a real taste for the director's chair.[17]

Kesey turned his attention to preparing for the University Theater's production of *Macbeth*. When it came time for casting, he was sure that he would do well, thinking himself the best actor by far. The director, one Horace C. Robinson, was not as impressed with Kesey as Kesey was with himself. Robinson offered him the part of Ross, a significant role in the play but not the lead that Kesey believed he deserved. He briefly fantasized about turning the part down in a show of bravado, but in the end he accepted it with good grace. He worked hard to master the role, and despite some dress rehearsal skitters, he seemed happy with his performance when the play opened on Friday, December 2. The show itself garnered such good reviews that the play was resurrected for another weekend of performances the following February. The program made much of Kesey's summer adventures. "He has also tried his hand at motion pictures and T.V. in Hollywood," it reported. Given what we know of his time in Los Angeles, this was something of an overstatement, but—to steal one of the more famous lines from *Cuckoo's Nest*—it was the truth, even if it didn't happen.

Kesey's next venture put him back in the place he felt most comfortable: in charge. After the success of the U of O orientation skit, Hinkson asked Kesey to write and direct a play that would give high school students "a good sample of college entertainment," as the program put it, and "provide a realistic glimpse of Oregon's personality."[18] This was essentially another promotional device for the university, but Kesey threw himself into the project as if it were his gateway to Broadway. Never one to aim low, Kesey produced a two-act musical, *Fall Term*, set on the U of O campus. The plot followed the adventures of a group of new students, one of whom, Big Deal Biscario, just happened to be an escaped convict from Alcatraz. Rod Vlasak—a fellow student—wrote the music, but everything else, including the lyrics to the songs, came from Kesey's pen.[19] He also did the casting (which included Faye as a nurse), made the sets, played a bit part in the show, promoted the play to high schools in Oregon and on the East Coast, and directed the whole affair. Kesey did most of the writing over Christmas break and the New Year, hurrying to get ready for the first rehearsal in mid-January.

Kesey barely had enough time to devote to the project. He was taking a full load of classes this semester, rehearsing for the second run of *Macbeth*, penning a column for the college newspaper, wrestling for the school, and writing short stories. Somehow he pulled the show together, and by mid-February it was time to run through the production in front of a panel made up of invited high school officials and college administrators. The previous year's show had generated so much controversy that it had been banned from some schools. As a result, Portland's public school officials had let it be known that they were unwilling to stage any more offerings from the University of Oregon that were not supervised by faculty.[20] After a viewing of the show, the panel instructed Kesey to remove any reference to liquor in the show and to cut the terms "rear-end," "low hips," and "sexy" from the script. He did as he was told, but not for the last time in his life, Kesey queried the wisdom of authority figures, blasting the decision in the *Daily Emerald*, the campus newspaper, suggesting it was based on fear rather than reason.[21] In the end, the show was a big success, winning over the crowds in Bend and in Eugene. John Herman, one of Kesey's Beta brothers, saw the show at the Mac Court in Eugene. It "was just incredible," Herman remembered. "It was mind-boggling, an extravaganza, a huge celebration of the University."[22]

Kesey found little time to rest on his laurels. As soon as the performances of *Fall Term* were over, he started working on his Beta Theta Pi's effort for the upcoming U of O Vodvil show. This year, his fraternity had chosen to do something out of the ordinary: a musical adaptation of the biblical story of creation with Kesey as the narrator, backed by a male-voice chorus. This was hardly typical humorous fare, and though the Betas made it to the finals, Kesey was bitterly disappointed when the show's organizers decided to place their performance in a special category, outside of the main competition. Kesey complained of being censored and forced to conform, sentiments made only worse when some of his fraternity brothers raised doubts about his plan to wear blackface for the performance. Ignoring his critics, he wore it anyway. This would not be the last time he would be accused of being racially insensitive—some critics felt that his portrayal of the black hospital porters in *Cuckoo's Nest* were stereotypical caricatures of African Americans, for example—but Kesey was never a racist at heart.

On the night of the performance, the Beta chorus trooped silently out onto the stage of the McDonald Theater. Kesey followed moments later, taking his place at center stage behind the lone microphone. If his plan had been to produce a stark contrast between the narrator and the crew cut, tuxedo-bedecked chorus, then he was more than successful. There he stood, wearing a long black coat, white shirt, and black lariat tie. With his blacked-up face framed by an Amish-like beard and a shock of receding white hair, he looked, if not exactly godlike, at least like a preacher from another planet. To a hushed audience, Kesey began reading from the Bible held in his left hand, gesturing with his right as the chorus began to sing. The piece was impressive, winning an award for Most Original and Excellent Performance, and praise from a reviewer who wrote, "the Betas added a serious note to the program with their excellent presentation of a difficult number."[23] None of which was good enough for an ambitious Kesey, who dismissed the award as unworthy of all their effort. He was hurt that his piece did not win the coveted Best Performance award.

Kesey's hectic schedule continued for the rest of the semester. Early in May, his play *Confinement* went into production with the University Theater. Kesey had written this piece the previous year, but it does not seem to have been a production to which he devoted much time thereafter. In mid-May he auditioned for the next U of O theater production but wasn't offered the part he wanted. The approach of his wedding day gave him little time to fret about this latest blow to his ego.

Kesey and Faye Haxby had been dating since junior high. She was quiet and shy—the opposite of Kesey—but there is no doubt that she was his dream girl: beautiful, supportive, compassionate, and enthusiastic about life. Kesey really loved and appreciated her, and thought that she brought out the best in him. While he enjoyed his "sport" with other girls, his love for Faye was something different altogether. She came from a family of relatively modest means who also lived in Springfield. Her father, Melvin, sometimes struggled to find work. Faye spent a lot of time with the Kesey family growing up. Who wouldn't? There was always something going on with the Keseys—golfing, hunting, football, wrestling, boxing, swimming in the river at the swinging bridge, riding the rapids in canoes, kite fights (with sharp pins on the kite frames intended to pop the balloons fixed to their tails)—and lots of gatherings and outings to which Faye was always invited. She was already a part of the Kesey family before she married into it.

After high school, while Kesey travelled the five miles from Springfield to Eugene to attend the U of O, Faye went sixty miles northward to Corvallis, where she enrolled at Oregon State College (OSC). She lived in Azalea House, a women's cooperative residence that had been opened in 1953 as part of an initiative to provide low-cost housing to students. Faye was also a member of Talons, a sophomore scholastic and service honorary club. For their first year and a half at college, she and Kesey maintained a long-distance relationship, though he often drove up to Corvallis in his old Ford to bring her home for the weekend or vacations. Faye came back from OSC for Christmas in late 1954, but she had some health problems and never went back for the spring semester. Instead she worked at the Darigold creamery and tried to get healthy. She would eventually transfer to the University of Oregon in the fall of 1955, majoring in dietetics.

Kesey had been planning on proposing to Faye for a while. By today's standards, he was pretty young—twenty—to be getting married, but not by the standards of the mid-1950s, which found most people marrying in their early twenties.[24] Kesey's friend Boyd had gotten married the previous year, setting the precedent for his old roommate to follow. In late October 1955, Kesey and his father drove over to Crescent Lake to buy the engagement ring, the best he could afford. And then, on Christmas day, in front of both families, Kesey gave Faye a large, wrapped package as a Christmas gift. Kesey, ever the prankster, had hidden the diamond ring deep inside the package. When Faye found it and realized what was happening, she blushed and started crying, placing the ring onto her finger with shaking hands. The wedding was planned for the following spring, May 20, 1956, at the First Congregational Church in Eugene. It almost didn't happen. When Kesey and Faye showed up at the courthouse to buy the license, the office was closed because of an election. With much begging and pleading, they finally found someone to help, but the clerk had to make a special license because the official ones were all locked away. The wedding went ahead, but it subsequently turned out that the license was invalid, so Kesey and Faye had to get officially married all over again later on.[25] Kesey had his bachelor party at the Beta house a few days before the wedding. Downing whatever was handed to him—gin, rum, beer, bourbon—he was quickly very drunk. He crawled under one of the house rugs and then peed out of one of the office windows. Staggering outside, he made his way over to the Gamma house, where he serenaded the occupants with poetry and a ragged version of "Danny Boy." His Beta brothers dragged him back to their house, where he passed out.

At the ceremony a few days later, Faye wore a long, flowing dress of her own creation; Kesey wore a white tuxedo and a black bow tie. The church was decorated with flowers: white snowballs and red peonies. Kesey's brother, Chuck, was the best man, with Boyd Harris and a few other Beta brothers acting as ushers. One of Faye's sisters acted as her matron of honor; the other, Myrna, was one of the bridesmaids, along with a selection of Faye's friends from school and college.[26] The cute kids acting as ring bearers and flower girls stole the show, just like at every wedding. While the packed church awaited Kesey's arrival—he was late—they were entertained by a male tenor singing "Believe" and "Whither Thou Goest." Kesey winked at Faye as she walked down the aisle arm in arm with her father. They exchanged vows, put rings on each other's fingers, and the deed was done. Married. Well, actually, that is not quite true. Unbeknownst to most of the people in the church, Kesey and Faye were already married, having previously eloped. Even in marriage, Kesey chose to rebel.

At the reception in the Wheeler Room at the church, guests sipped coffee or punch while munching on cake and listening to the Beta chorus serenade the happy couple with "Without a Song," a tune dating from the late 1920s but popularized by Perry Como in the early 1950s. When Kesey and Faye got ready to leave, they found their car—a 1953 Nash that was a wedding present from Fred and Geneva—decorated with crepe-paper ribbons and smeared with red, yellow, and blue paint. It was also disabled (one of the Beta brothers had loosened three spark plugs). Once they got the car going, Kesey and Faye headed to the Pacific Coast, where they planned to honeymoon. They stopped at Cannon Beach (which is a little seaside resort to the west of Portland), then on up to Astoria, where they went to see a local landmark, the Astor Column. After that, they caught the ferry across the bay to Washington and hung around there for a few hours before making the return crossing. Once back in Oregon, they drove south down the coast road, ending up at Cannon Beach again. They rented a cabin for the next few days, spending their time getting tanned on the beach, fishing, and relaxing. They were back at their place, 1234 Fifth Avenue, Eugene, by May 26, to start preparing for another summer in Los Angeles.

Hollywood: The Return

By June 20 Kesey was back in LA. This was another speculative quest. If the right opportunity came his way, then Kesey was prepared to seize it and run with it. If not, finishing college was not a bad option to fall back on. This time he was joined in California by Faye and by Boyd Harris, his old roommate from the U of O. Harris also brought along his recent bride, Sandy, to share in the adventures. None of them had any immediate prospects for auditions, so Faye and Boyd found themselves some other work while Kesey determined that he would stay at home and write. He also signed up for night classes at UCLA, as did Harris and Cap, Kesey's acquaintance from the previous year. Kesey quickly discovered that things were not going to be any easier the second time around. Jean Haliburton, the agent, seemed disinterested in doing much to further Kesey's ambitions, and Dr. Lumsden, who had made calls on Kesey's behalf in the past, seemed unwilling to do the same again. Within a week of his arrival, doubt and depression were eroding Kesey's usual optimism and exuberance. His confidence was shaken even more when Dr. Lumsden told Harris that he did not think Kesey was going to make it, and that he had seen people with much more talent than Kesey fail in the movie industry. Wounded, Kesey reminded himself that people with half his talent had made it all the way to the top, but this was small consolation when he was so obviously all the way down at the bottom. He sought strength from the one individual whom he felt he could always rely on: himself.

But Kesey still needed help and at this point Cap was the only one offering to do anything. The situation did not sit well with Kesey, given the previous year's events, but he had no choice but to endure Cap's continuing advances on the off chance that the older man would live up to his grand promises. Kesey doubted that Cap was being sincere, but he could not be sure because he seemed to mock and joke about everything. This was obviously a friendship of convenience for Kesey, and not a very good one thus far. Cap did eventually arrange to go to a studio with Kesey, but after an incident when Kesey forgot to make a late-night telephone call to Cap's mother requesting help after his car had broken down, Cap got mad and stood Kesey up. The studio meeting fell through and the odd friendship fizzled out.

Help then came in the bizarre form of a man called Gene Maltese, someone Harris had met on the street one afternoon and invited to stay at his house. The man immediately settled into Harris's home as if it were his own and demanded hospitality as if Harris and Sandy were his servants. Summoned by Harris, Kesey arrived later that first evening to encounter this loud, insensitive braggart, playing his guitar, trying to sing, and spouting off to no one in particular. Over the next few days, Maltese succeeded in getting on everybody's nerves, particularly when he used the small apartment to practice for a *Moulin Rouge* audition that he ultimately flunked.

However, Maltese had one saving grace, and that was his tenacious capacity for self-promotion. Kesey was amazed to watch this fearless character work the phone for an afternoon and generate more leads than he had been able to in a month. One of these calls led to a meeting with an acting coach called Griffith, the nephew of D. W. Griffith, the so-called father of film who had directed the controversial first cinematic masterpiece,

The Birth of a Nation, back in 1915. Kesey tagged along with Maltese and managed to impress the younger Griffith enough to be invited to meet with him again the following day. An argumentative Maltese got no such invitation, succeeding only in annoying Griffith to the point of anger. Within a week or so, Kesey and his friends got together and decided that Maltese had to go. A group of them cornered him at Harris and Sandy's apartment. Kesey tore into him, others cussed and shouted, while even Sandy landed a few low blows. Maltese got the message and left, thus ending an irritating though colorful episode.

Griffith invited Kesey to participate in his actors' workshop. Kesey took Faye along, and they sat and watched some other performers go through their paces. When it was their turn, the Keseys ran through a routine that they had put together over the previous couple of days. They both made mistakes—flubbing lines and missing cues—but Griffith was impressed enough to ask them both to join his clientele. He was particularly impressed with Faye, telling Kesey that she was a very saleable commodity. Kesey was encouraged by Griffith's enthusiasm but troubled by the price tag of twenty-two dollars and fifty cents per month that went with it. As a comparison, the rent for their apartment, including utilities, was just sixty dollars per month. Desperate for any sort of opening, though, Kesey and Faye decided to sign up despite the high price, and joined the workshop at the end of June.

After just a month of classes, Kesey was increasingly concerned that the workshop was a waste of money. While the classes themselves were enjoyable, Griffith had so far failed to generate much in the way of work or even auditions. Kesey had also come to dislike Griffith personally, particularly when the old man criticized his work. Kesey never would learn to take criticism easily, but the conflict between him and Griffith was as much about his mounting frustration as it was about anything else. July had been a particularly difficult month. With no obvious progress being made, and no help from any quarter, Kesey was feeling listless, gaining weight and writing little. He was increasingly disheartened by the prospect of another summer in Los Angeles slipping by without much to show for it. His one job that month had been as a model for a drawing class. He had spent a day sitting in a series of strange positions in front of a class of about twenty people. He received twelve dollars and a stiff neck for his troubles, as well as plenty of posing time to mull over his predicament.

August, at last, brought an audition and a break. The audition was not a very promising one—an open session at the Hal Roach studios—but at least it was better than posing naked in front of a bunch of art students. Kesey, Faye, and hundreds of other contenders turned up, hoping to get themselves noticed, but no one made the grade, at least as far as Kesey could tell. The break came shortly thereafter, through a combination of luck and opportunism. One Tuesday, Faye's day off, she and Kesey visited an agency. While in the office, Kesey overheard a conversation between the agent and a writer on the other end of the phone. The agent told the writer that some guy at a studio by the name of Newt Arnold was looking for a story about American Indians, and a quick-witted Kesey memorized the producer's name and ran back to his apartment and started typing.[27]

Kesey based his story—titled "Sunset at Celilo"—on the real-life struggle then faced by the Celilo Indians in northern Oregon. He knew that the government was in the process of building Dalles Dam on the Columbia River, an act that would destroy the spectacular Celilo Falls, submerge much of the traditional homelands of the area's native people, and put an end to their salmon-fishing practices. Kesey was familiar with the region, since his family had lived near there for a while, and they used to go to the Pendleton Round-Up every year, a rodeo that was held not too far away from the site of the dam. The young Kesey would occasionally see local American Indians standing on makeshift scaffolding over the churning water, using long tridents to spear the salmon that were trying to leap up the falls. He once saw a man with lipstick on his face like war paint, and blood on his face and shirt. Kesey had only limited contact with Native Americans otherwise. One of his teammates on the high school football team was a Native American student called Wayne Redhorse, a stocky character who earned Kesey's respect by playing with a cast on his arm throughout his senior year. A member of the U of O wrestling team was Native American, as was an older man by the name of Charlie Buzztree, who came to do odd jobs around the Kesey household when Ken was just a child. But that was about it, personally speaking. One particular encounter with a man he had never met, though, left a lasting impression on Kesey, shaping his perception of Native American culture and later influencing his depiction of Chief Bromden in *One Flew Over the Cuckoo's Nest*. Late one summer, the teenage Kesey was riding the bus home from the Round-Up when the police pulled it over to the side of the road, close to where the dam was being built. The traffic was all backed up because an Indian had apparently taken a knife between his teeth and charged out into the highway in some desperately futile gesture of resistance against the building of the dam. Tragic as the incident was—the man ran head-first into the grill of an oncoming diesel truck—Kesey saw it as an act of great bravery and fortitude. "It was really the beginning of *Cuckoo's Nest*—the notion of what you have to pay for a lifestyle," he recalled years later. "It started an appreciation in me for the Indian sense of justice and drama. I mean, it's dumb and nasty, but that's class, and the fact that he had a knife between his teeth, that's style."[28] Like a "fabulous yellow roman candle exploding across the sky," as Kerouac might say.

"Sunset at Celilo" foreshadowed many of the themes of Kesey's later novels. It featured a plot that pitted brother against brother, and underdog against authority. The main character, Jim, is headstrong, stubborn, and proud of his Indian heritage. It would be easy to make too much of a connection between Jim and Chief Bromden, but Jim is clearly an antecedent to some extent: a heroic Indian figure whose integrity and strength of character is set in stark contrast to the avaricious, duplicitous nature of the White Man. Kesey has Jim returning from a stint in the army to find the dam almost completed and the tribe resigned to their fate. Chief Tommy Thompson—a real-life figure, 103 years old at the time of Kesey's writing in 1956—had negotiated a financial settlement with the federal government, but Jim questions the real value of the expensive and gaudy consumer goods that it has bought. Jim's younger brother, Joey, thinks it a waste of everybody's time to try to save a cause that is already lost. The two brothers get into a fight, during which one of them accidentally falls into the churning waters of the falls and drowns, his death an obvious metaphor for the demise of his culture (and a precursor to Joe Ben's drowning scene in *Sometimes a Great Notion*). The story ends with the old men of the tribe watching the floodwaters rise over their ancient lands, until sunset when the falls are submerged under the calm waters of the new lake.[29]

Kesey presented the piece to Arnold, who told him it was not quite what the studio was looking for. Still, he encouraged Kesey to bring him some more of his work and Kesey quickly rattled off something else, this one called "War Chief Joseph." It was a well-researched, fictionalized account of the battles between the Nez Perce Indians and U.S. Army General

Howard (who is portrayed as an Indian-hating bible thumper who comes grudgingly to respect Chief Joseph). Again, this story was not to the studio's liking—clearly Hollywood was not yet ready to recast American Indians as the good guys in their Western fare—but Kesey's encounter with Arnold was the one bright spot in what would otherwise be another fruitless summer adventure. As in the previous year, Kesey had failed to find many opportunities to prove his mettle as an actor, but this time at least his screenwriting efforts had given him a chance to flex his talents as a writer. He would never completely relinquish his performative ambitions, but once he returned to Oregon for his senior year at college Kesey devoted more and more of his energies to writing. It was out of failure in Hollywood that Kesey the writer emerged.

THE YOUNG WRITER

As a child, Kesey always had the ability to write well, but it was not something he loved to do. He was not even much of a reader, preferring comics to books or the popular press, in part because he found them less pretentious. "A single *Batman* comic book is more honest than a whole volume of *Time* magazines," he explained to Gordon Lish in 1963, "because of their honest, open-handed bullshit."[30] This fascination with comics and superheroes would find free expression during the later Prankster era, from the Marvel-inspired murals that graced the interior of Further to the poster for the Acid Test graduation ceremony that featured a caped superhero with a steely jaw that Superman himself would have envied. But Kesey did not just read comics. By the time he got to college, he had definitely started reading more literature. He read Faulkner and clamored to hear him when he visited the U of O. He liked Hemingway enough to send him some of his own work. Hemingway wrote back and encouraged him to keep writing.[31] Kesey enjoyed a good Ray Bradbury sci-fi novel, and he was intrigued by J. D. Salinger's *Catcher in the Rye*. His favorite author at college was probably John Steinbeck. Kesey read *Tortilla Flats*, *The Grapes of Wrath*, and *East of Eden* one after the other in the spring semester 1955. He added *Sweet Thursday* to the list within a year. Maybe Kesey was reading all these books for a class, but regardless, he really enjoyed Steinbeck's gritty realism and easy writing style. He also admired Steinbeck's ability to tell a good powerful story without seeming like he was moralizing or preaching. Kesey certainly tried to emulate Steinbeck's style in his own early writings. One could even say that the fashion in which Kesey conveyed his antiauthoritarian message in *One Flew Over the Cuckoo's Nest* owed a debt to Steinbeck's nonconfrontational approach.

Kesey sometimes wrote for his high school newspaper and penned the occasional report for the *Darigold News* (a newssheet his father sometimes mimeographed for the co-op members). His earliest publication was a brief piece about a film shown in his science class—"It was a very educational picture, though some of the students, especially girls, thought it sort of 'erkey,'" he concluded—that was printed in a local Springfield newspaper in March 1949. The press continued to publish an occasional poem or letter from Kesey in the early 1950s, but it was not until his sophomore year at college that he embarked upon his most notable early literary endeavor: a weekly column called "Gulliver's Trifles" for the university newspaper, the *Daily Emerald*. Kesey's efforts in this column were usually fairly irreverent and somewhat random in their choice of topic. Some of them were laugh-out-loud funny, some a bit too clever for their own good, and more than a few read like they were written hurriedly as the print deadline approached. Mostly, they were quirky exercises in humorous fiction rather than journalism, a chance for Kesey to test his wit and vent his spleen on the printed page.

Kesey's columns usually focused on issues relating to college, though he sometimes addressed current events, and occasionally simply used the opportunity to tell a story about himself. Whatever he chose to write about, it was usually in a manner that allowed him plenty of creative freedom. His commentary, for example, on the university's plans to increase the number of parking lots on campus came in the form of a sarcastic fake letter signed by one "J. C. Feathernest, Pres. Eugene Taxi Lines."[32] Another fake letter, from one "Velma Dustigutt, President, WCTU," allowed Kesey to berate the student senate for its criticism of student drinking at college sporting events.[33] One particularly bizarre column addressed the then-burning issue of race and civil rights in the South by recounting the tale of a salesman who tries to sell an amazingly efficient team of cotton-picking monkeys to a poor southern farmer. The farmer refuses, explaining that "just as we start gittin' attached to 'em the damn Yankees would come down here, free 'em, edjecate 'em and put 'em to votin'."[34] Though Kesey excused himself in his introduction—"This story in no way reflects the beliefs of its writer"—the piece is in poor taste and would have struggled to get past an editor today. The fact that it was published in 1956 without a second thought says as much about the racial insensitivity of the times as it does about Kesey's judgment.

Accusations about Kesey's own insensitivity toward matters of race (and gender) would dog him for most of his life. While it is true that Kesey sometimes relied a little too heavily on one-dimensional stereotypes in his novels—perhaps intentionally—his greater sin probably lay in his inability to relinquish the language, humor, and imagery of his youth when such sensibilities were no longer considered socially acceptable. We might certainly fault Kesey on his use of stereotypes, but let us not condemn him as a racist (as some have done) on this point alone.[35] In actual fact, as a young man, Kesey was surprisingly enlightened on matters of race and civil rights, at a time and a place where such liberalism was not the norm. In a high school poem called "Oil and Water and Blood," for example, the young Kesey imagined two soldiers, one black, one white, stuck in a foxhole together during a firefight. Though they are initially hostile to each other, the black soldier heroically rescues the injured white man, getting himself shot in the process. He awakes to find a tube running from the arm of his foxhole companion into his own, a symbolic mixing of the blood, showing that the two share a common humanity much deeper than their skin color.[36] A second poem, called "Get You Together," further demonstrates Kesey's youthful commitment to racial and ethnic equality, calling upon people of all colors and creeds to join together to strive for a better future. Kesey always denied that he was in any way racist and he usually reacted to all such accusations with defensiveness. In the mid-1990s, when some students from the Naropa Institute, Colorado, complained that the black characters in his musical play *Twister* were stereotypical, he dismissed all such criticism as "PC BS."[37]

Such concerns were way in the future for the college-era Kesey. His early column in the *Daily Emerald* had given him a chance to test the waters as a writer, but his later screenwriting adventures in Hollywood during the summer of 1956 seem to have propelled him to take his craft more seriously. Back at the University of Oregon after that summer, Kesey submitted "Sunset at Celilo" as a proposal for a documentary television drama for his radio and TV writing class. A note to his professor, attached to the end of the story, reveals a very real concern for the plight of the

Celilo Indians, with Kesey stressing that the story was true even if his account was fictionalized. The professor, Dean Starlin, encouraged Kesey to do more with the piece, and so Kesey turned "Sunset at Celilo" into a screenplay. The plot was similar to the story, but there were a few significant differences: there was no love interest, for example, in the screenplay, and the ending was slightly different. Foreshadowing the style of *Cuckoo's Nest*, Kesey also introduced a narrative voice in the screenplay— "Wacanda Agua, the Great Spirit"- to tell the story from a Native American perspective and to link the various scenes together. It is not entirely clear what happened to this screenplay. In late February 1957, in what was likely a boastful moment of self-promotion, Kesey told the *Eugene Register-Guard* that the Otto Preminger agency was still trying to sell two screenplays that he had written while at UCLA.[38] In all likelihood, he was referring to "Sunset at Celilo" and, perhaps, "War Chief Joseph."

What we do know for sure is that Kesey increasingly focused on writing in the second half of his four years at the University of Oregon. His major required him to take a number of playwriting and TV screenwriting classes, but he began to feel increasingly constrained by the types of scripts that these courses demanded (*I Love Lucy*–like situation comedies or dramas in the style of Paddy Chayevsky, an Oscar- and Golden Globe–winning playwright whose work was influential during the 1950s "golden era of live television"). When Kesey started including too many descriptive passages in his assignments for these classes, one of his teachers suggested that he forget about stage direction and camera angles and concentrate on his fiction writing instead.

Kesey took a short story class from a professor called James B. Hall, a published poet and the author of *Not by the Door* (1954), a story about an Episcopalian clergyman and the conflict between his faith and his natural desires. Hall was a somewhat controversial character at the University of Oregon because he wore white shoes, a clear indication at the time, according to Kesey, that "you were either a faggot or a commie, or maybe both."[39] The class read a Hemingway short story called "Soldier's Home" about the struggles of Harold Krebs, a man trying to readjust to society after having fought in World War I. Toward the end of the story, Krebs's mother fixes him a meal of bacon and eggs and, not for the first time, tries to encourage him to leave the house and find a job. Hemingway described the event in his characteristically terse prose, "Krebs looked at the bacon fat hardening on his plate."[40] Hall pointed to this line and told the class, "Now that's it—there's the story, it's there in that line. Everything is built around it. You don't notice it as you read by it, but it takes effect inside of you."[41] It was a moment of epiphany for Kesey, a moment when, in his recollection, "a door opened up to me and it's never been closed."[42] What appealed most to Kesey about the insight that Hall provided was the idea that good literature and good magic employed similar simple tricks to great effect. "Without even noticing it, a writer, or I think magician, can work into his routine that essential trick," Kesey explained some forty years later. "You have contained within what seems to be simple, ordinary stuff, a really high-powered phrase that passes right by the reader, or the viewer, or the audience. But when the story takes effect, that little thing inside the person goes off like a bomb. At the very end of the story you find yourself very affected, and you can't put your finger on why."[43]

Hall was more than just a good teacher to Kesey. He recognized his young protégé's natural abilities and he encouraged him to utilize them. Hall told the local newspaper, the *Eugene Register-Guard*, that Kesey was a "sensitive writer [who] shows great promise."[44] At one point he actually told Kesey privately that he was an "artist," and that as such, he need not worry about his future. That is not something professors say to many of their students. Kesey never forgot the lessons that Hall passed along, and he remained forever grateful to his old teacher for revealing the magic of literature. "[He] really taught me the best things that I was ever taught about writing," Kesey reflected years later, "how wonderful it is."[45]

That fall term of 1956 was one of Kesey's busiest. He took twenty-one hours of classes (earning a 3.5 GPA for the term, his college best) in addition to working at his father's creamery, sometimes for forty hours per week. That would have been more than enough for most people but Kesey also continued to pen his column for the *Daily Emerald* and he wrote a play concerning safety for telephone linesmen (a piece commissioned by the Oregon Power Company—a utilities company—which hoped to turn it into an educational movie for their industry). More significant, Kesey began working on his first full-length work of fiction, "End of Autumn," a sporting novel that focused on the exploitation of college athletes by telling the tale of a football lineman who was having second thoughts about the game. By the middle of January 1957, a first draft of the book was finished, all 293 pages of it. It was set on an unnamed campus, though the appearance of familiar Eugene landmarks such as the millrace suggested that Kesey's imagination had not strayed too far from home. Hall agreed to help edit and revise the first draft, and an excited Kesey told a journalist that he hoped to have the book published "sometime in the spring."[46] It never happened. By September 1957 Kesey had resorted to offering publicists half the profits from the book in exchange for them agreeing to push his novel to publishers, but even this attracted no offers. "End of Autumn" never was published, to Kesey's eventual relief. "[B]y the time I had finished," Kesey told Beat scholar Tom Clark, "I had learnt so much in the course of the writing, that I knew that the novel really wasn't that good."[47]

After graduating from the University of Oregon in June 1957, Kesey spent another fruitless month in LA, knocking on the same doors that had remained closed to him the previous two summers. He was back in Oregon by August. At the end of the year, Kesey returned one more time to LA to talk to the agent who was handling his scripts—and to watch the University of Oregon football team play in the Rose Bowl—but this meeting with his agent proved as futile as all the others. At least his team won. Hollywood's resistance to the young Kesey's advances left a bad taste in his mouth that would never really leave him. Over the years, he would return again and again to LA to pursue various projects (including the making of the *Cuckoo's Nest* movie and his efforts to turn the footage of the 1964 bus trip into a movie), but he usually left disappointed and frustrated. Not a little bitterly, he told *Esquire* magazine in 1992, "I've never left LA with more than I came with."[48]

Kesey's first real publication, a short story titled "First Sunday of September," appeared in the *Northwest Review* in the fall of 1957, and that same season, with the encouragement of James Hall, Kesey applied for a Woodrow Wilson scholarship to take him to Stanford University to join Wallace Stegner's famed creative writing class. Kesey never would let go of the theatrical or cinematic aspirations of his youth, but for a while they took a back seat as he explored the world of letters and much beyond. Hollywood's loss was literature's gain.

3

Sin Hollow

THE HOODED TERROR

The extended Kesey clan loved nothing more than a good competition. Brother against brother, cousin against cousin, father against son; sports bound the family together. Family gatherings often featured wrestling, boxing, races, touch football, or kick the can. Even funerals could turn into sporting occasions as the older folks kept their kids busy by throwing them all into a big ring to see who was the fastest or the strongest. Once, they even staged a competition to see which kid could stay on top of a four-hundred-pound cow the longest. "Man oh man, was that terrifying," remembered Chuck Kesey.[1] Ken Kesey was a particularly good football player, a standout right guard on the Springfield High School varsity team. He made all-district as a senior and consistently won acclaim for his ability to recover fumbles and block punts. Kesey would often call the plays— mostly because he was the only one on the team who had taken the trouble to learn them—and he liked to boast that his team never lost when he played quarterback (though he would usually neglect to mention that he filled this position only twice).

Kesey's main athletic pursuit, though, was wrestling, a sport that he declared gave "the little guy a chance to show he's as much an athlete as the 220-pound football player."[2] He shared his passion for the mat with his brother Chuck, a high school district champion and collegiate competitor in his own right. The two spent a lot of time wrestling each other as they grew up. Three years older, Kesey could usually hold his own against his brother, but Chuck gave as good as he got. Ken Kesey had a very strong high school wrestling career. His senior yearbook pictured him in a classic wrestling stance, with a caption that listed his accomplishments: "Ken Kesey, the 'Hooded Terror,' was perhaps just what the name indicates. Ken took third in District 6, first in Big Six, and third in State. He won 17 out of 20 matches during the season and wrestles in the 178 class."[3] This winning record helped Kesey gain admittance to the University of Oregon, where he established himself as one of their best grapplers. In a four-year career with the "Oregon Ducks" he was easily their top wrestler in the 177-pound division. Strong and skillful, Kesey "wrestled with the seeming intent to dismantle his opponent," the college newspaper once reported.[4] It was a style that won him all but six of his thirty-three starts in Oregon's trademark green and yellow kit. His coach, Bill Hammer, sang Kesey's praises as "one of the outstanding leaders of the team."[5]

In his junior year (1954–55), Kesey won the George Lowe scholarship, an award given to wrestlers who had demonstrated their abilities both on the mat and in the classroom. He repaid the honor by placing a more-than-respectable third in the Pacific Coast Intercollegiate (PCI) wrestling championship at season's end. The following year, Kesey went undefeated until the PCI final, where he lost to Barry Billington of UCLA, dislocating his shoulder in the process. It was a tough loss for Kesey. Billington was a large man—not for nothing was he nicknamed "Big Barry Billington"—who smoked cigarettes and happily fooled around while everyone else seemed wrapped up in the supposed great significance of the event. Kesey was shocked by Billington's approach, but he saw in it a valuable life lesson. "He just *beat* my ass, walked all over me, wound up 13–2. And one of the things I found out about Billington was that *he* was out there winning because he was having his fun. For me, it was necessary; I mean I needed it and was working at it." Thereafter, Kesey determined that "having fun" was one of the most important ambitions a person can have. "Whatever it is has got to be fun," he explained to Gordon Lish. "I want to write a *good* novel instead of a *poor* one just because it's *fun* to write a good novel. . . . Our society says you're going to have to hurt a whole lot before you do *anything* good. Well, if in most cases it turns out that way, it's because it *has* to. We've just come to *believe* that it must."[6]

The injury was certainly not fun, but Kesey returned in his senior year with every prospect of finally winning a PCI title. Unfortunately, as another undefeated season drew to a close, Kesey re-separated his shoulder in a

match against local rivals Oregon State University. As he lifted his opponent, Bud Geister, high off the mat, the two fell to the canvas and Kesey
landed awkwardly on his bad shoulder. He had to default the match due
to the injury and sit out the rest of his senior season, an inglorious end
to an otherwise stellar collegiate wrestling career.[7] The damaged shoulder eventually contributed to his failure to make it through the Olympic
wrestling trials in San Francisco in 1960. "I was on top of this guy," Kesey
recalled of his first and only bout, "and he popped me around my shoulder just for an instant and it was over. The guy got a watch for getting the
fastest pin in the tournament."[8] It was the first time that Kesey had been
pinned since way back in high school.

The loss spelled the end of his Olympic ambitions and his competitive
wrestling days, but we should not ignore the impact that wrestling had on
the young Kesey. In the words of renowned wrestling coach Dan Gable,
"Once you've wrestled, everything else is easy." Just "making weight" is
difficult. In his undefeated junior year, Kesey wrestled at 167, a tough
weight to get down to given his natural build, but an advantage over skin-
nier opponents. Kesey struggled to reach and maintain his weight, striving to lose pounds at a time through diet and dehydration. The fact that
he made it shows great self-discipline and self-sacrifice. And while the
sport is intensely physical in nature—the sport of gladiators in ancient
times—wrestling is also intellectual, requiring deep knowledge, patience,
and quick wits. It's almost like a violent game of chess. Kesey liked to call
it the sport of reason. "Football, boxing, they are all trying to decrease the
reason and intelligence of the opponent by knocking them out," Kesey
explained to one interviewer. "But the wrestler doesn't try to knock anybody out. He gets them by the arm and sits them back there and says,
'Now listen carefully to me or I'm gonna break your shoulder' and you
reason with them." His easiest opponents were the big brawny footballers
who were all muscle and no skill or experience. Kesey likened his writing
to wrestling: "[W]riting is the same for me. You get them by the brain and
you put a half Nelson on them and you say. 'Listen, I'm gonna reason with
you, I'm gonna tell you something that might be a little hard for you, but
its correct."[9]

Kesey's shoulder injury had an unexpected consequence: it kept him out
of the armed services. Like every other American male who made it to his
eighteenth birthday, Kesey had to register his name and permanent address

with the local selective service board in readiness for being called up. The rules stated that as long as college students maintained an above-average academic rank, they qualified for a deferment. Once Kesey graduated in 1957, however, his college deferment ended and he became eligible for induction into the military. At this point in time, Kesey was deciding what to do next with his life. Though he still had acting and screenwriting ambitions, Hollywood had been a complete bust, so he had few other choices than to work for his father. The only other iron that he had in the fire was the Woodrow Wilson scholarship that he had applied for the previous fall. If he were successful and went to graduate school, he would earn another deferment. He had no way of knowing what his chances were for the scholarship, but it certainly seemed like a long shot, especially given the fact that his grades had not been that great. Kesey settled restlessly into a job at the Darigold creamery while he honed his acting skills in local productions. He also kept up with his wrestling, training at the university and entering tournaments whenever he could. He had no interest in a military career, and so it was with some dismay that he found himself called up for a physical exam in the spring of 1958.

Kesey had dreamed up a typically crazy scheme to try and fail the medical.[10] He had bought a bottle of glucose at a local health food store and stashed it, along with an eyedropper, in his pants on the day of the physical. His plan was to surreptitiously drop some glucose into his urine sample, throwing off his sugar count and raising suspicions that he was diabetic. Of course, he had no idea how little or how much glucose to add, so when the time came to urinate in the cup he chickened out rather than risk making a fool of himself. His back-up plan was to volunteer to become an officer in the coast guard. This, he knew, would involve signing up for four years during which he would have to attend the Coast Guard Academy in New Haven, Connecticut, but he figured that was preferable to being sent off to some army boot camp.

As it turned out, all this frantic planning was unnecessary. Kesey had taken part in an AAAU wrestling event the weekend before his date with the selective service medical team and had weakened his shoulder ligaments again. The X-ray that was taken as part of the armed services physical a few days later showed what looked like a dislocation. The following Monday, he received a package containing an AAAU wrestling trophy, which was welcome, and a letter asking him to go back up to Portland for

more tests, which was decidedly not. Luckily for Kesey, the doctor assigned
to him at Portland was a sympathetic ex-wrestler who could see that he
had absolutely no interest in joining the military. The following Wed-
nesday, an anxious Kesey received another two pieces of mail. One letter postmarked from Portland informed him that he had been classified
as 4F: unfit for military service. The other, postmarked from Seattle, told
him that he had won a Woodrow Wilson Fellowship to Stanford to study
creative writing with Wallace Stegner. That night, Kesey and Faye's little
place in Eugene—they had now moved to 1795 Columbia Street—saw
quite a celebration.

The fellowship that Kesey won can trace its origins back to 1945, when
a Princeton professor persuaded a private donor to support a graduate
fellowship program whose aim was to create a new generation of college
professors to meet the postwar growth in higher education. At first, the
program was fairly small, even after the Carnegie Corporation granted
Princeton $100,000 to expand its scale. Only after the Ford Foundation
chipped in a staggering $24.5 million in 1957 did the program become a
significant source of graduate student funding. Kesey's timing could not
have been better. Renamed the Woodrow Wilson National Fellowship
Foundation, Ford stipulated that their money be used to support one
thousand fellowships per year over the next five years. Eventually, after
the Ford Foundation twice renewed their funding, the program would
support more than fifteen thousand fellows, a number of whom would go
on to win Pulitzer Prizes, nine would become Nobel laureates, more than
five hundred would be Guggenheim fellows, and many others would continue on to successful careers in academia, business, government, and the
arts. The fellowship was a good deal for Kesey. It offered him full tuition
at Stanford, a $1,400 stipend, and additional money for Faye. The scene
was set: after a summer of relative uncertainties, Kesey and Faye were
moving to California, Stanford bound.

THE CREATIVE WRITING PROGRAM

A few weeks before Stanford's 1958 fall semester started, Faye Kesey traveled from Oregon to California to find a place for her and Ken to live. She
found a small apartment above a garage on California Street in Palo Alto,
accessible via a gravel walkway that seemed to double as a litter area for

local dogs. It was not exactly four-star accommodations, but it was more than good enough for a graduate student and his wife. Faye and Kesey packed up all their earthly possessions, and their dachshund pup, and drove down to Palo Alto in a U-Rent truck. Kesey set about decorating the apartment. He pinned his collection of famous paintings on the wall—no originals, of course, just reproductions cut out of glossy magazines—carefully stacked his collection of records next to the record player, and cleared a corner for a desk and a typewriter. He was ready for business. Faye's sister, Myrna (Wilma) Haxby, came to live with them in the apartment. Family was always important to Ken and Faye and they were excited to start one of their own. They would eventually adopt a baby girl—Shannon—in early 1961. To everyone's pleasant surprise, Faye had found herself pregnant shortly after arranging the adoption. Zane Kesey joined the family just a few months after Shannon, in the spring of 1961.

Palo Alto was originally just a small summer vacation resort for wealthy San Franciscans, but over the years its identity had merged with that of Stanford University. The place changed rapidly in the early sixties, its economy bolstered by the influx of money generated by military and aerospace technology research at companies like Lockheed, the Stanford Research Institute, and Watkins-Johnson, but when the Keseys arrived it was still pretty much a sleepy little town. In 1958 it had a population of only about 48,000, and its downtown boasted a small J.C. Penney's department store, one restaurant, and not much else.[11] One of the few local hotspots was a place in nearby Menlo Park called Kepler's Bookstore. Opened in 1955 by Roy and Patricia Kepler, two local pacifists and civil rights activists, it supplied textbooks to Stanford's students. It also functioned as the mid-peninsula's version of San Francisco's famous City Lights bookstore, stocking paperback Beat novels and leftist magazines. A local ordinance forbade the sale of liquor within one mile of the university, but you could get a cup of coffee in Kepler's and sit in the reading section where they had a few tables and chairs. In April 1959 Palo Alto got its first real coffee shop venue—St. Michael's Alley—opened by Vernon Gates at 436 University Avenue. The place was a hit right from the start, with crowds so big on opening day that the doors had to be locked at noon. Within a few years, this venue would play an important role in the region's music scene, hosting early gigs by the likes of Joan Baez, Jorma Kaukonen (later of Jefferson Airplane), and various members of the Grateful Dead.

Kesey was intimidated by the Stanford campus. "[C]oming out of the University of Oregon," he recalled, "it was like I'd been in high school. What a shock it is, going to graduate school and finding out that all of the undergraduates know more than you do, they're twice as sharp. It was a whole different world. I still knew what pi-r-squared was, but they were talking about literature and about art, about politics, about stuff I didn't know existed, and yet they all knew about it, coming from all over the United States."[12] He met most of the participants in that year's creative writing program at a welcome cocktail party thrown by Professor Richard Scowcroft. Kesey was not exactly a cocktail party sort of guy, so the event was a little unsettling, particularly when he found that his prospective colleagues all seemed polished, sophisticated, and miles ahead of him in terms of literary knowledge and accomplishments. He had some catching up to do, he realized, and then some.[13] The only character in the room that he felt comfortable with was another recipient of a Woodrow Wilson Fellowship, a six-foot-four fellow from Ohio named Ken Babbs.

The Stanford creative writing program was Wallace Stegner's baby. In 1945 he had been hired away—headhunted, we would call it now—from his instructor position at Harvard to be the professor of creative writing at Stanford University. When he arrived, Palo Alto was still not much more than a dot on the map. Most people still referred to the university campus as "the farm," a reference to the fact that the land originally served to house the horse farm of the university's principal founder, ex-governor of California Leland Stanford. Stegner was charged with finding ways to enhance the university's fledgling School of Humanities. He proposed a creative writing program that would attract and nurture America's best young writing talents by offering them a supportive environment and string-free fellowships of two thousand dollars per year. The average wage in the United States in the early 1950s was approximately three thousand dollars per year, so this was a pretty generous deal for students.[14] With a five-hundred-thousand-dollar private endowment secured from the oil-rich brother of the head of the English Department, Stegner was able to build the program unhindered by budgetary concerns and departmental politics. His first step was to hire an assistant professor to help run things. Richard Scowcroft joined the Stanford faculty in 1946 and helped Stegner prepare for the first batch of students, who began in the fall of 1947. The project was an immediate success. Within four years, members of the program had published an astonishing forty short stories and three novels. It was a taste of things to come.[15]

For the 1958–59 academic year, Kesey's first, Stegner chose three writers to receive the fellowships that had been named in his honor: a Kentuckian named Wendell Berry, Chicago native Mitch Strucinski, and the program's first successful black applicant, Ernest Gaines. Former Stegner fellows were encouraged to attend the program's workshops, an option taken up by activist Tillie Olsen, who had been a fellow in 1955. Nonfellows could also attend as long as they submitted an acceptable writing sample ahead of time. Ken Babbs, a young woman called Kay House, and a well-read writer from Alabama named Nancy Packer were admitted under these conditions, as was Kesey, who sent in an extract from his college football novel, "End of Autumn." In all, Wendell Berry remembers, there were about twenty people in the class that fall.[16] It was led by Scowcroft (Stegner took over in the winter quarter), and they met one afternoon a week in the Jones Room on the fourth floor of the old Stanford Library. The room had been furnished by Mary Stegner, Wallace's wife, with stylish Danish furniture, imposing bookshelves, a large hexagon-shaped table, and even a record player and a coffee machine. It was elegant but comfortable; a reading room rather than a classroom, which ideally suited the nature of the seminar.

This was not a lecture class, and hardly anyone took notes. Every week, a few people would read from their works in progress while the rest of the class would discuss their merits and suggest improvements. Students would submit work to Scowcroft ahead of time, and he would choose which papers would be read aloud by the usually nervous author. Since there was no photocopying technology, the class had to listen attentively if their comments and suggestions were going to make sense. Under different conditions, this type of seminar format might be brutal, but Stegner and Scowcroft were insistent that comments remain helpful rather than overly critical, especially since they took more of a backseat role in the process. Stegner believed that "the best teaching that goes on in a college writing class is done by members of the class"; Scowcroft also ran his seminar according to the same principles.[17] "In general I would try to direct discussion rather than express my opinion," Scowcroft told one interviewer. "The teacher plays a part, but his main role is to galvanize the others."[18] To foster goodwill, Scowcroft and Stegner worked hard to generate a sense of community among the class members. They welcomed the students into their homes for the occasional party and/or audience with celebrated visiting authors, such as Robert Frost.

The atmosphere in the seminars remained mostly congenial and supportive, though naturally, divisions and alliances materialized. Kesey and Babbs emerged almost immediately as the loudmouth rebels who did not take their craft or their studies quite as seriously as some of the other members of the class. This was probably true, but it was also something of a defensive posture, since Kesey and Babbs lacked the literary qualifications and experience possessed by many of their peers. Nancy Packer, who went on to teach at Stanford and chair the writing program, remembered how the seminar seemed to be divided between "the intellectuals who had read some stuff and the barbarians who had never read anything . . . [and] were proud of it; [they] thought you sullied your style if you read anybody else." Kesey's arrogant air could sometimes rub people up the wrong way. Packer recalled one occasion when Kesey felt that the class had missed something in one of his readings: "he said, 'Yeah, I didn't think you'd get it,' with a very proud tone to his voice that somehow showed a superiority over all of us because we hadn't been able to understand what he was driving at."[19]

Kesey's personality got him noticed in the class, but his work was not particularly outstanding, at least until he started working on *Cuckoo's Nest* much later on. Scowcroft had mixed feelings about Kesey's abilities and had doubts about the quality of "Zoo," the Beat novel that Kesey wrote during his first couple of years at Stanford. "Although the book didn't seem to have any promise at all," Scowcroft told one interviewer, "there were little jewels in it. My feeling about Kesey was that he was capable of doing the worst and best writing of anyone in the class. And he couldn't tell the difference." Stegner's relationship with Kesey was initially cordial, even though there were clear differences between them. "I was never sympathetic to any of his ideas because I thought many of his ideas were half-baked." Stegner recalled. But "we got along in the class perfectly well. I liked his writing most of the time."[20] Even when Kesey submitted a paper titled "On Why I Am Not Writing My Last Term Paper"—a clever, but ultimately self-serving assertion of superiority—Stegner maintained his patience, offering Kesey words of encouragement while at the same time chiding him for confusing self-expression with self-indulgence.[21]

These comments hint at the real difference between Stegner and Kesey: one of sensibility. While Stegner is remembered as a superb Western writer, his biographer Jackson J. Benson notes that for much of his life, Stegner "fought a battle to dispute the Western myth of rugged individualism, particularly as it has been embodied in the lone horseman."[22] Kesey, on the other hand, spent most of his existence living out that myth, both in his work—the leading characters in all his novels are "rugged" individuals of one stripe or another—and in his personal life. Whereas Stegner valued order, cooperation, and convention, Kesey seemed to him to be intentionally wild and reckless, the embodiment of the Beat culture that the young Oregonian had embraced and that Stegner had rejected. "Kesey got blown by the San Francisco hip scene when he came down from Oregon,"[23] Stegner told one interviewer, implying that it set the young Oregonian off on the wrong track. When Kesey started to act out the role of the rebellious "lone horseman," Stegner must have felt that all his advice about "discipline" and the dangers of "self-indulgence" had fallen on deaf ears. "It was his extracurricular activities after he left the class . . . that kind of teed me off," Stegner admitted, especially when Kesey seemed set on encouraging some of the other students in the seminar to join him in those activities. "Stegner saw Kesey and what he represented as a threat to civilization and intellectualism and sobriety," explained author Robert Stone, a member of the seminar in 1962. "But for those of us who were there, what was going on around Ken was so exciting, and just plain fun that we were not about to line up against each other on ideological grounds."[24]

The real break between Kesey and Stegner occurred in 1963, several years after Kesey had left Stanford. In an interview with a literary journal, he criticized his former teacher and his role at Stanford: "He's not writing to people any longer," Kesey expounded dismissively. "He's writing to a classroom and his colleagues. . . . A man becomes *accustomed* to having two hundred people gather every day at one o'clock giving him all their attention. . . . That can't happen without affecting a man's writing—the wrong way."[25] Stegner was hurt by the comments, and despite various efforts to smooth things over by mutual friends like Ed McClanahan and Wendell Berry, the famous professor never really forgave his former student. When Kesey heard that Stegner was angry, he went to the professor's office to explain himself—telling McClanahan that his words had been taken out of context—but Stegner instructed his secretary to turn him away. They never spoke again. Though Kesey later felt bad about the ill will his words had caused, Stegner represented precisely the type of old-school authority figure that Kesey felt compelled to challenge. "I have felt kind of impelled into the future by Wally, by his dislike of what I was doing, of what we were doing. That was the kiss of approval in some way," Kesey told a college audience in 1993. "I liked him, and I actually think he liked me. It was just that we were on different sides of the fence. When [my friends and I] got together and headed off on a bus to deal with the future of our synapses, we knew that Wally didn't like what we were doing and that was good enough for us."[26]

At Stanford, both Kesey and Babbs felt this outsider status from the start. When Babbs threw a party early in the fall quarter, some of the more scholarly types were notable by their absence. It took a while for friendships to emerge among the different personalities in the group. Wendell Berry, for example, eventually became a lifelong and devoted friend to Kesey, but he was initially unimpressed with the young man from Oregon. Mitch Strucinski, the debonair pipe smoker, was friendlier, oftentimes regaling Kesey and Babbs with tales of his time in the army. Mitch could be something of a rebel in class himself. He once shared a story that contained a graphic description of a man chopping up a dead pig with an axe so that it would fit into an incinerator. Scowcroft, who was shaky at the best of times, was shocked by the gory account, as were some of the others in the class. Babbs and Kesey loved it, enjoying its black humor and vivid imagery. They saw the mixed reaction in class as a revealing moment, separating those who had gone through life protected from its harsher realities and those who had lived lives sufficiently close to nature to recognize that violence and death were both intrinsic parts of human existence. Mitch was not the only one to experience disapproval in the seminar. In later years, Babbs would speak glowingly about his time at Stanford but he had mixed feelings in the moment. He often felt unfairly criticized by the people sitting around the table in the Jones Room, and he concluded that the program had ultimately undermined his confidence in his abilities as a writer.[27]

Kesey remembered thinking at first that Babbs was something of a "gleef"—a midwestern term for someone "who's not quite an oaf but is on his way there"—but he soon came to recognize that beneath Babbs's rough-edged, fun-loving exterior was a sharp mind and a sharper wit.[28] Babbs had been raised in Mentor, Ohio, a small town on the shores of

Lake Erie, about thirty miles east of Cleveland. His father was the editor of a weekly local newspaper; his mother was the librarian at Babbs's high school, where he played trombone in the band and earned a little extra pocket money by helping out with cleaning and maintenance duties. Once, Babbs and a schoolmate were walking down a corridor when one of the big translucent globes that covered the ceiling lights fell and crashed down between them. A couple of inches either way and disaster would have struck. Babbs took the incident as deeply meaningful, an indication that he was destined to do something significant with his life.[29]

In the classroom, Babbs excelled in the humanities—he occasionally wrote for the high school newspaper and the yearbook—but after he graduated in 1953, he turned his back on writing and elected to pursue a career in engineering, mostly because that seemed to make good financial sense. He won a basketball scholarship to the Case Institute of Technology in Cleveland, but after two years he decided that the math required for his engineering degree was too much for him, so he transferred to Miami University in Oxford, Ohio, to study English literature. At that time, Miami was known as the Cradle of Coaches because of the strength of its athletics programs. Even though its basketball team was one of the best in the nation, Babbs was good enough to make the team as a walk-on, initially playing forward, later switching to guard. Led by future NBA Hall of Famer Wayne Embry, the team twice made it to the NCAA finals but they never advanced past the third round. Playing with Embry, an African American, was an eye-opener for Babbs. When the team went on the road to play tournaments in and around Pennsylvania, West Virginia, and Kentucky, Embry was usually refused service at the restaurants where they stopped to eat. "Boy, did that piss me off," Babbs remembered.[30]

Sports were an important point of contact for Kesey and Babbs, but the two also shared an interest in the Beat movement. Babbs had arrived in San Francisco in good time to register for his classes at Stanford, but he was so enthralled with North Beach and all it had to offer that he made himself late. "It took me two weeks to get the thirty miles down the road to Stanford," he remembered. "I loved the scene in North Beach so much I just kept putting it off."[31] On one of their weekend trips to "beatnik central," Babbs impressed Kesey by commandeering an open mike and blabbering a stream of consciousness into it for what seemed like an eternity. Their friendship was cemented from that point on.

Babbs moved into a barnlike house hidden among some apricot tress in an area known as Whiskey Gulch. The place was some fifty yards off the Bayshore Freeway, the main thoroughfare connecting San Jose, Palo Alto, and San Francisco. A bachelor, he shared the place with his dog, Gus, a black-and-white cross between a German shepherd and a Saint Bernard. Gus had about a dozen metal tags attached to his collar, and much to the amusement of Kesey, the tags clunked and clanked like a cowbell every time Gus walked anywhere. Babbs had decorated his home with the type of homespun art that would later grace the interior of Further and La Honda. A collage consisting of newspaper and magazine cuttings was pasted on one wall. Roman chariots, football players, cars, motorcycles, herds of horses, airplanes, and trains all charged across the scene, all facing in the same direction, all led by a couple of cartoon cops blowing their whistles like pop-art pied pipers. Balloon dinosaurs and weird yellow sparkly dogs hung from the ceiling. A huge picture of Goodwin "Goody" Knight, then Republican governor of California, dominated one of the other walls, a characteristically ironic political statement from Babbs. His satirical approach to politics found free expression again during the 1964 bus trip when the Pranksters painted the slogan "A Vote for Goldwater is a Vote for Fun" on the side of Further as they drove the bus backward down a street in Phoenix, Arizona, Goldwater's hometown.

Kesey shared and appreciated Babbs's lowbrow artistic sensibilities and his irreverent, playful sense of humor. Early in the fall quarter, Gus turned up outside the Jones Room, baying and scratching at the door, looking for his master. As Scowcroft surveyed the room, trying to work out who was responsible for causing this disturbance, Gus pushed the door open, lumbered over to the table, and slumped at Babbs's feet. To Kesey's amusement, Babbs feigned innocence, asking around the table if anyone knew the owner of the dog.[32] In the years to come, as often as not, it was Babbs who put the Merry into the Pranksters.

PERRY LANE

Sometime during the fall of 1958, Kesey ran into a former Stegner fellow (1956–57) by the name of Robin White. He was a Yale-educated, "hail fellow, well met" sort of guy who was enjoying some success with his recently published first novel, *House of Many Rooms*. His second, *Elephant*

Hill, would win the Harper Prize in 1959. White and his wife, Marny, quickly hit it off with Kesey and Faye, and after a gathering at Wallace Stegner's place, they invited the Keseys to meet some of their friends. All four crowded into the Whites' car and drove to a narrow, unlit street just off what is now Sand Hill Road on the west side of the Stanford University golf course. The street sign identified the unpaved road as Perry Lane (it was changed to Perry Avenue in 1962, but that seemed a little pretentious for such a rustic, tumbledown place, so most people continue to call it Perry Lane). A series of small, single-story wooden cottages ran on either side of its one-block length, most of them clad with wooden shingles, each boasting a stone chimney that seemed to be the only thing holding some of them up. At one end of the Lane, a courtyard with five cottages scattered around its perimeter interrupted the simple symmetry of the street. A giant oak tree occupied the center of the open space. Gnarled and scarred, it was easy to believe the local legend that it was four hundred years old. Some thirty feet off the ground, the tree forked, offering the adventurous a place to "contemplate the heavens or escape from their wives," according to one press account.[33] Someone had dragged an old mattress up there to make the experience a little more comfortable, if no less risky. Another old oak stood right in the middle of Perry Lane itself, defying logic as well as traffic, and declaring to all who passed by that this was no ordinary place.

Perry Lane was in an unincorporated section of Menlo Park, on land that still belonged to the university. It had a long history well before Kesey arrived. When the United States entered World War I in 1918, the military took over parts of the old Stanford family farm to use as a training camp. The houses on Perry Lane were the last surviving examples of the small timber frame cabins that the army built to house the soldiers. In the 1920s, when various artists, writers, and fringe-dwellers moved in, looking for inexpensive accommodation, the place began building its reputation as Stanford's bohemian left bank. Over the years, the place had been home to some famous residents. In 1909 economist Thorstein Veblen, author of *The Theory of the Leisure Classes*, moved into a house called Cedro Cottage just around the corner from what became Perry Lane. He had come back to Stanford, his alma mater, to teach and write, publishing a lesser-known work called *The Higher Learning in America: A Memorandum on the Conduct of Universities by Businessmen* (1918) during this period. He left Stanford in 1919 but returned to die in Cedro Cottage in 1929.[34]

Veblen's residency in Cedro Cottage lent the location a certain left-wing eminence, but he was not the only important historical figure to reside on and around Perry Lane. Felix Bloch, physicist and Nobel laureate, lived on the Lane; as did Big Sur author Dennis Murphy; Jon Lindbergh, the son of the famous aviator; renowned psychologist Louis M. Terman; Lincoln Moses, a noted Stanford scholar in statistics and high-ranking administrator; and a stream of artists, poets, and students, two of whom—Mr. and Mrs. Byron Johnson—bought the cottages around the courtyard, the location of their honeymoon. By the 1950s Perry Lane's reputation was well established as a quirky, bohemian oasis. Hughes Rudd—later an award-winning TV news reporter and anchor for *CBS Morning News*—lived on the Lane in the early part of the decade. On one memorable occasion, he found a goat hanging by its tether in the courtyard oak tree, a victim of its own overly ambitious tree climbing efforts. "There aren't many crackpots at Stanford," Rudd noted dryly, "but they all live on Perry Lane."[35] One of the "crackpots" who followed in his wake, Vic Lovell, subsequently declared of Perry Lane: "In the late fifties and early sixties it was the only liberated ground in the Mid-peninsula."[36]

When the Whites and the Keseys arrived at Perry Lane, it was to Vic's house, number 5, that they went. The windows lacked curtains, allowing outsiders to view the room within. Kesey looked in and saw a group of people sitting around in a circle of mattresses scattered on the floor with not a stick of furniture in sight. The room was illuminated by a single bright light. The scene looked weird to Kesey; this was not how people lived in Oregon, or anyplace else he knew, and it struck him that these people were from another world. Once inside, introductions were made, and Kesey met Vic Lovell for the first time. It was an important moment. Though Lovell's role in the events to come would eventually be obscured by the sheer magnitude of Kesey's success and celebrity, without Lovell, many of those events might never have happened in the first place.

Kesey and Vic came from very different backgrounds. Vic's father was a career navy man, the commanding officer of a destroyer, a participant in the Operation Overlord landings at Normandy in World War II. His mother was born into the well-established Klauber family of San Diego. The family made its fortune in business, mostly operating wholesale groceries that initially catered to the needs of the Gold Rush economy. Typical of old-money families, the Klaubers had their fair share of genius eccentrics, and so Vic was not the first to pursue interests outside of the commercial world. Alice Klauber (1871–1951), Vic's aunt, was an artist who trained with Robert Henri in Spain and spent a lifetime promoting the arts in San Diego. Even more notably, Lawrence Klauber (1883–1968) somehow managed to be one of the world's leading authorities on rattlesnakes—his monumental 1,533-page study on them remains the definitive textbook in the field—while holding down a day job as the CEO of San Diego Gas & Electric Company. Vic's mother and his grandfather had both attended Stanford, so it was assumed that he would follow in their footsteps. He did, majoring in philosophy as an undergraduate and eventually earning a PhD in psychology, his chosen career.

Vic's first encounter with Perry Lane came during his undergraduate days at Stanford in the midfifties. There were a few other similar artistic enclaves close to Stanford, such as a row of rundown cottages along Alpine Road in Portola Valley, but generally speaking, as Vic explained, "those of us of a Bohemian inclination hung around Perry Lane."[37] He had been introduced to the Lane's existence in 1955 by a Stanford friend who lived there: Jim Spencer, an ex–bomber pilot in World War II turned scientific editor and sometimes fiction writer. It was wild even then, at least for its times, influenced but not dominated by the Beat movement then germinating in the North Beach parts of San Francisco. Vic and his friends would go to try and score pot from the Beat parts of the city. They were occasionally successful, but not enough for the drug to become a staple on the Lane in these early years.

Vic moved permanently to the Lane in 1957, and he quickly became one of the leading characters in the community, along with Robin White. Vic shared his house with Dirk Van Nouhuys, and Jim Wolpman, a law student he had been friends with since their sophomore days together at Stanford. For Wolpman, Perry Lane was a refreshing alternative to college dormitories and the mostly staid, "oppressive air" of the campus. At that time, Stanford had a reputation for being apolitical. This changed somewhat with the onset of the war in Vietnam, but before that, Stanford bred only a few civil rights activists or committed Ban-the-Bomb pacifists (Roy Kepler, of Palo Alto's Kepler's Bookstore, was a notable example). The student body was generally as nihilistic as it was conservative. In 1956 they elected as their student president a Perry Lane character called George Ralph. Ralph ran a satirical, derisive campaign centered on what he called "a motor-biker platform," which argued in part that the student body government should be eliminated because it served no useful function. This sort of anarchistic irreverence influenced the atmosphere on Perry Lane, but generally, people there were a little more left-leaning in their outlook and bohemian in their sensibilities. Mostly, they were intellectually motivated graduate students investing, as Wolpman recalled, "a lot of premium on being smart, being brainy."[38]

Kesey met another important Perry Lane figure on that first visit to Vic's house. As he chatted with Vic and the others scattered around the mattresses on the floor, a tall, graceful woman with striking red hair appeared at the doorway. This was Chloe Scott, a professional dancer and dance instructor who lived in the cottage across from Vic's. She was English, an evacuee from London during the days of the blitz when it seemed as if Hitler was on the verge of invasion. Chloe initially settled in New York with some of her extended family, and she eventually married an American whose name she still bore. The marriage did not last, and to escape the messy aftermath, Chloe and her daughter, Jennifer, moved to Palo Alto. They settled on Perry Lane at the end of 1956, moving into one of the smaller cottages, paying $50 a month in rent. This was pretty inexpensive, at least compared to the $150 per month she would have had to pay for a two-bedroom College Terrace apartment or the $27,000 she would have had to come up with to buy a three-bedroom house in Crescent Park.[39] People moved around the lane as it suited them. When someone moved out of one of the larger, $80-per-month cottages, Chloe moved in, freeing up her old place for Jim Wolpman and his new bride, Anita.

Chloe's first encounter with Kesey cast a long shadow over their relationship; it was a shadow that Kesey regretted having caused, but one that Chloe could never quite shake. Showing off in front of Vic's friends, Kesey blurted the first thing that came into his head as Chloe entered the room. "Why, Harriet Selsdon, I live and breathe," he said, making an obscure reference to the fact that she looked a little like the actress who had played the character of that name in the movie *The Man Who Came to Dinner*. "Who?" replied Chloe, befuddled by this brash stranger. "Harriet Selsdon is the girl who took an axe and gave her mother forty whacks," Kesey replied, quoting the famous playground rhyme as it is paraphrased in the movie. "And when the job was done, she gave her father forty-one." This was another obscure reference to the movie, which loosely based the Harriet Selsdon character on Lizzie Borden, the young woman who had been accused of brutally killing her father and stepmother in Massachusetts back in 1892. Chloe raised an eyebrow and left, forever wondering what sort of man would rudely compare a woman he had never met before to a supposed axe murderer.[40] Chloe was always a part of the scene, but she briefly moved away from Perry Lane in 1960 when things started to get a little too wild for her tastes. Her move came after she came home one day to find four people sleeping in her house, none of whom she or anybody else had ever seen before.

The cast of characters on the Lane was long and constantly changing. Anne Atkinson was around in the early years, as were Ron Bondoc, Dick Bolin, Norm Giddan, and Nancy Hirshberg. Jack and Beverly Richardson lived across the street from the Keseys and were two of the first people they got to know. Suzanne and Irving Thalberg—son of Hollywood legend Irving Thalberg—lived on the lane but mostly kept to themselves. A close friend of theirs, analytical philosopher Donald Davidson, then an assistant professor at Stanford, was an occasional visitor to the Lane but an important influence on its intellectual climate, since he taught many of its leading residents. Phil Wilson, a star tackle on the Stanford University football team, who gave up the game to pursue an interest in Zen Buddhism, was part of the circle for a while. Jim Spencer, Vic's friend, still lived on the Lane. Jim and Vic and other Perry Lane figures all went on to play a significant role in the creation and administration of a nontraditional institute of higher learning, the Midpenisula Free University. Carl Lehmann-Haupt lived next door to the Keseys. Carl had connections to the New York publishing world and would later try to help get some of Kesey's early efforts in print. Carl's younger brother, Sandy, joined Kesey in some of his later adventures. Jane Burton, a philosophy graduate student and good friend to Chloe, lived at number 7 Perry Lane. She would be an important constant on the scene, maintaining her friendship and involvement with Kesey long after he had moved up to La Honda and immersed himself in Pranksterism. She was one of the few Perry Lane veterans to make the 1964 bus trip to New York, but pregnant and highly uncomfortable, her recollections of the event are far more sober and circumspect than most of her fellow passengers. Jane never considered herself a

Prankster and would likely agree with Vic's comment that "a fine line divides revolution from decadence," his critical assessment of the difference between Perry Lane and La Honda.[41]

A young graduate student physicist by the name of Lee Anderson lived at number 1 Perry Lane. Lee's humorous and analytical way of thinking would often serve as a welcome grounding during some of the more outlandish philosophical discussions that took place late at night on the Lane.[42] He was also a good drummer, a rarity among a crowd who thought that mere ownership of a bongo automatically made one good at playing it. Lee would supplement his meager income by giving drumming lessons to local kids on Saturdays. One of his regular students was a teenager called Bill Kreutzmann whose mother taught dancing at Stanford. Kreutzmann later recalled his good luck having a drum teacher who was "very hip, a very lose soul who wasn't interested in teaching by the book, more by feeling."[43] By all accounts, it did not take Kreutzmann long to become one of Palo Alto's hottest drummers. By 1964 he was keeping time in a rhythm and blues group called the Zodiacs that played the occasional Stanford fraternity party. In early 1965 two of the guys from the Zodiacs, Jerry Garcia and Ron "Pigpen" McKernan, asked Kreutzmann to join them in a new musical adventure that they were putting together called the Warlocks (later the Grateful Dead).

Kreutzmann was not the only link between the Grateful Dead and Perry Lane. By the time the Warlocks were getting together—late 1964, early 1965—Kesey's scene had long since shifted to his new place in La Honda, but Jerry Garcia and some of his friends had been part of a coterie of local kids and drop-outs who had occasionally crashed the parties at the Lane in 1962 or 1963 when Garcia and some other notables (like his lifelong songwriting partner, Robert Hunter, and future Prankster Page Browning) were living in a large rooming house called the Chateau, a few blocks from Perry Lane. Garcia and his buddies were not exactly welcome. Alan Trist, a friend of Garcia's whose house backed on to Perry Lane, remembered arriving at some event on the Lane and being "thrown out on our ear."[44] Phil Lesh, bassist in the Grateful Dead, was not initially part of that circle, but he had his own early connection to Kesey's scene. Lesh had met a young guy called Charles "Mike" Lamb while both were students at the College of San Mateo in late 1958. Mike, it turned out, had been raised in and around Palo Alto—one of his parents was an administrator at Stanford—and his bohemian inclination had led him to Perry Lane. He took Lesh with him to the Lane in late 1960 or early 1961. They had gone to visit Vic Lovell, whom Mike had befriended, but they also ran into Kesey, who was busy writing *Cuckoo's Nest* at the time. Lesh's first impression of Kesey was not too positive. In fact, the exact phrase he used to describe his later Acid Test buddy was "blustering asshole."[45]

Mike Lamb would go on to have his own role in San Francisco's music explosion with his band, Freedom Highway, and he also introduced a couple of other notable figures to Perry Lane. One was Roy Sebern, the person responsible for the light shows at the Acid Tests, who moved onto the Lane after first accompanying Mike to a party there. The other was Sally Demma, a teenage runaway who found friendship and shelter on the Lane. Vic Lovell described her as "the original teenybopper[;] . . . the first, and the acknowledged leader of a long line of teenage girls on the lam from straight society."[46] Unfortunately, she was also one of the Lane scene's first casualties, dying in a car crash in 1963. Her brother, Peter, was also part of both the Perry Lane and Prankster circles, later running the Hip Pocket Bookstore in Santa Cruz with Merry Prankster Ron Bevirt.

Its parties and bohemian reputation attracted all sort of young renegades to Perry Lane, most of whom just wanted to get in on the action, though there were a few who would create the odd problem, occasionally stealing bits of stuff here and there. There were plenty of young women— "nymphets," the Lane residents used to call them—who would "kiss their straight dates chastely goodnight, and then come over to the Lane, get high, and ball somebody," as Vic Lovell recalled.[47] Others had more innocent ambitions, adopting Perry Lane as their home away from home and the residents as their surrogate parents. On the weekends, some of these local kids and their older Perry Lane friends would pile into cars and head in a convoy up to San Francisco to play "Beat tourist" around various North Beach haunts like Lawrence Ferlinghetti's City Lights bookstore, various coffee shops, and occasionally Allen Ginsberg's San Francisco apartment. Other weekends would involve trips into Palo Alto to watch a young local talent called Joan Baez perform at St. Michael's Alley, or an unknown Jerry Garcia playing around Palo Alto. Chloe Scott once led a mass outing to an exhibition at the San Francisco Museum of Modern Art. The collection was a revelation to most of them. It was inspirational and cutting edge, and it somehow felt connected to their own experimental sensibilities. A trip to the first West Coast performance of Samuel Beckett's groundbreaking *Waiting for Godot* generated similar empathies, though this time they were filtered through the additional lens of peyote. When, during the second act, one of the cast members looked out into the audience and asked, "Where are all these corpses from?," the Perry Laners were convinced that he was talking to them. They immediately got the giggles and struggled to maintain their composure for the rest of the performance.

Passing through Perry Lane on their way to adulthood was an important and enlightening moment in many of these youngsters' lives, but it was also instructive to the slightly older residents who entertained them. As Vic Lovell noted of the young women that hung around the lane: "[T]hey were flamboyant proof of our capacity to corrupt the youth, and thus to affect the world from which we were alienated."[48]

HERE COME THE KESEYS

Faye and Kesey did not come back to the Lane for a while after that first visit with the Whites, but in their absence, Robin White sang Kesey's praises to its residents. When one of them, Ray Waddington, decided to move on, White let the Keseys know that they should rent Waddington's cottage—number 9, not far from Vic's—before anyone else did. Kesey came to look at the place and found it inches deep in debris, the electricity cut off, and the inside painted an off-putting light blue color. The outside had been badly clad in fake bricks. Despite the ramshackle appearance of the place, Kesey and Faye had no hesitation in signing the lease, attracted by the scene at Perry Lane more than the quality of the accommodation.[49] Faye's sister, Myrna (Wilma), had recently reunited with her boyfriend, and so the Keseys let the pair move into the Perry Lane house for a week on their own. The plan was to give them some space to sort out their differences and make plans for the future. The hope was that they would also fix up the place a bit. Unfortunately, when Myrna and her boyfriend set about clearing away some greenery around their cottage, some of the existing residents were upset about losing a little shrubbery. This somewhat tainted the Lane's initial reception to Faye and Kesey when they eventually moved in—aided by Babbs—but at least the house had been cleaned and the bedroom repainted (though in an equally dreadful yellow color).

After this shaky start, the residents of the Lane quickly warmed to Faye and Ken. The young Oregonian was just another graduate student at first, one among many, but his house gradually became the focus of activities on the Lane, and he emerged as one of its leading characters. "[Faye and Ken] were a very friendly, country type couple who moved in and wanted to get things going and have parties," explained Jim Wolpman. "It became very much more lively. . . . We were very close, kind of like a family even before Ken arrived—there were so few of us, and we got very close; we meshed very nicely, some people closer than others. Ken liked that and wanted to build on that."[50] Faye was quiet and attentive, possessed of a character strong enough to keep Kesey in line if she had to, but she rarely exercised her power in that way. Kesey was a force of nature. He had "such an enormous and powerful presence," remembered friend Ann Lambrecht, "that it was almost like being in the same room with a supernatural being; he had such an extra dose of human magnetism."[51] He was quite capable of being loud, sexist, judgmental, and arrogant, but he was rarely boorish; he was always too interesting and too funny to be that. Even with his quirks, he was a fun guy to hang out with. When Vic used to try and get him to take a Rorschach test or the Thematic Apperception Test, Kesey would use it as an opportunity to flex his imagination and oratory skills, weaving long complicated tales full of wild tangents about what he could supposedly see in the symmetrical inkblots or ambiguous pictures before him. Kesey also treated politics and philosophy as a competitive sport, as intellectual jousting, where winning the game depended on how creatively you could play it. Much of the time it seemed that he could find a way to agree with you and disagree with you at the same time. Kesey's frontier-style libertarian politics set him apart from the progressive and skeptical politics of some of his contemporaries, but they made for some lively conversations. Vic and Jane Burton were Ken's main intellectual interlocutors on the Lane, and both were profoundly influenced by the analytically precise thinking of Donald Davidson, their former professor. Davidson admired Kesey's creative zest, but the two were not close, and their modes of thought were very different. "Ken was well aware of [Davidson's] influence on the rest of us," remembered Jim Wolpman, another of Davidson's students. "In fact, it was the intellectual friction engendered by their contrasting outlooks that best captures what was happening . . . during those years. Ken, of course, never gave in, but [Davidson's] very opposition forced upon him a certain rigor that he never would have achieved otherwise."[52]

On one occasion—this would be later, around 1962–63—the discussion turned to the causes of war and the alternatives to bloody mass conflict. One person suggested that the world's problems could be better served by getting all the world's leaders together in a big muddy ring, making them strip to their underwear, and letting them fight out their differences. Kesey, ever the contrarian, dismissed such notions as totally wrongheaded, insisting that the people, not their leaders, should be held accountable for the existence of wars.[53] Typical all-American Kesey. "People were constantly arguing with Ken," Wolpman recalled. "He loved it and people loved it back because he was so much fun to argue with. . . . [His] arguments were not logical arguments—they were stories and metaphors. You never could quite pin him down, but it was fascinating the directions he would take. . . . You couldn't help but be taken with his sheer, bubbling creativity."[54] Another friend, Larry McMurtry, felt the same way. "There was a lot of the frontiersman in him, an unwillingness to accept conventional answers to a lot of profound questions," remembered McMurtry. "We argued and debated a lot of things. But I never would not listen to him, even if I thought some of what he said was gobbledygook, because there would always be the perception of genius if you waited him out."[55]

Robin White was not so impressed. He was less than thrilled about having his position on the Lane usurped by this country upstart. "When Kesey took over the role of head honcho from poor old Robin White," Chloe Scott remembered of her former neighbor, his "nose was put out completely because everybody started going over to Kesey's instead of his house."[56] White came to dislike Kesey intensely. When he and Marny hosted a house-warming party at their new place later in the year, everyone on the Lane was invited except Kesey and Faye. As a result, a few Perry Laners came to the conclusion that Robin White needed taking down a peg or two. At a book-signing event in Stanford shortly after the party, a few of them dressed up in outrageous beatnik costumes and harassed White mercilessly. White got his revenge by publicly castigating Kesey whenever the opportunity presented itself. In the midsixties, White told a reporter from the *Village Voice* that his former protégé was a needy, dominating coward. "If Kesey was in isolation, he'd disintegrate," White fumed. "He's got to have buttressing, weak individuals he can exploit. . . .

Perry Lane was [originally] made up of nonconformists. After Kesey came on, it became very conformist. There had to be sex parties, marijuana smoking, and you had to dress and speak a certain way. Kesey became master of ceremonies. He has a real capacity to perform, which quite exceeds his capacity to write."[57] Ouch.

White was right about one thing: Kesey was a born performer, and any stage would do. He was an excellent raconteur, oftentimes regaling his friends with elaborate stories about his youthful days in Oregon. He could go into incredibly detailed descriptions of the cheese-making process or offer hilarious portraits of some of the characters who worked at the creamery. There were stories about Kesey's family too, like the one about his brother, Chuck, and the time he caught a skunk and lay down with it in a cage with his face near the dangerous end (of the skunk, that is). Another story related the tale of Kesey and Chuck finding an injured owl on a trail. They decided to walk around and around it to see if its head would pop off as it twisted its neck around trying to follow their progress. Failing in their childish cruelty, the two brothers adopted the owl as a pet, only to see it killed when another of their wild menagerie, a jealous raccoon, pushed a huge jar off a high shelf and killed it.[58]

Stories like these kept Kesey's friends on the Lane endlessly amused, but they also made obvious the stark differences that existed between his rustic, rural origins and most of their suburbanite backgrounds. These differences should not be overstated, but they would be writ large by Kesey in *Sometimes a Great Notion*, much of which concerns the conflict between two main protagonists, the Stamper brothers: Lee, a sensitive intellectual, and Hank, a roughhewn logger. Asked about the book in 1963, Kesey acknowledged that in part this conflict was about his own personality. "For one thing, I want to find out which side of me really is: the woodsy, logger side or its opposition," he told his friend Gordon Lish. "The two Stamper brothers in the novel are each one of the ways I think I am."[59] This conflict between the two brothers could also be understood as a reflection of the differences that existed between Kesey and many of the people on the Lane.

These obvious cultural differences were not enough to stop Kesey involving everybody in his driven determination to have a good time. Whether it was a game of pick-up basketball, "people croquet" in the Perry Lane courtyard, playing a dartboard baseball game that he had devised, or diving into an elaborate game of charades complete with costumes and props, Kesey was usually at the center of things. The Halloween party in 1959, for example, was a theatrical extravaganza. Everybody's costume was colorful and creative. Faye dressed as a dance-hall girl, Vic Lovell came as a mummy, Chloe Scott appeared as Reba the bird girl, and Jane Burton turned up as a yogi. Others dressed as Attila the Hun (Norm Giddan), a flapper (Nancy Hershberg), or Dracula (Dick Bolin), but stealing the show, at least in his own estimation, was Kesey. He had gone to a lot of effort to transform himself into a *Wild One*–era Brando, with the black leather boots and a black leather jacket bearing the lettering BRMC (Black Rebels Motorcycle Club) on the back. He was convinced that his friends did not even recognize him at first. Gone was the beard that he had worn for the previous six months. He had also dyed his hair black and used his old theater makeup skills to concoct a Brando-like broken nose. By the time the party ground to a halt at six the next morning, Kesey's hair dye had begun to run, and the putty on his nose had started to slip, but at least he had been Brando for a night.[60]

Dinner parties on the Lane would often turn into crazy ad-libbed poetry sessions. There were many musicians on the Lane, so evenings of music and singing were commonplace. Kesey was learning to play guitar, and he would sometimes lead a sing-along of the sort of old-timey folk songs and "Okie" standards that his family sang at their get-togethers. It was also very much a literary scene, the location of many late night sessions where books would be read and discussed and dissected. It became common for some of the members of the creative writing seminar to retire to Perry Lane after class to continue their ruminations. "Frequently, the seminar would go on half the afternoon," remembered Gurney Norman, a Stegner fellow in the 1960–61 seminar class (Larry McMurtry, Peter Beagle, and James Baker Hall received the three other fellowships that year). "We would then go to the campus coffee shop for two more hours of talking and then the real hardcore element—one of whom I became as time went on—would go back to Ken's house where Faye would cook up rice and beans, and it would go on into the night. . . . That's how we gravitated to Ken's house, and his house became the center of one side of the socializing among campus writers."[61]

Sometimes the Lane's activities could get just plain silly, the way they do when adults indulge in childlike games. Vic, for example, had an old toilet bowl that he would set in the middle of his living room, and people would use it as a basketball hoop. On another occasion, Jim Spencer recalled "walking into a cottage and there were forty or fifty people lying on their backs with their feet up trying to keep a bunch of balloons in the air."[62] Lane residents used to have spectacular water fights during which people would climb into trees and onto roofs to get the best shot. During one such battle, Kesey found a large number of horse chestnuts piled up behind the chimney where he was hiding. He kept the water-mob at bay with this ammunition for a good few minutes, but the game came to a premature end when Vic went crashing through a skylight and fell into Jane's bathtub below. At another get together, the players all armed themselves with a rolled-up newspaper and ran around swatting one another, laughing and giggling at their own childishness. When the papers had virtually disintegrated, the partiers gathered them together in the fireplace and set them alight. The bravest of the revelers then moved to the roof, where they danced among the glowing paper embers that were floating up the chimney and out into the night sky.[63] Sometimes things would get rowdy enough to attract the attention of the local police, but never to any great consequence, even after drugs became part of the scene. "The police knew something was going on and really wanted to bust somebody," Jim Spencer remembered, "but all they found were people playing darts, playing volleyball, doing normal things."[64]

Sometimes the Lane hosted giant street parties. One of the most spectacular took place in the spring of 1959 when Kesey staged a massive luau cookout.[65] This was no ordinary barbecue. Kesey decided to teach these college kids how they did things where he came from, and in this case, that meant roasting a whole pig on a spit. He dug a pit in Chloe's yard, filled it full of rocks, and fashioned it into something that looked like a huge birdbath. Then he and Dirk Van Neuhause poured four bags of charcoal briquettes into the lined pit before trying to get the rust off the old spit contraption that they had borrowed for the occasion. Kesey and Babbs mounted the carcass on the spit while Faye, Jane, and Anita (Babbs's girlfriend and future wife) set about stuffing it. The fire lit, Kesey left Jack in charge while he went off to the city with Bev to pick up his old college buddy, Boyd. All three then hurried to North Beach, where Kesey set about looking for a pianist friend of his, Joe Elias, whom he hoped would play at the party. They found him—skinny, toothless, already drunk, and sporting an earring in one ear—propping up a table in the Coffee Gallery. Kesey lured him to the party with the promise of lots of friendly women and good times. They picked up a gallon bottle of cheap Golden Chablis and headed back to the Lane. It was getting late, already past nine-thirty.

The scene at the party was already swinging. The pig had been almost completely destroyed, picked to its bones by hundreds of sticky fingers. The jazz combo was already wailing, its music competing with an "Okie" record that was blasting out of Vic's place and an unknown guitar player who was struggling to play along with both. Kesey found Jane lying down drunk on a bed, waiting to feel well enough to start drinking again. Hundreds of people milled around the cottages and up and down the Lane. Kesey recognized and greeted many of them, but there were others he had never seen before. He spotted some members of the Stanford wrestling team that he had been working out with and occasionally helping to coach. A group of bongo players showed up and set about doing their thing at Kesey's place. Dick Bolin grabbed his bongos and joined in the rhythmic racket, and a red-headed beatnik chick started swaying and weaving to the beat. From out of a crowd of suntanned fraternity types, a big guy stepped forward and started dancing suggestively with her. Kesey recognized him as the best wrestler on the Stanford squad, a guy called Art Spiegel, and as he danced with the girl his buddies yelled out their encouragement, "Go, Art, Go." Art spotted Kesey and came over to greet him. The two started wrestling playfully, but Kesey stopped the fight short, much to the disappointment of Art's cheering buddies, who seemed to be fixing for a fight of one sort or another. Babbs was walking around the place in his marine fatigues, looking to quell just such an eventuality.

Vic called Kesey over. The police had just arrived and were busy telling Robin that it was illegal to hold a street dance without a permit, that the neighbors were complaining about the noise, and that under no circumstances should the street be blocked. The usual complaints. While Kesey and the others set about moving the piano and the band into Chloe's yard, one cop started yelling to no one in particular, urging the owner of the station wagon blocking the street to move it. Quick as a flash, Kesey noticed that the police car was causing a similar obstruction so he started responding in kind, calling on the owner of the car with the spotlight on it to move it out of the way. The cops left laughing, but not for long. They would come back two more times before the night was out.

Shortly after the cops left that first time, things turned a little ugly. The wrestling crowd and their equally drunken crew-cut buddies had taken exception to the beatnik elements at the party. They had broken up the bongo scene, and Art, Kesey's old wrestling pal, had landed a punch on Dirk. A diplomatic Kesey calmed the situation by appealing to the young guns' egos by asking them to help provide security for the party. Nice trick, but it only worked for a while. Not much later, Babbs had to rescue Jane Burton from three of Art's buddies who had maneuvered her into a bedroom and locked the door. Babbs threw them all out, much to the relief of Jane, but even then Kesey caught them plotting to trash his house because Babbs had interrupted their "fun." And so the evening went: a strange combination of revelry and aggression, like a scene from *The Wild One*. When Kesey stumbled out of bed the next day, the dogs had dragged what was left of the pig off the spit and were lugging it around the dusty courtyard, tearing it up like Kesey and his friends were about to tear up the staid old fifties script that their parents had bequeathed them.

Roll over Beethoven

The straight-laced Whites—Robin the son of missionaries, Marny a practicing Quaker—objected to the wild parties. They also disapproved of the drug use that would later develop on the Lane, but they particularly disliked the Keseys' liberal sexual attitudes. It was not as if Perry Lane had previously conformed to the conservative sexual mores of the day—far from it—but the Keseys pushed those already extended boundaries a little further. Soon after they arrived, they made it known that they had an open marriage, and it did not take long for them to start exercising their sexual freedom. They befriended a young couple who lived across the street from their cottage. After a party during which Kesey had been necking with the woman and Faye with the man, they came back to the Lane and each couple paired off to separate houses. Thus began a brief, mutually satisfying exchange that ended only when the other couple started to feel that it was becoming a strain on their marriage and on their friendship with the Keseys. This wasn't the only extramarital fling on the Lane. "What's wrong with a little sex," said a female character in Hughes Rudd's story about the Lane in the early 1950s. "That's what Perry Lane is for, isn't it?"[66] Not for nothing did some disapproving locals call it

"Sin Hollow."[67] Over the years, the line between friend and lover on Perry Lane was often difficult to discern in a social milieu that Jane Burton once described as "an incredibly supportive group love affair."[68] Chloe Scott put it even more succinctly: "Everybody was sleeping with everybody."[69]

Nudity and sex became part of the social experiment on the Lane. When a couple of inches of snow fell on the Lane briefly during the winter of 1962—a very rare occurrence on the mid-peninsula—Kesey, Vic, and the others quickly scraped up all the snow they could and lined their side of the street with snowmen and women copulating in Kama Sutra poses. "They didn't last very long; you had to live on the street to see it," recalled resident Paul De Carli. "Even with snow, [Kesey] would show a little bit of defiance of the norm."[70] Strip poker was not that unusual on the Lane, nor was the occasional topless moment or nude sunbathe. Even before drugs entered the fray—which tended to lower people's inhibitions even further—things could get pretty loose. After another Hawaiian-style cookout in the summer of 1959 turned into a three-day marathon party, Kesey emerged from his bedroom early one morning to find at least five or six couples scattered around his living room floor. Most of them were just trying to sleep off their hedonistic endeavors, but much to Kesey's voyeuristic delight he saw that two of the couples were engaged in breathless, frantic love-making, impervious to the people around them.[71] The Whites would have been appalled, just as they would have been at the decorum of Judy, a young woman who participated in the opening ceremony of an event that their former neighbors dubbed the First Annual Perry Lane Olympics. "The torch consisted of a plumber's helper with a burning rag stuffed in the cup," Vic Lovell recalled. Judy "held it high, sitting naked on the back of a convertible which was driven around the block before its triumphant arrival."[72] Shocking stuff for some locals, but within a few years, nudity would become almost fashionable among a certain social set in the region. One of the most talked-about occasions involved a Passover celebration in which about forty naked people marked the traditional Jewish holiday in the living room of Group House, a Menlo Park office complex of psychologists.[73]

Later in the sixties, organizations such as the Sexual Freedom League and the influential liberal sexologist Dr. Albert Ellis (author of *American Sexual Tragedy* [1954], *Creative Marriage* [1961], and *Sex without Guilt* [1966]) would be at the forefront of the sexual freedom movement, but the sort of open sexual behavior that these people advocated was already being practiced by small groups of progressive artists, musicians, writers, and intellectuals scattered around the United States. Perry Laners knew they were not alone in these pursuits: Chloe Scott had been part of Jackson Pollock's artistic circle when she lived in Long Island, and she was well aware that plenty of those people had engaged in the same bed-hopping "free for all" that some people enjoyed on the Lane. Nevertheless, Kesey's promotion of sexual freedom among the Perry Lane community made a few individuals feel a little uncomfortable. "We were young people, there was some of that going on already," Jim Wolpman remembered, "but it seemed like it became more so. . . . There was some pressure toward it." While everything was above-board and consensual, there is a lingering sense among some of the participants that circumstances conspired to push them to engage in activities that they probably would not have done otherwise. Kesey could certainly be a womanizer, but it would be too easy to dismiss his promotion of sexual freedom as merely a symptom of his raging hormones. "I think he thought it had to do with creating that large group that he wanted to create," Jim Wolpman explained. "It seems to me that he didn't just want to get women. . . . It seemed to be a higher motive than that."[74] Higher motive or not, Kesey discovered at his own cost that not every couple was capable of living with the consequences of an open marriage. In one instance, a friend and past resident of the Lane burned a draft of *Sometimes a Great Notion*, along with some other manuscripts that he found in Kesey's writing room, after he discovered that Kesey had slept with his wife.[75] Kesey was unrepentant, claiming that his friend had engaged in similar errant behavior. Still, the experience left its mark. "I was always for as much 'free sex' as you could get," Kesey told one interviewer much later in life, "but I learned really quickly that it wasn't all that 'free,' that you paid for it some place."[76]

The sexual experimentation on the Lane was part and parcel of a broader rebellion against what were seen by the Lane residents as the constraining cultural and social mores of the day. Chloe Scott recalled that from their perspective, "the fifties were pretty staid and there was a lot to rebel against . . . or refuse to go along with." Sexual inhibitions were seen as just something else to rebel against, to challenge, or to leave behind. This is important if we want to understand what happens next. Well before drugs came on the scene, Kesey was already rebelling against the standards of the day according to his own understanding of what it meant to be an American. If this was the land of the free, then Kesey wanted to be free: free to challenge what he saw as dogmatic rules and conventions, free to express himself as an individual, free to live up to the ideals that America promised. The problem was an American Cold War culture that denied people the very liberty it was supposedly fighting to preserve. America had taken a wrong turn, it seemed to Kesey, and therefore, any right-thinking American should do what they could to set it back on track.[77]

Perry Lane is important to this story not only because many of its residents went on to be Pranksters—most did not, and a few would be offended to be called such—but also because it gave Kesey an opportunity to test himself and his ideas among a fascinating group of people, many of whom were his intellectual equals. The free-thinking, curious, questioning temperament of the Lane offered Kesey a stimulating environment in which to develop his own ideas and his craft. He matured as a writer, as a thinker, and as an individual on Perry Lane. He was never a dogmatic, anti-American lefty, but he was always something of a rebel, distrustful of authority, and enough of an American to challenge that authority when it seemed to him to be wrong. We should not overstate this rebellious ambition, but let us also note its presence. Over the course of the next few years, events would conspire to push it to the fore, making Kesey the somewhat unlikely public face of a social movement from which he actually felt quite removed.

And the significance of the parties and the hedonism? Well, on one level, a party is just a party and hedonism is just hedonism, but given what would happen next—the drugs, La Honda, the bus trip, the Merry Pranksters, the Acid Tests, and the wider emergence of a fully blown counterculture—these gatherings take on some historical significance. The larger street parties on the Lane were remarkable in their scale, but their beer-keg and pig-roast sensibilities suggest that they were as much a product of Kesey's family traditions and his fraternity history as they were a precursor to the parties at La Honda and the Acid Tests that followed. Their major significance is that they served as a point of first contact for a number of individuals who would go on to play a role in the Merry Pranksters. They also served as a point of connection between the Perry Laners and other like-minded scenes in the region.

The smaller, intimate parties on the Lane seem far more historically important than the larger ones. The Perry Laners were an incredibly tight-knit group of people who were well aware that their relationship was special. They even took to reciting their own pledge of allegiance: "I pledge allegiance to Perry Lane, and to the vision for which it stands. One consciousness, indivisible, with liberty and justice for all."[78] Their get-togethers were opportunities to gather in a setting where all rules and social conventions were consciously challenged, if not abandoned altogether. Add a healthy measure of playfulness, a willingness to act out or perform, some good food, and stimulating conversation, and you have the setting for an interesting and maybe revealing historical event. Add pot and powerful psychedelic drugs to that mix, and the future starts to take shape.

4

A Royal Road to Insight

CROSSROADS

By the fall of 1959, after just one year at Stanford, Kesey was becoming somewhat despondent about his situation and his prospects. He and Faye were desperate to start a family but they were struggling to get pregnant, despite their best efforts.[1] The Keseys were also pretty broke, getting by on the money that Faye brought home from her job at one of Stanford's libraries and a fellowship that Kesey had been awarded for the upcoming year (his Woodrow Wilson Fellowship had expired at the end of the 1958–59 school year). Unknown to Kesey at the time, that fellowship was not guaranteed. "One day this rough-looking fellow turned up to talk to us," recalled noted literary critic Leslie Fiedler, who sat on the committee that awarded the fellowships. "Everyone else on the committee hated him. 'One person we don't want to give this fellowship to is the wrestler,' they said. I fought them to the death and finally won."[2]

Searching for additional income, Kesey and Faye hit upon the notion of opening up a coffee house at a dingy location in the back streets of Palo Alto. They got as far as finding a potential partner for the deal—a woman whose primary qualification seemed to be that she was prepared to put five thousand dollars into the venture. Kesey hatched some half-baked idea about serving nutmeg tea instead of coffee because he had heard or read, probably in William S. Burroughs's *Naked Lunch*, that it could get you high, but the coffee shop plan eventually fizzled out without amounting to anything.[3]

Kesey had more than just domestic and money woes. The fellowship allowed him to keep his coveted position at the long table in the Jones Room of the Stanford Library, the location of the creative writing program's weekly meetings, but Kesey was not at all happy with the way his writing was going. His contributions to the seminar that fall came from his Beat novel in progress, "Zoo," but he was having a devil of a time getting it finished. Losing confidence, he wrote to Babbs, telling him that he was increasingly concerned that all his efforts to date had produced little of redeeming value.[4]

As the winter of 1959 closed in, some brighter news appeared on Kesey's doorstep. Earlier in the year, he had submitted a few chapters of "Zoo" to a literary competition staged by Harper Brothers Publishers. By late November he had pretty much forgotten about it, but then a letter arrived informing him that he had won a Saxton Grant, giving him two thousand dollars tax-free and thus bragging rights on the Lane as an award-winning writer. The letter warned Kesey that the grant did not carry any assurance of publication, but in his reply he gushed enthusiastically: "The letter is a first of its kind, and whether anything comes of it or not I shall cherish it always among my pile of short story rejection slips."[5] The news infuriated an increasingly antagonistic Robin White, who refused to believe Kesey's claim to fame and even threatened to go to the Saxton office to disprove it. When Kesey threw a huge champagne celebration in his own prizewinning honor, he pointedly excluded the Whites from the invitation list.

The Saxton money was welcome, but the award didn't help get "Zoo" published. Putnam turned it down in April 1960, so Kesey sent the complete manuscript to Harper Brothers, where it was warmly received—"one of the most interesting entries. . . . Fresh in its handling of language and easily the best statement (if that is the word) we have seen on the Beats and their world"—but politely rejected.[6] Kesey considered trying at Viking, but he already seemed to be losing faith in the quality of his manuscript. Looking around for new material, he eventually started thinking about writing a novel based on his experiences on Perry Lane.

Those early months of 1960 were hectic for Kesey as he found himself busier than at any time since his period at the University of Oregon. He took a part-time job at a day-care facility, helping to look after about twenty-five four-year olds. He would start at 9:00 a.m. and work until after lunch. In the afternoons, he spent his time writing, helping coach the wrestling team at Stanford, and working out in training for the Olympic trials. A trip back to Oregon in April produced an interesting proposal: Kesey's old English professor, James B. Hall, offered Kesey a job editing the *Northwest Review*, a literary journal published by the university. The position paid two thousand dollars per year, plus tuition for as long it took Kesey to get a master's degree. Kesey was tempted, but not enough to say yes. Babbs, by now a Marine in flight-training school in Florida, was also trying to tempt Kesey and Faye away from California by encouraging them to come and join him in the Sunshine State. Kesey refused, mostly because he and Faye had entered into a two-hundred-dollar-per-month agreement with a woman who was willing to offer her as-yet-unborn baby for adoption, but also because he had just recently chanced upon a new source of income and inspiration. Vic Lovell had told Kesey about some drug experiments being carried out at the Menlo Park Veterans Administration (VA) hospital in Palo Alto. Kesey could not have known it at the time, but his decision to become a paid volunteer in these experiments would shape the rest of his life.

New Frontier, Old Frontier

Kesey and his friends were on the cutting edge of psychedelic drug use in the 1960s. Their use of these drugs at quasi-ritualistic events like the Acid Tests was a modern continuation of much older traditions that make good use of a myriad of naturally occurring plants and fungi. Amazonian peoples employ a vine called yagé; practitioners of the ancient Vedic religion of the Indian subcontinent used a number of plants to create a drink that they called soma; and pagan witches of Europe made potent brews incorporating belladonna, thorn apple, and henbane, or made hallucinogenic ointments from the roots of mandrake. As part of their celebration of the Eleusinian Mysteries, citizens of classical Greece (including Socrates, Plato, Sophocles, and Aristotle) drank kykeon, a beverage believed to have contained barley ergot (LSD is a synthesized version of ergot); and Australian Aborigines ate a desert shrub called pituri. The Aztecs ingested ololiuqui (a small seed containing lysergic acid) and peyote cactus buttons, as did certain tribes that lived in what is now the Southwest of the United States. So widespread was the historical use of mind-altering substances that author Charles Hayes concludes that "[v]eneration for the induced use of visionary experiences has roots in virtually every culture on earth."[7] These cultures used all these psychotropic substances for a variety of purposes, including, as pharmacologist Leo Hollister noted, "religious or magical celebration, for increasing sociability, for treating or understanding emotional disorders and for simply making an arduous life more pleasurable."[8] Since the Pranksters and the broader psychedelic movement of the 1960s employed LSD for very similar purposes, they were, whether they knew it or not, treading a well-worn path.

The same could be said of the prohibitive tendencies of the United States legal and political authorities. Although the current "War on Drugs" originated in the 1960s—in part symptomatic of a broader conservative cultural backlash to the period—the puritan urge to deny people the right to engage in drug-fueled activities has a much longer history. The Judeo-Christian tradition especially has generally frowned upon the use of mind-altering substances, mostly because such practices were associated with paganism and seen as a threat to the doctrines of the church. Once Christianity became the official creed of the Roman Empire in the fourth century, the church brutally suppressed all remnants of the "pagan drug cults" of Europe, including those Eleusinian Mysteries of the ancient Greeks. A millennium later, the Holy Inquisition exercised similarly lethal retribution across Europe, torturing and killing any "witches" accused of making and imbibing "magic potions." European colonial powers continued these prohibitory policies against the indigenous cultures that they encountered around the world. Officials of the British Empire, for example, outlawed the use of kava in Tahiti, just as the Spanish Conquistadors banned the use of peyote and other such substances in the Americas.[9]

An extensive literature now exists regarding these ancient practices and their prohibition, but special mention should be made of the work of Gordon and Valentina Wasson, since they played an important part in bringing this history to the attention of the modern world. The Wassons were among the first to document the ways in which numerous cultures used mushrooms as vision-inspiring agents in their spiritual practices.[10] An article describing one of Gordon Wasson's research expeditions to a remote Mexican village appeared in the May 13, 1957, edition of *Life* magazine. Formerly a vice president of J. P. Morgan & Co., Wasson was an improbable candidate to play the role of an Indiana Jones–like adventurer seeking spiritual wisdom from the ancients, but that made his claims for

the properties of the mushrooms he encountered all the more fantastic. "We chewed and swallowed these acrid mushrooms, saw visions, and
emerged from the experience awestruck," he wrote. "When it seemed to
us that a sequence of visions had lasted for years, our watches would tell
us that only seconds had passed."[11] This piece provoked significant interest among an American readership that included the CIA (who were so
determined to learn more that it sent an undercover operative with Wasson on his next expedition), and an up and coming psychology professor
called Timothy Leary, who was also prompted to investigate further.[12]

THE MOST DANGEROUS MAN IN AMERICA

Leary actually came to the psychedelic party pretty late, yet it would eventually fall to him to embrace the spotlight and lead the public dancing. In
the summer of 1960, while vacationing in Cuernavaca, Mexico, Leary took
some "magic mushrooms" that an anthropologist friend had procured.
It was an earth-shattering experience for Leary, someone who had never
even smoked marijuana before. "In four hours by the swimming pool in
Cuernavaca," he wrote in his memoirs, "I learned more about the mind,
the brain, and its structures than I did in the preceding fifteen as a diligent
psychologist."[13]

Once back at Harvard University—where he had been hired at the Center for Personality Research earlier in the year—Leary and a colleague,
assistant professor of psychology Dick Alpert (who later changed his name
to Ram Dass), set up the Harvard Psychedelic Research Project to investigate how to best utilize that key. By Thanksgiving 1960 Leary and Alpert
had procured four small bottles of psilocybin pills from Sandoz Laboratories in New Jersey (psilocybin is the psychoactive element in magic
mushrooms). Within a matter of weeks, fifteen or so staff members at the
Center for Personality Research had tried the drug in a "session" under
the guidance of Leary, Alpert, or one of their colleagues. News of these
initial experiments prompted many of the center's graduate students to get
involved with the psilocybin project, as both participants and researchers
in their own graduate work. Word of Leary's and Alpert's activities quickly
spread beyond Harvard's campus boundaries, and they found themselves
inundated with inquiries from the already extensive international network of scientists, philosophers, and scholars involved in similar studies.

According to Leary, many of these people urged him to work within the system, to keep the experiments low-key and "in-house," the fear being that if the political and legal authorities suspected that Leary was promoting the nonmedicinal use of these substances, then these authorities were likely to respond with prohibitive measures that would set back everyone's research into the possible value of psychedelics.[14]

Keeping quiet was not really Leary's style, and nor was being told what to do. After a December 1960 session with Allen Ginsberg—who had learned of Leary's project from a psychiatrist friend—Leary decided that the possibilities offered by psilocybin deserved to be experienced by more than just the mentally ill or an intellectual elite. The plan was to initiate a broad range of influential people into the "wonders of psilocybin" in the hope that they would help generate "a wave of public opinion to support massive research programs, licensing procedures, training centers in the intelligent use of drugs," and voilà, an evolution in human consciousness would result, leading to world revolution, world peace, and a new beginning. Aided and abetted by Ginsberg and his boyfriend, Peter Orlovsky, Leary gave psilocybin to such Beat luminaries as Neal Cassady, William Burroughs, Jack Kerouac, Gregory Corso, and Allen Ansen. Ginsberg also lined up sessions with Pulitzer Prize–winning poet Robert Lowell and famed avant-garde publisher Barney Rossett. Leary initiated Huston Smith, chair of the MIT philosophy department; Dorothy Norman, a well-known scholar and friend of Indian prime minister Jawaharlal Nehru (who subsequently offered to set up a research center in India for Leary); and a group of eight prominent psychologists associated with J. B. Rhine's parapsychology studies in Durham, North Carolina. By his own account, Leary "turned on" literally hundreds of people during his three years at Harvard.

While Leary was running around seeding what he thought was the next stage of human evolution, his research program at Harvard was producing some seemingly remarkable results. An experimental rehabilitation program at Concord State Prison in Massachusetts, for example, cut recidivism rates from an average of 70 percent down to 10 percent for the thirty-five convicts who volunteered to take part in the program. Leary came to believe that psilocybin, used in the right fashion, could rewire, or "re-imprint," the brain and generate dramatic changes of behavior in individuals. The apparent success of the prison project was welcome, but it raised the public profile of Leary's work in precisely the manner that he had been warned to avoid. Leary's group also facilitated a famous experiment run by Walter Pahnke, a doctoral candidate in the Harvard Divinity School. Pahnke arranged for five small groups of test subjects—mostly divinity students—to gather in the basement of the Boston University chapel on Good Friday, 1962. The idea was to investigate the supposedly mystical aspects of the psilocybin experience by giving some spiritually oriented individuals the drug in a religious setting. Only half the subjects received a pill containing psilocybin—the rest a placebo—but those who took the psilocybin reported going through a series of remarkable mystical experiences. An article in *Time* magazine about the Good Friday Experiment introduced the Harvard Psychedelic Research Project to the nation. The article was positive, but the responses to it were not. Established religious figures condemned the idea that enlightenment was attainable through a pill; the Harvard Divinity School discouraged its graduate students from pursuing similar studies; and though Pahnke was awarded his degree, he was not allowed to continue with this line of research, and his grant proposals were denied.

Initially, Leary's experimental quest for a "neurological revolution" was fueled solely by psilocybin, but in the spring of 1962 an Englishman by the name of Michael Hollingshead turned up at Leary's house bearing a mayonnaise jar full of LSD-laced sugar.[15] One spoonful was enough to shatter Leary's reality all over again. His introduction to LSD corresponded with the beginning of the end of his tenure at Harvard. Some of Leary's faculty colleagues in the Center for Personality Research came forward with complaints about the legitimacy of the work being carried out by the Psilocybin Research Project. A staff meeting was called to air grievances. The school newspaper, the *Harvard Crimson*, ran a lurid account of the contentious meeting, a story that was picked up by the Boston newspapers and the national wire services. The press coverage attracted the attention of the Massachusetts State Narcotics Bureau, at which point Leary and Alpert decided that if their work was to continue, they would need to keep a lower profile on the Harvard campus and try to sever their financial dependence on the Center for Personality Research.

Leary and Alpert spent six weeks of the summer in 1962 in Zihuatanejo, Mexico, investigating the world of LSD with a group of about thirty friends and colleagues. On any given day, a third of the group would ingest the drug, and each ingester would be guided and assisted by someone who remained straight. The remaining members of the group would spend their day resting, recuperating from their last trip, and writing up their experiences. In Leary's and Alpert's absence, certain members of the Harvard administration became increasingly concerned that the activities of the Psilocybin Research Project put the institution's reputation at risk. Seeing the writing on the wall, Leary, Alpert, and their associates began setting up an independent organization—the International Foundation for Internal Freedom, or IFIF for short—with the intention of creating a network of research centers across America to conduct psychedelic research and training. In May 1963 Harvard fired Leary, ostensibly for failing to show up for his classes, and they dismissed Alpert for violating an agreement that stipulated that he not supply psychedelics to any undergraduates. Leary and Alpert joined Ralph Waldo Emerson as the only professors ever fired from their posts in Harvard's long history.

Leary learned of his dismissal while he was in Mexico trying to set up another psychedelic summer camp. Before those plans could be finalized, he and his IFIF compadres were deported by the Mexican authorities on the charge that their tourist visas did not allow them to run a business in Mexico. After an aborted attempt to set up a research center on the island of Dominica in the Caribbean, Leary and IFIF finally set up shop on a large estate in Millbrook, New York, about a two-hour drive from Manhattan. The estate belonged to Billy Hitchcock, the son of Thomas Hitchcock, a legendary American fighter pilot, world-class polo player, and heir to the fortune of American financier Andrew Mellon. Billy's sister, Peggy Hitchcock, had been part of Leary's circle since spring 1962, and it was she who had arranged for Dick Alpert to give Billy LSD. Enthused by the experience, Billy graciously agreed to let IFIF use the sixty-four-room four-story mansion on the estate as their headquarters. Stung by all the adverse publicity surrounding their departure from Harvard and their deportation from Mexico and Dominica, Leary and Alpert scrapped their plans to create a national network of psychedelic training centers. Instead, they determined to lower their profile but continue their research into "altered states" within the gated protection of the Millbrook estate.

Leary's profile did not remain low for very long. A marijuana bust for the possession of a few joints (it was actually his daughter's pot, hidden in her underwear), on the way back from Mexico in December 1965, put him back in the national and international spotlight, especially when he was sentenced a few months later to thirty years in jail and fined forty thousand dollars. Another attempted bust in May 1966, this time a raid on Millbrook led by local prosecutor (and later Watergate criminal) G. Gordon Liddy, only added to Leary's celebrity status, as did an appearance before a Senate committee hearing in the early summer of 1966 that was deliberating whether to make LSD illegal. Leary was never one to avoid center stage, but he always felt that the rebellious role he came to play in the 1960s was forced upon him by the actions of the establishment (Kesey felt similarly about his own notoriety). Leary's lawyer told him the prosecutor wanted to make an example of him, but all he actually succeeded in doing was making Leary a martyr, and an internationally famous one at that. It was a role that Leary embraced, and by 1966 he was far and away LSD's most prominent spokesman, its most recognizable public face, and its media-anointed high priest. Inspired by a conversation with Marshall McLuhan, Leary even offered the masses a catchphrase for the times, "Turn On, Tune In, Drop Out." He spent a lifetime denying that the phrase urged people to just get stoned and abandon all worthwhile social activities, but that is how it was interpreted by a mainstream "silent majority" who were increasingly fearful that LSD spelled disaster for all they held dear. No wonder Richard Nixon, their mouthpiece, eventually dubbed Leary "the most dangerous man in America."

Though Kesey and Leary became good friends later in life, their paths crossed only rarely during the heyday of their notoriety. "The famous professor had always been a more distant phenomenon than a close friend," Kesey admitted after Leary died in 1996, talking about their earlier years.[16] Some of the Perry Lane residents actually had much closer ties to Dick Alpert. Before being hired at Harvard, Alpert's first professionally accredited job had been as a part-time therapist at the Stanford Counseling and Testing Center (he had earned his PhD in psychology in 1957). Alpert had obtained some funding from a national magazine to investigate what Stanford students wanted out of life, and Vic Lovell was one of the few who did not provide the stock answer: "I want a good wife/husband and a well-paying job." Alpert found Vic interesting, and Vic found talking to someone about himself rewarding, so Vic became Alpert's first-ever therapy client. The two became friends and occasionally saw each other socially. Indeed, Alpert's first taste of marijuana came courtesy of Vic at one of the parties on Perry Lane. Vic's friendship with Alpert was

an important point of connection between East and West Coast psychedelic scenes.

Kesey first learned of IFIF through Vic and Jane Burton in the spring
of 1963. Vic was advocating signing on with Leary and Alpert down in
Mexico, but Jane was not so sure. Vic produced a piece of yellow paper
and pinned it to the wall, telling Kesey and the others to sign up if they
wanted to join him on a trip to Mexico to turn-on at one of Leary's seminars.[17] Kesey was initially lukewarm about the prospect—he was too much
of an individualist to ever want to join anybody else's scene—but he was
also never one to miss a party either, and so by the time May came around
his reticence had been replaced by excitement. He and Faye and a selection of their Perry Lane friends booked their spot at the IFIF seminar
down in Zihuatanejo, but Leary and Alpert were expelled by the Mexican
authorities before they had a chance to get there.

WEAPONS OF MASS DISORIENTATION

Although Leary, Alpert, Kesey, and a few other countercultural icons are
generally blamed for "turning on" America, the fact is that the psychedelic era was in many ways an unintentional product of the Cold War
and the post–World War II emergence of a pharmacologically inclined
mental health industry. Indeed, more than twenty-five years before Leary
and Kesey embarked on their first psychedelic voyages, various U.S. government agencies, the pharmaceutical industry, and certain members
of the medical community had been busy expending millions of dollars
and thousands of hours exploring the potential of a vast array of mind-
altering natural and synthetic substances. Reviewing all this activity, Martin A. Lee and Bruce Shain came to the astonishing conclusion that "nearly
every drug that appeared on the black market during the 1960s . . . had
previously been scrutinized, tested, and in some cases refined by CIA and
army scientists."[18]

Little of this was common knowledge in the early 1960s. "Ginsberg
said this was all coming from the CIA," Kesey told one interviewer, "but
nobody believed that, like nobody believed a lot of other conspiracy
stuff."[19] A Freedom of Information Act (FOIA) request filed by author
John Marks in the 1970s and some revealing Senate hearings in the fall of
1977 proved Ginsberg correct. The hearings, chaired by Teddy Kennedy,

confirmed that various U.S. government agencies had carried out an extensive series of tests involving LSD and other substances going back as far as World War II. These government agencies had a number of ambitious goals. The U.S. Navy's Project CHATTER (1947–53), for example, set out to develop a "truth serum" for use in its questioning of captured enemy combatants. The U.S. Army had even grander ambitions. Its Chemical Corps sought to develop "psychochemical weapons" that would revolutionize battlefield combat by giving U.S. forces the ability to temporarily incapacitate or disorient the enemy. Between 1955 and 1958 alone, the army administered LSD to more than a thousand volunteers in tests that were usually carried out at the Army Chemical Warfare Laboratories in Edgewood, Maryland.[20] In 1962 the U.S. Army's Operation DERBY HAT commenced a series of field tests carried out in the Far East that actually administered these experimental drugs to seven unwitting individuals—all foreign nationals—as part of an investigation into their supposed involvement in various spying or smuggling activities.[21]

Though the U.S. military had a significant role to play in investigating the weapons and intelligence potential of mind-altering drugs, the main protagonist in this pursuit was the CIA (and, to a limited extent, its predecessor, the Office of Strategic Services). Early CIA projects such as Operation BLUEBIRD (which evolved into Operation ARTICHOKE) tried to develop drug-induced "behavior modification" and interrogation techniques. An interest in Manchurian candidate–like "brainwashing" techniques was a major focus of attention during and following the Korean War. These projects were relatively small scale compared to Project MK-ULTRA, which ran from 1953 through 1964 with a budget that ran into the millions.[22] Richard Helms, then CIA Assistant Deputy Director for Plans, initially proposed the establishment of MK-ULTRA, but it was actually run by Sidney Gottlieb, chief of the CIA's Technical Services Division. Helms went on to be CIA Director (1967–73).[23] MK-ULTRA functioned primarily as an umbrella organization, funding and coordinating at least 149 different subprojects that studied all aspects of "behavior modification." Of these projects, twenty-five involved drug tests on human subjects, six of which involved the administration of drugs to unsuspecting participants.[24]

The CIA ran some of these projects themselves—including one that involved surreptitiously dosing male clients with LSD at brothels in San

Francisco and New York—but most were carried out by more than 185 nongovernment researchers whose work was closely monitored by the CIA. Forty-four colleges and universities, fifteen research foundations or pharmaceutical companies, twelve hospitals or clinics, and three penal institutions received MK-ULTRA money. The CIA often invested heavily in these projects. On one occasion, the agency provided $375,000—which triggered $1 million of federal matching funds—toward the cost of constructing a new wing at Georgetown University Hospital, perhaps with the intention of facilitating its own particular research interests.[25]

All these U.S. government sanctioned or operated drug programs experimented with numerous substances—marijuana, alcohol, barbiturates, caffeine, peyote, mescaline, cocaine, amyl nitrate, PCP, heroin, amphetamines, and nitrous oxide (laughing gas)—but the drug that initially elicited the most excitement was a synthetic derivative of ergot—a fungus that grew on diseased kernels of rye—that went by the laboratory name of lysergic acid diethylamide-25 (LSD-25). A Swiss chemist called Albert Hofmann was the first to synthesize this drug.[26] Hofmann began working for Sandoz Pharmaceuticals in Basel in 1929, and by the mid-1930s he was leading a project that isolated and tested numerous ergotamine molecules with the intention of generating new uterotonics (which enhance the ability of the uterus to contract after a child is born and thus help prevent postpartum hemorrhage).[27] Of the many compounds that Hofmann synthesized, an ergobasine marketed under the trade name Methegine continues to find global application as a dependable uterotonic. In 1938 Hofmann began synthesizing a series of lysergic acid compounds whose chemical structure suggested that they might possess similar properties to ergobasine. Hofmann also hoped that these new synthetic compounds might generate a useful analeptic (a circulatory and respiratory stimulant). LSD-25, the twenty-fifth in the compound series, was tested by the pharmacological department at Sandoz but found to be less effective as a uterotonic than ergobasine. The lab report noted in passing that animals subjected to the drug became restless, but generally speaking, LSD-25 aroused little interest, and its testing on animals was discontinued.

Five years later, acting on what he later called "a peculiar presentiment," Hofmann decided to go back and look afresh at the properties of LSD-25. On Friday, April 16, 1943—known to some LSD aficionados as "Better Friday"—Hofmann made up a fresh batch of crystalline LSD-25 and dissolved it in water. During the final step of the process, he began feeling "unusual sensations" and so he decided to take the rest of the day off. By the time he had made his way home, he had begun to hallucinate, experi-- encing what he later reported to his supervisor was "an uninterrupted stream of fantastic images of extraordinary plasticity and vividness and accompanied by an intense kaleidoscopic play of colors."[28]

Suspecting that the strange experience was caused by his coming into contact with LSD-25, Hofmann returned to work the next Monday and set out to test this hypothesis. He dissolved what he thought would be a safe amount of the compound in water—250 micrograms (250 millionths of a gram)—and drank it down. Within less than an hour Hofmann had began to embark upon the first intentional LSD "trip" (a phrase first coined a few years later by the U.S. Army). This time his experience was not so pleasant; he had difficulty speaking, his motor skills became un- coordinated, and he endured hellish paranoiac visions. Hofmann worried that he had caused himself permanent brain damage, but by the next morning he felt fine, in fact invigorated. "A sensation of well-being and re newed life flowed through me," he wrote in his autobiography. "Breakfast tasted delicious and gave me extraordinary pleasure. When I later walked out into the garden, in which the sun shone now after a spring rain, every- thing glistened and sparkled in a fresh light. The world was as if newly created."[29]

Sandoz Pharmaceuticals set out to find a use for this wonder drug, a tiny speck of which seemed capable of producing incredible experiences similar to, but even more intense than, those produced by mescaline, a semisynthetic extract of the peyote cactus. Tests on animals produced inconclusive though interesting behavioral results. Spiders, for example, given a low dose of LSD-25 spun perfectly symmetrical webs, while at higher doses they lost interest in weaving all together. Later animal stud- ies with LSD showed that mice became more aggressive under its influ- ence; monkeys tended to become tamer; Siamese fighting fish became less inclined to fight; pigeons became better able to distinguish between light and dark colors; rats improved their climbing abilities; guppies changed color; and so-called waltzing mice lost their ability to dance.[30] Unsure what to do with a chemical that had such bizarre effects, Sandoz turned to some recent studies involving mescaline that had suggested it produced schizophrenia-like symptoms in anyone that took it. These studies concluded that mescaline might be useful in treating mental disorders, or at least in providing some insight into their nature. A psychiatrist with family connections to Sandoz tested LSD on some of his patients and generated similar results to the mescaline studies. He concluded that low dosages of LSD might be used to facilitate psychotherapy by allowing repressed thoughts and feelings to come to the surface. By the late 1940s, Sandoz had begun marketing LSD-25 under the trade name Delysid to researchers, promoting it as a drug that might help individuals deal with their psychological problems and give psychiatrists insight into their patients' condition.

The first batch of Delysid arrived in the United States in 1949, and within a few years a dozen or so research projects had sprung up to investigate its properties. By the mid-1950s, numerous such studies had been carried out. Initially, most of them focused on testing LSD-25's supposed ability to temporarily induce or mimic insanity—which is why researchers began to refer to the drug as a "psychotomimetic"—while later studies increasingly incorporated LSD-25 into therapy sessions. Some of these research projects showed promise. Alcoholics, for example, seemed to respond to a high-dose treatment of LSD better than they did to any other type of therapy. One report concluded that "properly used, LSD therapy can turn a large number of alcoholics into sober members of society. . . . [T]his can be done very quickly and economically."[31]

Beyond the scientific import of all this research, the work carried out by the medical and scientific communities on these substances inadvertently served as a conduit for the gradual spread of knowledge and excitement about them to the wider world. The first "pied pipers" or promoters of psychedelic drugs as tools of enlightenment generally encountered these substances at the hands of doctor and researchers. For example, the celebrated English author Aldous Huxley experienced his first trip courtesy of a psychiatrist, Humphrey Osmond, then clinical director of Saskatchewan Hospital in Canada. In early 1953 Huxley had read an essay by Osmond and his colleague, John Smithies, in a small scientific publication called the *Hibbert Journal*. The essay mostly concerned the current state of twentieth-century psychology, but it also mentioned the potentially valuable clinical properties of mescaline. Intrigued, Huxley contacted the authors, praising their work and expressing an interest in personally trying mescaline. Early in May 1953 Osmond visited Huxley at his Los Angeles home and granted the Englishman his wish. Huxley's reverent account of his mescaline-inspired visions were published a year later as *The Doors of Perception*, a book that initially sold slowly but one that played an important role in promoting the notion that mescaline and other such substances offered fantastic, transcendent flights for those willing to seek them out. Read widely in the 1960s—and the inspiration for the naming of the rock group the Doors—*The Doors of Perception* became an important landmark in what would eventually be called the "psychedelic movement."[32]

A significant proportion of the money funding the medical research into psychedelics came from the CIA. Some recipients of the U.S. government's largesse were aware of the source of their funds. According to Martin Lee and Bruce Shlain, a number of prominent psychiatrists and research scientists—including Louis Joylon, chair of the Department of Psychiatry at the University of Oklahoma; Ewen Cameron, director of the Allain Memorial Institute at Montreal's McGill University; Harris Isbell, a leading research scientist at the Addiction Research Center in Lexington, Kentucky; and Carl Pfeiffer, a pharmacologist from Princeton University—functioned as "scholar informants," channeling information directly to the CIA regarding the "aboveground" LSD scene. At the CIA's bidding, the Indianapolis-based Eli Lilly and Company had developed the capacity to synthesize LSD in significant quantities by mid-1954, but if something more exotic was required, the CIA could always turn to its friends in the research arena to help procure samples from European pharmaceutical companies.[33] Most researchers actually remained unaware that their work was being funded and closely monitored by the CIA, a fact that led Senator Ted Kennedy to accuse the CIA of having engaged in activities that "involved the perversion and the corruption of many of our outstanding research centers in this country."[34]

THE VA HOSPITAL

One of those research centers was the VA Hospital in Menlo Park, located not far from the Stanford campus and Perry Lane. Leo Hollister, MD, had been working there since the early 1950s, developing new psychiatric drugs and new ways to test them. He had created a technique called "double-blind controlled evaluations" that brought him some degree of recognition within the profession.[35] In late April 1959 Hollister went to an LSD research conference hosted by the Josiah Macy Foundation, an organization with close ties to the CIA. This particular conference brought together many of the leading LSD therapists of the day. These therapists dominated the conference program, mostly because they represented the then cutting edge of LSD research (which increasingly meant carrying out research in the psychotherapist's office rather than the laboratory or mental ward). Hollister was disturbed by the unscientific nature of much of this work,[36] later dismissively claiming that "not one single report in all the burgeoning literature regarding the therapeutic employment of these drugs meet the criteria for an adequate evaluation by modern standards of clinical pharmacology."[37] He resolved to initiate his own clinical research program back at the VA hospital in Menlo Park, focusing mostly on a careful analysis of the pharmacological and physiological impact of psychotropic drugs on the "normal"—that is, not mentally ill—individual.[38]

Within a year of the conference, Hollister's own project was up and running, much of it funded by grants obtained from official bodies such as the National Institute of Mental Health and the National Institute of Health, both of which had previously "served as conduits for channeling money" from the CIA to aboveground drug researchers.[39] The trials occurred at weekly intervals, using volunteer subjects, all of whom had been screened to ensure that they were in good general health and to "rule out overt psychiatric disorders."[40] First-timers were paid twenty dollars per session; returnees got paid increasingly larger amounts up to a maximum of seventy-five dollars depending on how many times they came back. Volunteers were told to fast for at least eight to twelve hours before the scheduled 8 a.m. start of the tests, and no food was allowed during the trials themselves.

The tests took place in small, private rooms that looked out onto a psychiatric ward in the VA hospital. Typically white and sanitized, the rooms were austerely furnished with just a cot or chaise longue, a table with a glass of water on it, and a tape recorder or whatever testing equipment was required on that particular day. The door was locked—Hollister didn't want his test subjects mingling with the people on the ward—but a tiny window, reinforced with a chicken-wire screen and toughened glass, allowed hospital inmates to see in and Hollister's guinea pigs to see out. Attendants stood by, but they left the subjects alone unless needed or when tests were being administered. Blood and urine samples would be routinely taken before the tests and at regular intervals during them, except for the first ninety minutes, when interruptions were kept to a minimum. Interns or orderlies also carried out a whole array of tests designed to record the effects of the drugs on the test subjects' motor skills, their memories, their creative abilities, their breathing, their reflexes, and their imagination. These tests varied in their complexity. An assessment of a subject's motor coordination, for example, might simply involve the person being asked to place a finger on his or her nose. At the other extreme, an investigation into how different drugs affected the perception of color required test subjects to organize eighty-five colored buttons according to their hue and to stare at a spinning black-and-white disk while identifying any colors that they saw.[41] The good doctor ensured that his subjects were aware of the nature of the drugs that they had volunteered to take, but he would not tell them in advance what drug they were being given on any particular day, nor would any subject necessarily receive the various drugs in the same order. The occasional placebo functioned to keep the experiments honest.[42]

Vic Lovell, Kesey's good friend and neighbor on Perry Lane, was an intern at the hospital and one of Hollister's test subjects. Lovell only lasted a few sessions, however, finding the clinical setting and constant tests frustrating. "I was all turned on," he remembered in hindsight, "with no place to go."[43] Lovell told Tom Wolfe of one occasion in which he drew a huge Buddha on the wall of the hospital room as some sort of expression of his drug experience, but the orderly administering the tests simply ignored the artwork and just carried on with the trial as if nothing had happened.[44] Hollister found Vic's type of response to be problematic. He was in the game of generating scientific data through careful testing and observation, while oftentimes his test volunteers seemed set on seeking (or receiving) something else entirely: some sort of spiritual enlightenment. "Testing under even moderate doses of drugs," Hollister later wrote, "is complicated by poor motivation of subjects, who often view the whole procedure with disdain as they search for a royal road to insight."[45] When Lovell dropped out of the tests, he arranged for Kesey to take his place. Kesey went to a few sessions as a replacement for Lovell, but then he became an enthusiastic member of the regular Tuesday morning VA crowd in his own right, as keen as any of them to travel as far as that "royal road" would take him.

Kesey's involvement in the VA experiments began early in 1960 and lasted for approximately two months. He remembered the setting well: "It was a ward. All the other people in it were nuts. I went out and looked through the window, a little, tiny window, and the door there with a heavy, heavy screen between two panes of glass. There was no way to break out. You could barely see out through it. I'd look out there and see these people moving around, and I could understand them a whole lot better than I could understand the doctors and the nurses, or the interns—and they knew this. They would come in and look at me in there, and I'd look at them through this little window."[46] Even at this early stage, one can easily imagine the seeds of *Cuckoo's Nest*—set in just such a ward—germinating in Kesey's mind as he looked out through that chicken-wire plate glass window.

Kesey turned up every Tuesday, week after week, working his way through a whole range of drugs (at least "eight or ten" according to his own estimates),[47] running the gamut from well-known psychedelics such as LSD-25, psilocybin, and mescaline to more obscure pharmaceuticals such as IT-290 and MP-14. Kesey's first experience at the VA hospital was, as they would soon be saying in the parlance of the day, "mind-blowing," sending him off on a trip full of indescribable visions and auditory hallucinations. Kesey later told Tom Wolfe that he first realized he was high when a squirrel that he had been watching play in the grounds of the hospital dropped an acorn and the thud of it exploded on Kesey's senses. Given its lowly origins, the sound seemed extraordinarily loud and clear within the room. Stranger still, the sound seemed to have a visual component, creating a blue resonance that bounced around the room.[48] Six hours later, collecting his check for twenty dollars from the doctor's office, Kesey asked what was in the little blue pill that had caused such remarkable sensations. "It's called lysergic acid diethylamide twenty-five," the doctor told him. Kesey said he would be back the following week.[49]

A tape recording of one of Kesey's sessions from early 1960 survives and is featured in *Magic Trip*, a documentary about Kesey and the 1964 bus trip. The recording offers a fascinating glimpse into Kesey's mindset during this critical moment in his life, and the nature of the experiments themselves. Questioned by a nurse at the beginning of the test, Kesey admitted to being more excited than anxious about what lay ahead, open and waiting to see what was going to happen. Over the course of the next four hours Kesey was subject to a whole battery of tests administered by a psychologist, various nurses, and trainee aides. Some of these were purely physical in nature: he was required to give both blood and urine samples, for example, and have his reflexes and his pulse checked at regular intervals. At one point, he was attached to an EEG machine to investigate how the drug might be affecting his brain's electrical activity. Other experiments looked to test his ability to add numbers, to draw straight lines, to complete a drawing by joining together dots, and to generate "after images." Kesey particularly enjoyed the test with a strobe light. "It was so great," he reported to the nurse. "[W]hen that thing started it became like the sun, like a huge vacuous sun that sucked into it all manners of colors, like a magnetic force field because everything that went into it was concentric . . . and the faster the light would blink, the faster these things would pour into it: shapes, bats, and hen eggs, and everything that had been drawn like a very delicate pen and ink drawing, cascading into the strobe light."[50]

At intervals Kesey recorded his thoughts into the Wollensak tape recorder on the table next to his bed, describing his visions and ideas as the drug took hold. He admitted to feeling drunk and woozy at first, like the room was spinning, but he did not feel any nausea. At one point he imagined the tape recorder to be a great toad and the microphone to be an electric shaver. Staring at the light above him, it turned into a great eye with optic nerves leading to all the walls. Approximately three hours into the test, Kesey's trip was reaching his peak. "It's quarter to one and I'm high out of my mind," he slurred into the tape recorder. "Wild color images. There's this great colored frog of a man outside standing at the door. . . . It's the most insane thing." Besides the visual effects of the drug, Kesey also reported its effect on his thinking and his feelings. "It's such a good drug," he insists, "in that I am suddenly filled with this great loving and understanding of people. . . . [The drug] seems to give you more observation and more insight, and it makes you question things that you ordinarily don't question." These comments are important because even though he recognized that his feelings might be simply an effect of the drug, he still could not help believing that it had also provided him with some insight that he had previously lacked. Kesey's belief that these sorts of drugs offered enlightenment is entirely in keeping with the view offered by Aldous Huxley in *The Doors of Perception*, and by the psychedelic movement to come. Also foreshadowing another familiar countercultural refrain, Kesey bemoaned the illegality of such drugs and their supposed danger to society: "No-one's gonna get high on this drug and rape somebody," he asserted in his usual blunt fashion. "They're more likely to give the girl a bouquet of flowers. Public support has to get behind it. We need a huge missionary; we need a messiah to tell the people." Toward the end of the test, the nurse asked Kesey whether this had been a comfortable or uncomfortable experience. "I think it was a good experience," he replied. "I think any time you see *more*, especially if you have a basic inherent love of most people, the more you see of them—the real person—the more you like." Asked in a later interview how the experience left him, Kesey responded, "It was like discovering a hole down to the center of the earth. You could see jewelry down there and you wanted people to go down and enjoy it."[51]

Hollister's interests were not limited to LSD-25; in fact, he designed a number of his studies to explore the similarities and differences among and between a wide variety of psychotropic drugs. Kesey was probably a test subject in a study that compared the effects of psilocybin, JB-329 (Ditran), and IT-290 (dl-alpha-methyltryptamine), all of which were obtained from Sandoz and/or a pharmaceutical company called Lakeside Laboratories.[52] Hollister's account of that comparative trial was published in late 1960 in the *Journal of Nervous Mental Disorders*. Sixteen volunteers participated in this experiment, most of whom, Hollister noted, were "graduate students who had been trained to make objective observations and possessed descriptive ability."[53] Tape recorders were again provided so that volunteers could record their subjective accounts of the trials. Over a number of weeks, they took various oral doses of the three drugs while Hollister and his assistants monitored a wide array of clinical and biochemical measures. The testing was extensive, and as scientific as circumstances allowed. Prior to each trial, blood pressure and pulse rates were recorded, as were pupillary size, muscle reflexes, and simple coordination. These tests were repeated two hours after the subjects took psilocybin and IT-290, and approximately four hours after the Ditran. Volunteers also had to complete a number of psychometric tests, each of which was administered before the drug trials began and at hourly intervals thereafter. One of these tests consisted of a series of basic arithmetical problems; another tested a subject's ability to copy four lines from a completed drawing; and a third tested his or her capacity to estimate various periods of time, anything from five to sixty seconds. Kesey recalled convincing an orderly during this test that he had developed an amazing ability to accurately gauge time. Unknown to the orderly, this ability had nothing to do with the properties of the drugs Kesey had taken and everything to do with Kesey's trickster personality. He knew from the pretest readings that his pulse was running at seventy-five beats per minute, so when the orderly asked him to estimate when sixty seconds had passed, Kesey just slyly counted off the requisite seventy-five beats of his pulse.[54]

Hollister's report made no mention of Kesey's newfound abilities, but it did reveal why Ditran played no part in the psychedelic movement to come. While psilocybin seemed to contain similar clinical properties to LSD—producing a "dreamy introspective state" according to Hollister—and certain similarities to IT-290, which had a "mood elevating effect similar to, but stronger than dextroamphetamine" (a speed-like substance), Ditran was a different creature altogether. Hollister wrote that with any sizable dose, "subjects were generally so incapacitated as to require staying in the hospital overnight, much mental confusion persisting throughout these hours." He also noted that "from one moment to the next, subjects had difficulty in remembering what they were talking about or what they had just said." The volunteers who took Ditran found the experience so unpleasant that few agreed to try it a second time, even though most had "only a fragmentary memory of the experience."[55] Kesey told Wolfe that even though the tests were blind (you did not know what you were going to get), he could tell when he had been given Ditran because the hairs on his blanket always seemed to turn into "a field of hideously diseased thorns."[56] Recalling such incidents, Kesey told a later interviewer, "[m]an, you don't want to give anybody a bad drug, no matter how much you want to know about it. If you're interested in it, take it yourself. But to give somebody a bad drug, it's a real mistake. When I could feel that it was going [in] that direction, I would gag myself, and get out of me as much as I could."[57]

Despite such moments, Kesey consistently described his first encounters with psychedelic drugs as the most profound experiences of his young life.[58] Here was a man who had been drunk only a couple of times in his life, taking drugs powerful enough to shake his understanding of reality to the core. In a rare, pre-*Cuckoo's Nest* 1961 press interview, Kesey told one Springfield reporter that he thought "[e]veryone should have a chance to experience these things. You see things from a completely different point of view, and discover things are not as you always thought them to be."[59] A couple of years later, a friend, Gordon Lish, asked him what had happened during the experiments, and Kesey responded in a similar fashion: "Another *world* happened. . . . It slowly becomes evident to you that there's some awful and unique logic going on, just as real, in some ways, as your other world."[60]

The CIA and the military never did find the truth serums or mind-bending weapons that they sought from LSD, psilocybin, and a vast array of other psychedelic drugs. Nor did the psychopharmacologists ever find in psychedelics the wonder drugs that they had hoped for (in part, perhaps, because the powers-that-be eventually put a premature stop to their research). However, this strange conglomeration of historical actors and forces—powerful drugs developed by a profit-driven pharmaceutical industry, well-funded and well-intentioned research scientists and doctors, and the anything-goes mentality of the Cold War intelligence agencies—did succeed in unintentionally spawning a cultural revolution that would, it is not an exaggeration to say, transform the United States and the world in its wake. At the VA Hospital in Menlo Park, the scientific community and the government lost their grip on the psychedelic torch to a bunch of hip graduate students and their curious friends. The youngsters grabbed it and ran.

5

Better Living through Chemistry

The Menlo Park VA drug trials had revealed a new frontier for Kesey to explore, and it was entirely in keeping with his personality that he leapt to the challenge with such gusto. Years later, he recalled that first moment of discovery: "When we first broke into that forbidden box in the other dimension, we knew that we had discovered something as surprising and powerful as the New World when Columbus came stumbling onto it. . . . We were *naive*. We thought that we had come to a new place, a new, exciting, free place; and that it was going to be available to all America."[1] It soon would be, though probably not in the way that Kesey might have predicted. "I knew that LSD couldn't be stopped," he explained to one reporter, but he never imagined that taking LSD would turn into a mass movement.[2] His role as that movement's "pied-piper of acid" is overstated in the historical record, but there is no doubt that he freely encouraged his circle of Perry Lane friends to investigate psychedelic drugs for themselves. And why not? The VA trials were legal and officially sanctioned, and the substances they were testing seemed harmless yet fantastic. It was typical of Kesey and his friends that they wanted others to share their good fortune with others. Initially at least, this is how the psychedelic revolution got its start, rippling out from the first few initiates to their circle of friends, and then out to *their* circles of friends, and so on.

The drug trials continued for several years after Kesey's participation, and eventually most of the people that he knew had made the early morning trek to the hospital to indulge their curiosity. Many of these people would go on to be players in the traveling road show that was the Merry Pranksters. Roy Sebern, creator of the Acid Test light shows, signed onto the dotted line at the VA. Jim Wolpman took part in a study run by psychiatrist Joe Adams at the Palo Alto Medical Research Foundation. Wolpman suspects CIA involvement in these trials. Ken Babbs's brother, John, first learned of the tests from a flyer hung on a billboard in the Stanford student union. His particular trial lasted four weeks, during which he was given psilocybin, LSD, mescaline, and a combination of all three. The sessions were not as much fun as he had hoped. The constant interruptions, the attempts at hypnosis, the inane questions, and the sterile environment all detracted from the drug experience itself. "The trick," according to John, "was to try to maintain the euphoria of my high until I was through for the day—around three in the afternoon—and take it back to Perry Lane."[3] One of Kesey's friends, Mike Hagen, remembered that this could make Tuesday afternoons on the Lane something of an event. Hagen also took part in the trials, and one afternoon, still loaded on God-knows-what, he went home to the Lane to find everybody else "just higher than Hell," spraying water everywhere, running around in their bare feet "just playing in the jungle."[4]

Barefoot they might have often been, but since most of the Perry Laners were graduate students, they also treated their drug taking as one big research project. They read anything they could get their hands on that might help them make sense of their newly discovered altered states, including ancient mystical texts, scientific journal articles, books by Joseph Campbell (particularly *The Masks of God*), Buddhist tracts, anthropological monographs, and lots of drug-inspired literature. Even though Tom Wolfe portrayed Perry Lane as a party scene—which it undoubtedly was plenty of the time—there also tended to be an intellectual aspect to many of the Lane's activities. These strange substances that offered fantastic flights of the mind were as interesting to the inquisitive bright sparks on Perry Lane as they were enjoyable. Kesey was as curious as any of them, spending time combing through the research journals at the VA hospital, seeking knowledge and, one suspects, new possibilities. This scholarly approach to the "exploration of inner-space" fell away as the scene shifted from Perry Lane to La Honda, but it served as a foundation of knowledge for those who made the transition.

Word of the VA drug trials filtered out from Perry Lane and the Stanford campus to others whose ears were open to such possibilities. While

Kesey is remembered as the most famous graduate of Leo Hollister's drug-testing experiments, those Menlo Park VA trials had a much wider regional influence, introducing psychotropic drugs to a significant portion of the peninsula's burgeoning psychedelic community. One of those who heard the call was a young man named Robert Hunter—soon to be the lyricist for many a Grateful Dead song—then living in a rooming house called the Chateau, just a few blocks from Perry Lane. Hunter earned $140 over the course of a four-week trial that introduced him to psilocybin, LSD, mescaline, and some combination of all three (as with John Babbs). Hunter had read a little Huxley in preparation for the effects, but he was still somewhat surprised to see Dracula stepping out of a locker in the VA hospital. "I knew I was hallucinating," recalled Hunter. "This was great fun." He also remembers experiencing a visit by "God and all that good stuff," and at one point, as tears flooded down his face, trying to explain to one of the clinicians carrying out the test what was happening. "I'm not crying," he said. "I'm in another dimension. I'm inhabiting the body of a great green Buddha and there's a pool that is flowing out of my eyes."[5] Hunter had taken a typewriter into the tests, determined to preserve for posterity a record of his first trips into the unknown. "By my faith," he wrote on one of the six pages of single-spaced notes that he produced in his first session, "if this be insanity, then for the love of God permit me to be insane."[6] When he showed his notes to his friends and fellow Chateau-dwellers, they were naturally intrigued. One of them, a young Jerry Garcia, later recalled, "[w]hen he came back with his reports of what it was like, I thought, 'God, I've *got* to have some of that.'"[7]

While the VA experiments allowed all these folks to actually experience these drugs, many of them had been aware of their existence for some time beforehand. That knowledge came partly from the reports about LSD and psychedelic mushrooms that had been filtering into the mainstream American media since the late 1950s. Prankster Ron Bevirt recalls reading about psilocybin mushrooms as a college student at Washington University in Saint Louis in the late 1950s and being assigned to write a biology paper on the subject. Kesey remembers being intrigued by an article in *Life* magazine that showed an LSD-dosed cat rearing back in fear from a mouse. Jerry Garcia was excited by his friend Hunter's VA tales, but he had first heard about LSD back in junior high school. "I saw a documentary showing a bunch of people who were taking LSD," he recalled. "The film showed this artist who was just drawing lines, and he was obviously very moved—like at a peak ecstasy experience. I thought, 'God that looks like such fun!' That image stayed with me a long time and that notion that there is some magical substance that corresponds to the best of your dreams."[8] Certain religious texts also served as an introduction to the psychedelic experience. Kesey told one interviewer, "[b]y the time I started taking peyote and LSD, I had already done a great deal of reading about mysticism—the Bhagavadgita and Zen and Christian mystical texts. They helped me to interpret what I was seeing, give it meaning. You don't just take the stuff and expect understanding."[9]

Another notable source of media coverage relating to these drugs came from movie star Cary Grant. He had been introduced to LSD in the late 1950s as a participant in some drug-therapy sessions run by Los Angeles psychiatrists Mortimer Hartman and Arthur Chandler. Grant was but one member of the Hollywood elite who was introduced to psychedelic drugs on a therapist's couch, but he was the most publicly enthusiastic. In a *Look* magazine article titled "The Curious Story behind the New Cary Grant," Grant confided: "All my life, I've been searching for peace of mind. I'd explored yoga and hypnotism and made several attempts at mysticism. Nothing really seemed to give me what I wanted until this treatment. . . . You're just a bunch of molecules until you know who you are."[10] On another occasion, he told reporters from the *New York Herald Tribune* that through LSD he had "been born again. I have been through a psychiatric experience that has completely changed me. . . . I am no longer lonely. I am a happy man."[11] Very few of those reading Grant's story actually had the opportunity to share his drug experiences—until the mid-sixties it was very difficult to get hold of psychedelic drugs without some sort of connection to the medical or research community—but the occasional article in the popular press and word of mouth allowed awareness of these wonder drugs to slowly filter out into the popular consciousness.

The Citadel of Culture Besieged by Barbarians

Another source of information about the illicit world of drugs came from the remnants of the Beat movement that still existed in San Francisco in the early 1960s. Though Kesey and the people around him were a little too young to claim to be Beats themselves—"too young to be a beatnik, and too old to be a hippie," Kesey once proclaimed—the Perry Laners' interest in drugs, not to mention their nascent countercultural take on the world, was certainly informed and shaped by the Beat culture that had gone before them. Beat literature was steeped in drug references, as was the jazz culture that accompanied and inspired it. Both offered tantalizing glimpses of altered consciousnesses and new perspectives for those who were reading and listening. Jack Kerouac's *On the Road*, for example, was well stocked with descriptive passages recounting the casual use of various drugs by a variety of colorful characters. Indeed, as writer Martin Torgoff notes of Kerouac's masterpiece, there is a "drug consciousness implicit in the entire inner journey of the book."[12] The same might be said of Allen Ginsberg's *Howl*, which included direct references to both marijuana and peyote, and it can certainly be said of William S. Burroughs's *Naked Lunch*, which is a fictionalized account of Burroughs's fifteen-year "oil burning junk habit," written in starkly revealing prose.

Naked Lunch made quite a splash on Perry Lane. Vic Lovell recalled that "it was incredibly influential to all of us in saying, 'There are new directions.' Especially Kesey. Ken read *Naked Lunch* a great deal. He was very much influenced by it. I recall us standing up, reading sections to each other so that we could *hear* the sound of it. We were amazed by it."[13] Though Kesey was a very different kind of storyteller, Burroughs's paranoiac style of writing left its mark on the younger man's work. In tone and sensibility at least, the opening few lines of *Cuckoo's Nest* bear a passing resemblance to those found at the beginning of *Naked Lunch*. Mike Hagen's response to *Naked Lunch* was a little more direct. On a trip to Europe in the fall of 1961, he crossed the Straits of Gibraltar to sample the pleasures of Tangiers for himself. Kesey was delighted when Hagen later turned up on the Lane bearing some North African marijuana to share with his friends.[14]

Kerouac left an even bigger impression on the young bohemians of Palo Alto. Jerry Garcia spoke for many in recounting, "I read [*On the Road*] and fell in love with it, the adventure, the romance of it, everything. . . . I owe a lot of who I am and what I've been and what I've done to the beatniks from the Fifties."[15] Ron Bevirt recalled that even as a high school student, he found *On the Road* to be fresh and appealing. "For those of us who had the background like I did, conservative middle class scene," he said, "*On the Road* was the most tremendous trip for us because we found out all about this gassy, groovy stuff going on. It was the first word that we got."[16]

Roy Sebern took that call literally, as did so many others of his peers. He put the book down and within days had set out for New York on an old motor scooter that he had. And when that stopped working after just forty miles, he ditched that idea and set out to hitchhike his way east instead.

Kesey read *On the Road* three times before he even left Oregon for Stanford, a move that he claimed later was inspired by a desire "to sign on in some way, to join that joyous voyage, like thousands of other volunteers, inspired by the same book, and its vision, and, of course, its incomparable hero [Neal Cassady]."[17] Kerouac was not Kesey's first introduction to Beat literature. "I had this record of [Lawrence] Ferlinghetti, [Kenneth] Rexroth and [Allen] Ginsberg reading beat poetry," Kesey recalled. "We used to play it out of our loudspeaker system over at the Beta house. Lots of people were into it. It was so new that it was really involved. All of the class, even the people that were down on it, were listening to it and had a lot to say about it."[18] Kesey even wrote a humorous take on the Beats titled "The Citadel of Culture Besieged by a Barbarian" for his weekly column in the University of Oregon college newspaper, the *Oregon Daily Emerald*. Foreshadowing his own rebellious future, Kesey cast the Beat character in this piece as a free spirit who had no place in the musty corridors of high culture. In this short vignette, a "tall, hep-eyed" saxophone player is turned away from the Music Department because he wants to play without supervision. "Plant me in the combo, pop," the character complains. "Leave me bleat, list me on the score and let me wail."[19]

Kesey's writing style was never much like Kerouac's, but he always acknowledged him as an important and influential figure, in much the same way that seeing Marlon Brando in *The Wild One* made Kesey want to be a movie star. And Kerouac loved *Cuckoo's Nest*. "I have to make a truly honest statement about this here Ken Kesey," he wrote to his friend Tom Ginsberg at Viking Press after reading an advance copy of Kesey's novel. "'A GREAT MAN AND A GREAT NEW AMERICAN NOVELIST!' . . . Tell him not to be ashamed of the dignity of his experience as a man in the world, the hell with the rest."[20] When Kesey saw the letter, he immediately dashed off a copy to Babbs, boasting that he had finally made it if he had earned Kerouac's admiration.[21]

Kesey and the Perry Lane crowd often took trips up to San Francisco to seek out what was left of the North Beach Beat scene. The multiethnic restaurants and the colorful local characters were big draws: Vesuvio's with its display of old-time slides on the walls, La Bodega with the "flamenco crowd," Dante's Billiards on Broadway where they sold enormous gorgonzola and salami French bread sandwiches, or the Pisa on Grant Street where for a dollar thirty-five you got to sit at long, communal tables and dine on soups, salads, and pasta dishes until you could eat not a morsel more. And while the scene was no longer what it once was—the disparaging glare of the media had cheapened its integrity and turned much of the area into something of a risqué tourist stop—its essence was still there if you knew where to look and if you knew the right people. Post *Cuckoo's Nest*, Kesey and his friends would converge on Ferlinghetti's place or Ginsberg's apartment, but even before Kesey's fame opened those doors, one could still occasionally run into one of the Beat literati just doing their thing right there on the streets. "I can remember driving down to North Beach with my folks and seeing Bob Kaufman," Kesey told one interviewer. "He had little pieces of Band-Aid tape all over his face, about two inches wide, and little smaller ones like two inches long—and all of them made into crosses. He came up to the cars, and he was babbling poetry into these cars. He came up to the car I was riding in, and my folks, and started jabbering this stuff into the car."[22]

Such encounters were enough to inspire Kesey to use the North Beach scene as the setting for "Zoo," the novel he wrote during his first couple of years at Stanford. "Zoo" was a semiautobiographical coming-of-age story, about a young man named Arnold "Arny" Mattheson, a liberal arts graduate from the University of Oregon who rebels against his father—an unsophisticated chicken farmer from Albany, Oregon—and takes up the Beat life. After graduating from college, Arny turns his back on the family business and heads down to San Francisco to find the bohemia that he had heard about. A Beat old-timer, Sagacious "Sage" Krail, befriends Arny and lets him lodge with him and his family in their North Beach apartment. Arny spends his time hanging out on Grant Street, visiting the coffee shop, and drinking Mountain Red wine with a bunch of other young misfits. He is determined to be a writer and a poet, but he achieves neither, instead getting by on the money that his father sends him every month. After a series of trials and tribulations, Arny ends up broke and broken on the streets of Tijuana, Mexico. In the last scene of the book, Arny makes his way back to Oregon, the prodigal son returning home, still bearing the beard and sandals of his North Beach adventure.[23]

Kesey's prose in this unpublished work is as colorful as ever, but his portrayal of the Beat scene is full of characters and circumstances straight out of a Hollywood beatnik B movie. Sage is presented as the genuine Beat article, a black painter possessed of cool and wisdom and tortured talent. Arny and his juvenile delinquent buddies come across as mostly Beat wannabes, wasting their time *acting* "hep" rather than *being* cool. Pot is illicitly purchased—where else?—from a black jazz saxophonist who dispenses bags of weed and green shield stamps from the restroom of a seedy San Francisco nightclub. "Zoo" reads like what it was: a story written from the outside by an innocent looking in. That was never more obvious than in the passages that dealt with drugs, since Kesey wrote them without much experience himself. His depiction of Arny's first marijuana high, for example, is giddily overblown. Kesey has him hallucinating after getting high from just a few tokes on a joint. A later scene finds the Arny character getting high on pot and trying to kill his father by stabbing him in the stomach with a bottle, like something out of *Reefer Madness*.

One Pill Makes You Larger, and One Pill Makes You Small

Bucking the usual trend, Kesey tried pot only after he had been exposed to far more powerful psychedelics during the VA drug trials. "The first time I smoked grass was in the Veterans Hospital doing the acid experiments," he recollected years later. "There was a little guy on the ward, a jazz drummer who immediately made me for a dope smoker, even though I wasn't. He turned me on. We used to stay up late at night watching black-and-white diver-bomber movies."[24]

Pot had been around on Perry Lane in the pre-Kesey era—Jim Wolpman remembers struggling to study while his friends indulged—but it became more of a staple after Kesey arrived. Kesey told a friend that the first time he got really high on pot on the Lane occurred at Norm Gaddam's house, with Vic Lovell and Dick Bolin (Gaddam was not actually there).[25] Kesey and the others locked themselves in the bedroom, closed all the windows, and pulled all the shades. A lone candle punctuated the darkness, giving barely enough light to roll and smoke a couple of joints. Kesey took one big toke and, not being a smoker, he immediately started coughing. The coughing fit blasted the pot smoke deep into his lungs, heightening the drug's effect and causing a sensation to travel up his spine and explode in his head, like a Fourth of July rocket. Kesey lay on the bed and let his mind drift to wherever the high wanted to take him. He imagined himself a tiny ball suspended from a huge dome by a little thin thread. The thread snapped, sending him falling into a shimmering lake of mercury. Before he could hit, Kesey opened his eyes and stood up. Over the objections of Lovell and Bolin, he headed out into the night air and, for no apparent good reason, grabbed a fencepost out of the ground and broke it over his knee. Then he stood nose to nose with a big jack-o'-lantern light, and when it went out a few minutes later, he told the others that he had extinguished the light through willpower alone. The three of them made their way over to Chloe's house. She was out, so they put on a record, Stravinsky's *Rite of Spring* (the music the dinosaurs dance to in Disney's *Fantasia*), and lay down to wait for her return. Kesey closed his eyes and returned to his imaginary world. This time he found himself at the bottom of the mercury lake, looking up to the surface. He watched as the sound of the music disturbed the lake's surface, sending what looked like brilliant icicles of sound darting through the surface of the lake in time with the rhythm. As Kesey lay still, the icicles got smaller and smaller and the music got quieter and quieter until he could no longer see or hear anything. He blacked out. He came to somewhere on the Stanford golf course, loping across it as if he were half man, half wolf. It was quite an experience.

Normally, the pot high is much milder than the one Kesey experienced here (this was the one and only time that he ever blacked out on the drug). It is certainly not as intense or prolonged as an LSD trip, though Kesey was still convinced that pot held important properties. "Good old grass I can recommend," he wrote in *The Last Supplement to the Whole Earth Catalog* (1971). "To be just without being mad . . . to be peaceful without being stupid, to be interested without being compulsive, to be happy without being hysterical . . . smoke grass."[26] He was not alone in such sentiments. Norman Mailer, one of America's most prominent young literary stars of the day, remembered that he "thought it was a wonder drug. A panacea for the universe."[27] By April 1960 Kesey was excitedly introducing the pot experience to his family back in Oregon. During a trip back to Eugene following the death of Faye's father, Kesey got his younger brother, Chuck, high for the first time.[28]

It was not long before Kesey started trying to grow his own marijuana on Perry Lane (and later in a ravine by the VA hospital and later still on the Stanford University golf course). Much to the annoyance of Anne and Paul De Carli, newcomers to the neighborhood, Kesey chose to plant his pot seeds in their backyard, rather than his own. Paul De Carli remembers, "there was a corner of my backyard that was hidden by shrubs from my view, [but] right across the fence from Ken's. He planted pot in my backyard because the cops were watching him. . . . Ken would do that kind of irresponsible thing, and so people were a little bit leery of him. Ken is a nice fellow, good company, but those of us who were somewhat more risk-averse kept our distance from some of the activities."[29] By August Kesey's homegrown marijuana crop was ready for harvesting, so he offered to send Babbs some pot hidden in a little hollow statue of Saint Jude.[30] Babbs now refutes much of this history, but his letters at the time seem to indicate he was a willing convert. In later years, U.S. soldiers in Vietnam could easily get their hands on pretty much any sort of drug that they desired, but Babbs got there well before that happened. He tried and failed to score in Saigon, and though he had heard they sold marijuana openly in the marketplace in Laos, he never made it there. Kesey kept him supplied with the occasional package from home—it was much easier sending illicit packages out of the United States than the other way around—much to Babbs's gratitude.[31]

Back on the lane, the De Carlis chose to keep their distance from their errant neighbor, but plenty of others joined Kesey in exploring the limits of drug-altered consciousness. The introduction of drugs to the Perry Lane scene inevitably changed things, forging strong bonds between aficionados and creating boundaries between those who were not inclined to experiment. Pot, especially, is a social drug, the enjoyment of which is augmented when it is shared with others. When sociologist Erich Goode notes that "[m]arijuana is not merely smoked in groups, it is smoked in intimate groups. The others with whom one is smoking are overwhelmingly *significant* others," he merely confirms what every pot smoker already knows from experience. Tom Wolfe made much of the ritualistic nature of the Pranksters' activities, but what he did not understand was that those rituals were characteristic of pot smokers in general. As Goode explained, "brotherhood is an element in the marijuana ritual, as is the notion of sharing something treasured and esteemed. . . . [T]he activity has strong elements of tribal ritual: it reaffirms membership in the sub-community of users, it recreates symbol and substance of the group, and it relives for its participants significant meaning, belonging, loyalty."[32] Sneaking off to share a joint in the bathroom at a Perry Lane party may not seem like much of a bonding ritual, but the shared experience was significant in both symbolic and very real terms, binding Kesey's group together and providing common ground with a larger community of pot smokers in the Bay Area.

This sense of community is important to the broader story here, because the San Francisco counterculture or hippie movement (or whatever else it has been called) that emerged later in the sixties was initially not much more than a few groups of people scattered here and there. These people tended to possess free-spirited, antiauthoritarian sensibilities and shared similar interests in drugs, literature, music, parties, and performance. It was a family of communities well before it became readily identifiable (or marketable) as a movement or culture, and pot was the secret glue that bound it all together. For these mostly white, well-educated kids, if you smoked pot, you were automatically enrolled into an underground club that came with its own language, its own rituals, and its own sense of the world. David Nelson, a musician and friend to Jerry Garcia from the Chateau days, remembered that it "hadn't come above ground then and so anything about pot was like the cat that ate the canary. Any time you laughed you'd cover your mouth because nobody knew what you were laughing about. Only we knew." Best of all, the "pot club" had an open door policy, so new members were welcomed, acknowledged, and applauded. Nelson recalled the excitement that he and his friends felt when they judged the zany humor in the Beatles' *A Hard Day's Night* movie to be clear evidence that the Fab Four liked to indulge. "A friend called me up and said, 'you gotta see it man. I think they smoke pot,'" Nelson told an interviewer. "So I went to see it and I went, 'Oh my God! I think they do. They're smoking it.'"[33]

Pot became the staple drug of choice for Kesey's crowd on the Lane, but it was certainly not the only substance that they were investigating. Though not commonly associated with Kesey and the Pranksters, various forms of "pep pills" with speedlike qualities also played a significant role in their early pharmacological explorations. The influence of the drug-taking habits of the Beats should not be underestimated here; every

wannabe Beat worth their salt knew, or at least believed, that Kerouac's
On the Road was the product of a three-week typing marathon fueled by
bennies (Benzedrine) and coffee. Kerouac's hero of *On the Road*, Neal
Cassady, was also reputed to gobble speed like candy, later earning him
Prankster nicknames like "Speed Limit" or "the fastestmanalive." In late
1967 the Pranksters had to take Cassady to a hospital because of a bizarre
growth on his elbow. An intern asked him what was wrong and, according to Kesey, Cassady was only half-joking when he replied, "Amphetamine, amphetamine. [I've been] on amphetamine twice a day since 1943."[34]

Kesey and the Pranksters were popping pills before they ever met Cassady. Early in 1960 Kesey's doctor had prescribed him some Preludin for
an undisclosed ailment—possibly related to his Olympic training regime—
but Kesey started using them for recreational purposes. These types of
drugs were relatively commonplace in mainstream American society during this period. Preludins were often prescribed as diet pills because of
their ability to suppress the appetite, but taken in sufficient quantities they
acted as a stimulant and offered an amphetamine-like "rush." Dexamyl
(dextro amphetamine and amobarbital) was a "mood elevator," promoted
by Smith Klein & French in the popular press as a quick working antidepressant. One advertisement showed a happy, vacuuming housewife and
promised, "Just one 'Dexamyl' *Spansule* capsule, taken in the morning,
provides daylong therapeutic effect. And mood elevation is usually apparent within 30 to 60 minutes."

Though the Pranksters did not treat speedlike pills with the same admiration as psychedelic substances, they were always a part of their scene.
The Pranksters' 1964 bus trip, for example, is remembered as an acid-
fueled odyssey, but in addition to the LSD-laced orange juice in the fridge
behind the driver's seat, the Pranksters also took along a jar containing
five hundred Benzedrine pills (as well as a shoebox full of joints rolled
specially for the occasion by Prankster Steve "Zonker" Lambrecht). Kesey
and the Pranksters were not the only ones popping pills. The Grateful
Dead and their fans—Deadheads—generally acknowledge that some of
the songs on the Dead's first album (*Grateful Dead*, 1967) sound a little
fast. This was not a case of first-time studio nerves but simply a product
of their relying on diet pills—belonging to Mountain Girl, Prankster and
girlfriend to both Kesey and later Garcia—to get them through the long
recording sessions in Los Angeles. "So we went down [to Los Angeles],"

recalled Garcia, "and what was it we had, Dexamyl? Some sort of diet-watcher's speed, and pot and stuff like that."[35] This was nothing new to Garcia; he had first gotten high on "bennies, things like that" in high school.[36]

Kesey incorporated amphetamines into his writing habits. Always something of a night owl—he struggled with insomnia for most of his life—Kesey did the bulk of his writing when everybody else had gone to bed, something that might not have been immediately apparent to some of the others on the Lane. Paul De Carli remembered one occasion when he was up late, frantically trying to finish an overdue project. At around 3 a.m. he glanced out of his window to see Kesey tapping away on a typewriter in the small outhouse behind his home that served as his writing getaway. "I used to be annoyed at Ken for leading people down a path," De Carli recalled. "They thought that life was all fun while Ken was basically hiding the hard work that he had to do. . . . Basically every night he would write . . . then sleep-in like the partiers and get up at midday and start his activities with his followers."[37] Kesey kept himself going through the long night hours by taking prescription drugs with amphetamine qualities. By the fall of 1960, he was encouraging Babbs to adopt similar habits, offering to send him some Preludens to help him write at night.[38]

Once in the Far East, Babbs took Kesey's advice to heart, spending whole days at the typewriter working on his Vietnam novel, buoyed by whatever pills Kesey had sent him or whatever he had been able to rustle up for himself. At one point, he got a prescription for some Dexedrine by conning a doctor into believing he was having weight problems. He then swapped these pills with a colleague who had some of the more powerful Dexamyl pills.[39] Babbs was eventually able to buy some Dexamyl Spansules in Hong Kong, some of which he sent to Kesey, hidden in the binding of an Alley Oops kids' coloring book.[40]

Sometimes a Great Notion, even more so than *Cuckoo's Nest*, was written under the influence of speed. By early 1963 Kesey had gotten into the habit of popping pills to help him alleviate the boredom of the long and lonely writing process. Bennett Huffman, a student and friend of Kesey's in his later years, reiterated this point in a recent news article: "Ken was taking speed for 30 hours a block when he wrote *Notion*. He'd stay up for a day and a half just doing nothing but writing nonstop and then sleep for 12 hours and then do it again."[41] Kesey's pill-popping routines even found their way into *Notion*'s text by way of one of the lead characters, Lee Stamper. In an early scene, Kesey describes Lee standing in his New York apartment surveying the contents of his medicine cabinet full of "chemicals waiting like tickets for whatever ride the heart desired." Unsure whether he wanted to go "up or down," Kesey had Lee compromise and take "two phenobarbs and two Dexedrines."[42]

Kesey's long hours of writing for *Cuckoo's Nest* and *Notion* may have been fueled by equal measures of ambition, talent, and prescription pills, but it was psychedelics that provided the inspiration. Without any way to get hold of the substances that they had experienced at the VA hospital, the Perry Laners turned their eyes toward Laredo, Texas, where shadowy operations such as Smith's Cactus Ranch or Magic Gardens sold peyote by mail order to anyone with a shipping address and a money order. Peyote is a very rare plant in the United States—it only grows naturally in four counties of southwestern Texas—but it has a long-established history as a religious sacrament for certain Native American tribes, including for members of the Native American Church, which was first established in the 1870s. The psychoactive element of the cactus is found in the little "buttons" attached to the roots of the plant, and for just thirty-five dollars anyone could order a thousand of these buttons via mail order. Residents of New York used to be able to buy peyote over the counter—Allen Ginsberg remembered buying some from a store on Tenth Street, off Second Avenue, and Robert Stone's first psychedelic experience came courtesy of some peyote buttons purchased from a nameless espresso shop on East Sixth Street that could be identified by a dollar sign hanging out front— but purchasing and possessing peyote was illegal in the state of California. Prohibition was not enough to stop the Perry Laners from their experiments. Vic Lovell jokingly recalled, "[t]here was an exclusion in the law that said [peyote] could be used for religious purposes and we felt kind of religious about it."[43] When it came time to sign for the package or pick it up from the post office, those who felt they had the most to lose or the least amount of money shied away, but they usually got stuck with the arduous job of getting the buttons ready for ingestion.

Preparing one thousand buttons of peyote is a huge endeavor—cut the spines off, cut off the buttons, dry everything out, grind what is left into a powder or paste—but it is a necessary task because eaten as it comes, peyote tastes disgusting enough to make most people retch and vomit.

Native American users generally ate their peyote in a powdery form or drank it in a form of tea, but even then, as Leo Hollister noted, "vomiting was the price of entry into paradise."[44] Kesey and the Perry Laners experimented with various ways to lessen this "price of entry." They finally settled on packing the foul-tasting substance into pharmaceutical gelatin capsules, swallowing ten, twelve, and sometimes twenty at a time. Kesey sent Babbs a batch of capsules that he had prepared himself. He took six baseball-size cacti buttons, scraped out the fleshy part of the plant, and crushed it to a pulp. Once the pulp had dried, Kesey ground it into powder and stuffed it into the capsules. Kesey warned Babbs that even with all these precautions, the peyote might still make him feel queasy at first, so he advised him to take it on an empty stomach, with a motion-sickness pill and a couple of glasses of orange juice to wash it all down. The degree of nausea varied from individual to individual. Kesey felt sick to the gills just thinking about the natural taste of peyote. Vic Lovell was also prone to vomit. Faye, on the other hand, got away with little discomfort. Kesey assured Babbs that despite the unpleasant initial side effects, there was nothing to fear from this powerful psychedelic and much to gain.[45]

CUCKOO TIME

By the summer of 1960 Kesey had started working as an orderly at the VA hospital. His training for the job lasted four weeks, starting every day at 7:30 in the morning and going until four in the afternoon. He began on the "circle wards," full of patients whose conditions were serious, but not acute, "where the men have enough marbles left to choose up sides and play the game," as Kesey described them to Babbs. The last two weeks of his training were spent on a different ward, working with "the vegetables, the geriatrics, the organs eating in and organs shitting and pissing and moaning and coming on in religious tongues, creatures that need spooned puree and paplum, infants growing backwards, away from civilization and rationalization, back to complete dependence, to darkness, the womb, the seed."[46] These were the same people that Kesey had first encountered while sitting alone in that stark white room just six months earlier, the same people that he thought he could understand better than the doctors because of his drug-changed consciousness. "While under the influence of the drugs you have tremendous empathy with other people," he told a reporter in 1961. "I could see the suffering and anguish in the faces of the mental patients as if it were written there in black and white."[47] Recalling the feeling much later in life, Kesey was even more explicit: "I could look out through the window and see the people in the hospital— the nuts—I could see them and knew from my altered state that they knew something that the doctors didn't. They could see a truth that the doctors couldn't see and I could see it too."[48]

Come August, Kesey's training was over and he had started working as an orderly on the wards, mostly pulling the Monday through Friday, midnight to 8 a.m. red-eye shift. By his own admission, his job was not particularly taxing. All he had to do was "a little mopping and buffing, check the wards every forty-five minutes with a flashlight, be coherent to the night nurse stopping by on her hourly rounds . . . and talk to the sleepless nuts."[49] The schedule gave him plenty of time to sit and type—five or six hours a night—which he put to good use writing *Cuckoo's Nest*. "Most of the time I worked the midnight to 8 a.m. shift," Kesey told a reporter in early 1962. "That's when I did most of my writing. It was completely without the rest of the staff's knowledge—they're not going to be happy about it when they hear."[50] Perhaps they knew more than he thought. One nurse who worked with Kesey on the wards was less than impressed with his work ethic, remembering him as "lazy—perhaps because he was more concerned with researching *Cuckoo's Nest*."[51]

Kesey was certainly more focused on his writing than his duties. The book drew heavily from his surroundings, his background, and his worldview. He set the novel in a mental institute in the Pacific Northwest. Its leading character, the classic antihero Randall Patrick McMurphy, is a likeable rogue who comes to the hospital from a work farm in Pendleton, Oregon, where he has been serving time for statutory rape. A self-described "gambling fool," McMurphy is pretending to be insane, betting that life on the ward will offer him an easy way to serve out his time. He soon realizes that his ruse might actually extend his sentence indefinitely. He finds himself ensnared in an institutional system of control—the "combine"—far worse than the criminal system he has left behind, and at the mercy of Nurse Ratched, the dominant figure on the ward who dislikes and distrusts him. The other men on the ward come to look up to McMurphy, lionizing him as a "legend" because he dares stand up to

Nurse Ratched and challenge the system. To them, McMurphy's bluster-ing self-confidence and his willful free spirit represent everything they see lacking in themselves. McMurphy's bravado ultimately costs him dearly—he undergoes a forced lobotomy—but even in his demise, he inspires one of the other inmates, Chief Bromden, to find his inner strength and escape from the hospital.

Kesey drew inspiration for the characters in the book from the people he encountered on the wards at work, sometimes literally taking the words right out of their mouths. "I dealt with people all night long, people crazy as hell," Kesey later recalled. "I'd sit in the nurses' room behind this big nice typewriter. One time this guy came in. I have a coke on the desk. He says, 'I see you're drinking from a glass bottle. You could do a lot of damage with this.' And I'm just nodding my head and writing it down, 'you could do a lot of damage with this.'"[52] Another patient on the ward, "old Chartes," routinely yelled, "F-f-f-uh the wife! F-f-f-k the wife!," an expression that is echoed by the Ruckly character in the book. Big Nurse was based on a woman called Lois Learned. Though not exactly a sym-pathetic character in his novel, Kesey strongly objected to the way the movie made her into the sole villain of the piece. "She's not the villain," he explained years later, recalling an awkward moment when Learned approached him after a stage performance in Portland in the early 1990s. "She might be the minion of the villain, but she's just a big tough old ex-Army nurse who is trying to do the best she can, according to the rules that she has been given. She worked for the villain and believed in the villain, but she ain't the villain."[53] In an earlier interview, he attempted to clarify his real intentions: "*Cuckoo's Nest* was supposed to be a revolu-tionary book. It was supposed to be about America, about how the sick-ness in America is in the consciousness of the people. Not the government, not the cops, and *not* Big Nurse."[54]

Kesey was quick to acknowledge that most of the characters in the book were composites of actual people, but he always denied that McMurphy was based on himself. "McMurphy is completely fictionalized," he claimed in 1962. "I used him to take out my frustrations by having him do the things I'd like to do."[55] Some of those frustrations came from seeing people on the ward behave cruelly to the patients. One patient in partic-ular was obsessive about cleanliness, yet Kesey saw an aide repeatedly "go out of his way to find an excuse to touch the man, which would send him into a frenzy."[56] According to one report, when Kesey eventually took exception to a fellow worker mistreating a patient, Kesey picked up his coworker and heaved him through a shower room door. The incident led to Kesey being fired a few months later, though the official reason given was that he was "not interested in patient welfare."[57]

While the characters in the book were inspired by real people on the ward, Kesey's insight into their condition came, he claimed, from his own psychedelic experiences. Those experiences often came courtesy of the peyote that Kesey and his pals had ordered from Texas just a short while earlier. In fact, Kesey claimed that the initial idea for the novel came to him during his first peyote trip.[58] If Kesey wanted anything other than peyote, he was not above stealing it from the hospital. "They put me on the same ward with the doctor that'd given me those early pills," Kesey explained years later. "He was not doing his experimentation anymore. . . . One night, I came back in with my keys and went into his room, into his desk, and took out a lot of stuff. That was the source of most of our—*all* of our drugs—for a long time. . . . I already knew a bunch of it. I could see he wasn't using it, and it was going to waste, getting old in there. So I liberated it. [laughs]."[59] Jim Wolpman recalls believing that Kesey had someone on the inside at the hospital, helping him get drugs and directing their usage. Kesey would never admit this to Wolpman or name names, but he just assumed that was a precondition of Kesey's agreement with his source.[60]

Kesey would occasionally sneak some drugs back into the hospital. One night, he sat at the desk in the nurses' room and wrote a letter to Babbs detailing the peyote trip that he had just embarked upon. "All over me are little bits of leaf, dirt, ants, buts, crushed moth wings," Kesey wrote, clearly entranced rather than scared by the experience. He imagined himself barefoot in the mud, with twigs in his hair, immersed in a primeval natural environment. He talked about the drug-inspired visions of his own childhood, telling Babbs that he could remember what it was like to be three years old again. And then he began talking about how his colorful visual hallucinations evoked images of ancient Native American Indian cultures. "All these shapes when I close my eyes are Indian blanket shapes of intricate geometric perfection," Kesey wrote, describing the bright neon shapes colliding in his mind. He found that he could actively change their movements and their patterns, like a child twisting a kaleidoscope, watching the colors dance together until they settled again into some sort of temporary regularity. Kesey was convinced that the peyote experience had inspired the desert Indians of the Southwest. "[O]ur Aztecs and Navahos and Mescal Indians had a drug which worked a universal pattern on the inside of their eyeballs," he wrote, "a message from the gods."[61]

The letter is illuminating, not only for the fearlessness and wonder with which Kesey describes his hallucinations but also because in expounding upon the connection between Native Americans and peyote, Kesey reveals how the drug turned his thoughts toward Indian culture just as he was starting to write *Cuckoo's Nest*. The most striking feature of the book—though not the movie, much to Kesey's disgust—is the use of a Native American character, Chief Bromden, as its narrator. At one point in the writing process, Kesey tried telling the story from the first-person perspective of an aide on the ward—that is, himself—but he was dissatisfied with the result. "Something was lacking," he wrote to Babbs, "so I tried something that will be extremely difficult to pull off. . . . [T]he narrator is going to be a character. He will not take part in the action, or ever speak as I, but he will be a character to be influenced by the events that take place, he will have a position and a personality. . . . Fair makes the mind reel doesn't it?" The issue of literary perspective, or point of view (PV), was something that had been extensively discussed in Wallace Stegner's creative writing seminar at Stanford. Though Kesey and Stegner had their differences, in writing *Cuckoo's Nest* Kesey came to acknowledge that Stegner's old-school insights were perhaps not as passé as he had once believed. "I am beginning to agree with Stegner," Kesey told Babbs, "that truly [point of view] is the most important problem in writing."[62]

The idea for Chief Bromden and the opening scenes of *Cuckoo's Nest* came to Kesey after he had choked down eight peyote buttons one night on the ward. In later years, Kesey would claim that that he did not deserve much credit for the creation of Chief Bromden, but he would never deny the *pharmacological* stimulant that allowed for that creation. "I don't own the soul of the Indian," he insisted. "He just appeared while I was on peyote, and the first chapter of the book was written by him. I know now that the Indian in *Cuckoo's Nest* is not my Indian. He was brought into being by some higher power to tell America where it's at."[63] All modesty aside, Kesey was well aware that Chief Bromden was critical to the success of the novel. He believed that by viewing events from Bromden's unusual perspective—he was supposed to be crazy, after all—readers would be shaken free from their conventions and moved to see the world differently.[64] This was not just a literary device for Kesey; it was also the personal philosophy that would inform all of his and the Pranksters' public activities in the years to come. By challenging people's perceptions of themselves and their reality—through the use of drugs, art, magic, pranks, or any sort of unconventional behavior—Kesey hoped that one by one, the scales would fall from people's eyes, their foolish hang-ups would be revealed, and the world might be a better place. "The real meaning of psychedelics," Kesey told a reporter in 1967, "is to know all of the conditioned responses of men and then to prank them. This is the surest way to get them to ask questions, and until they ask questions they are going to remain conditioned robots."[65]

Kesey worked on the wards for about nine months, practically the length of time it took him to complete *Cuckoo's Nest*. Despite the profundity of his recent pharmaceutical explorations, there seems to have been no notion at this stage that he was going to be anything else but a writer. This devotion to his craft only lasted a few more years, but the fact that it was there at all in 1961 is worth noting. Kesey had certainly embraced psychedelic drugs and incorporated them into his writing and his lifestyle, but there was no suggestion at this stage that he saw for himself any sort of public role as their advocate or promoter. Contrast that with Leary, who changed the focus of his academic career and the course of his life in pretty short order after his first exposure to the same mind-altering substances. Sure, Kesey spread the "good word" among his friends and peers, but this is hardly the same as setting oneself up as an "acid guru." Times and circumstances would have to change before Kesey found himself with a public voice, an attentive audience, and a revolutionary message, but before all that, he was mostly just a talented writer who liked to get high and have fun with his friends.

Sometimes a Great Notion

By the spring of 1961 Kesey had finished his manuscript for *Cuckoo's Nest* and had handed it over to his old teacher, Malcolm Cowley. Cowley had offered to help get Kesey published, and he worked hard on his former student's behalf. Cowley had occasionally welcomed Kesey into his home to mix with the likes of novelist C. P. Snow and poet Stephen Spender, and in return Cowley was invited to attend the occasional party on Perry Lane. At one large springtime gathering on the Lane to celebrate the birth of Zane Kesey, the long-awaited firstborn, Cowley encountered a steaming bowl of punch made with Kool-Aid, alcohol, and dry ice. "It looks like the sort of punch that Satan would serve," Cowley told Kesey, politely accepting just half a cup. Fearful of what the punch might contain, Cowley never even tasted it. Instead, he shared a bottle of bootleg Arkansas whiskey with Kesey's grandmother.[66] Such moments obviously revealed Kesey's decidedly "hick" heritage to Cowley, but as far as he was concerned, the young Oregonian's lowly origins made his natural writing talent and sharp intellect seem all the more remarkable.

Cowley thought "Zoo" had a weak, overly sentimental story line, but he had no such doubts about *Cuckoo's Nest*. Even before Kesey's manuscript was complete Cowley was freely expressing his enthusiasm to his young protégé. With Kesey about a third of the way through writing, Cowley called him into his office and sat him down for a little chat. "Ken, I want to talk to you," Kesey remembered the old man saying. "I think you may be a genius. . . . Now, nobody's ever gonna know. My advice to you is to *play* like you are. You'll have a better life."[67] Cowley was also spreading the word to his friends in the publishing industry. "[Kesey] hasn't ever learnt to spell and didn't even begin writing for pleasure until he was an upper-classman," Cowley explained to Pascal Covici at Viking Press. "[But] his manuscript might just turn out to be something that would HAVE to be published."[68] Cowley's report on the completed manuscript was even more effusive and incredulous. The manuscript "has enormous vitality and I think the youngsters are going to read and enjoy it," Cowley wrote. Kesey's "tough, sentimental, and inventive-experimental in matters of conduct— I could tell you about his diabolical punches made with dry ice, alcohol and lime juice . . . or about his experiments with hallucinogenic mushrooms. He'll probably end by corrupting the whole Stanford group of writers, among whom he's a leader. I'm sure though that he's going to be heard from and that he'll write many books."[69]

For his part, Kesey's expectations were not that high. "'That's it, I made my run,'" he remembered thinking once the manuscript had been sent to the publishers. "I didn't 'expect'; I didn't even think about it. . . . When the reviews and stuff started coming out . . . I realized 'Boy! I have written a great book!' But, it didn't occur to me when I was writing it. I had no idea it would be taken like it was."[70] Kesey and Faye did not hang around Stanford waiting to find out. They waited until Zane was born and then headed back to Oregon, where Chuck had offered him some money to work in his creamery while Kesey planned his next project. Faye and Kesey had already been talking about going back to Oregon. Kesey missed the greenness of the place and thought it would be fun to go diving in the lakes and rivers. Before he left California, Kesey paid one last visit to the Menlo Park hospital to pick up some more illicit psychedelics from the doctor's office to take home with him. This batch of drugs included a chemical called MP-14 ("a derivative of a mushroom's active ingredient," according to Kesey) and some IT-290, another of the pharmaceutical drugs that Kesey had taken during Hollister's trials.[71]

Back in Oregon, Kesey and the family moved into a house next to the McKenzie River in Springfield. He spent the spring and summer working with his brother, "the only legitimate work" he would ever do, he later remembered.[72] The job was long and hard, and not particularly to Kesey's liking.[73] While Kesey toiled in the creamery, Malcolm Cowley worked his own magic in New York. In the late summer he telegrammed Kesey to confirm that *Cuckoo's Nest* would be coming out with Viking the following January. This was an exhilarating time for Kesey, even though he still had no idea that *Cuckoo's Nest* would make the splash that it did. Viking paid Kesey their top advance of fifteen hundred dollars, giving him a much better deal than he had expected. He also sold the rights to a publishing company in England, earning him an extra five-hundred-pound advance. The money was welcome. Kesey had planned to work at the creamery until January, but he was anxious to get back to writing, and the money from the advances made that possible.

Kesey and Faye had been exploring various ways that they might live inexpensively for a year while he wrote his next book. They looked at a house on an island on the Columbia River that came with seven acres of land and a very reasonable fifty-dollars-a-month rent, but turned it down. They even considered high-tailing it to Mexico for a year (a recurring fancy of Kesey's that would infamously be realized under very different circumstances in 1966). In the end, Kesey decided to go to live in Florence, a small logging town on the Oregon Pacific coast, about a ninety-minute drive west from Springfield. Kesey thought this would be an interesting place to write about, in part because had read that Oregon had the highest suicide rate in the nation, and Florence held the dubious distinction of having the highest suicide rate in the state. "I knew that that little town was where what I was interested in was likely to be the most intense," he told an interviewer. "So I got a job over there, setting choker. A logging job."[74]

By October of 1961 Kesey had moved into a house in a remote location called Enchanted Valley near Lake Mercer in Florence. He lived there rent free—Kesey surmised that the recently widowed owner of the house just wanted someone around for company—but the isolation did not exactly suit his sociable nature.[75] Still, it was good for his writing; for the first time in a long time Kesey found himself free of the distractions of family and friends, just him and his typewriter, sketching ideas for the next book. He did not stay there long, however. Come the new year, Kesey and Faye went back to Perry Lane, both of them happy to return to the action and he keen to begin writing up what would eventually—two years later—emerge as *Sometimes a Great Notion*.

Kesey's stay in Springfield had not been all work and no play. During that time, he and his family and friends made good use of the pharmaceuticals that Kesey had liberated from his former employer's desk. In midsummer 1962 Roy Sebern, Vik Lovell, and Vik's girlfriend, Ann Atkinson, drove up from Palo Alto for a few days to visit Faye and Kesey. The highlight of the trip was a party fueled by MP-14, where Kesey, a few of his cousins and in-laws, and the Perry Lane contingent all joined in taking the powerful psychedelic. The most memorable part of the evening came when Kesey dropped an open coke bottle, butt first, down a short cardboard tube. The resulting spew of exploding liquid flew across the room like a carbonated mortar shell and landed fair and square all over Vik. He responded—as was his wont—by vomiting violently and dramatically across the room, laughing hideously as he retched, all to the amusement and horror of everybody else.[76]

Later in the fall, Kesey and Chuck took some more MP-14 and went duck hunting at a place that offered a few creature comforts for a small fee. The blinds—the place you hide while waiting to take your shot—were septic tanks buried in the ground with a covering lid that provided a small space from which to shoot. It was completely dark in the blind, with nothing to do except bide your time until some birds came into view. As the drugs started to come on strong, the two brothers started "seeing stuff," but the way Kesey tells the story, this only seemed to help Chuck's shooting ability. "We're standing up in there looking and here came 3 big ole, beautiful small teal, flying right straight toward us," Kesey recalled. "I was watching them and suddenly, BOOM, BOOM, BOOM. Chuck dropped them all. I said, "God, that's good shootin'." He says, "Out of a flock like that I should have got 10 or 12."[77]

Both these stories reveal the ways in which Kesey casually incorporated these powerful drugs into his everyday life. Not for Kesey the neo-religious, almost sanctimonious approach adopted by Huxley and Leary toward psychedelics. No, here was Kesey passing out these powerful substances to friends and family as if they were party favors or picnic treats. In hindsight, this seems incredibly reckless, but it is important to remember that neither Kesey nor his friends thought that these drugs posed any great danger. People had gotten sick occasionally, but that was almost seen as a rite of passage, nothing more. The experience was nothing to be scared of, whatever happened. The notion of a "bad trip" did not actually become an issue until one of Kesey's guests started having a bad time at another MP-14 party at his house on the McKenzie River. Up until then, these drugs had seemed both legitimate—sanctioned by the medical establishment and the U.S. government, no less—and relatively harmless. "These things can be keys, no more," Kesey told Babbs after sending him some IT-290, "not crutches as I once feared."[78]

Leary's group at Harvard regularly tried to counter suggestions that psychedelics were inherently dangerous. In an article published in, of all places, *The Bulletin of the Atomic Scientists*, Leary and his coauthors insisted that in their extensive experience, "[psychedelics] are not addictive, nor sedative, nor intoxicating. There is no evidence for any lasting and very few transient physical effects. . . . Set and suggestibility, expectation and emotional atmosphere account for almost all of the specificity of reaction."[79] The Harvard group did not encounter an extended bad trip until their first Mexican psychedelic summer camp in the summer of 1962. Two people experienced "temporary psychotic episodes" as a result of taking LSD during their stay at Zihuatanejo—one was an undercover federal agent sent to spy on the groups' activities, according to Leary—but both fully recovered and, despite their difficulties, subsequently thanked Leary for the experience.[80]

Doors Can Be Windows Too

But even for fun-loving Kesey, psychedelics were more than just party drugs. The idea that psychedelics could reveal your true inner self was also central to Kesey's understanding of these powerful and mysterious substances, and he remained convinced that it was their most profound property. "The first drug trips were, for most of us, shell-shattering ordeals that left us blinking kneedeep in the cracked crusts of our pie-in-sky personalities," he wrote in 1971. "Suddenly people were stripped before one another and behold! As we looked, and were looked on, we all made a great discovery: we were beautiful. Naked and helpless and sensitive as a snake after skinning, but far more human than that shining knightmare that had stood creaking in previous parade rest. We were alive and life was us. We joined hands and danced barefoot amongst the rubble. We had been cleansed, liberated! We would never don the old armors again."[81] Though Kesey and the Pranksters had their differences with Leary's camp, there was clearly a significant degree of agreement about the transformative and therapeutic value of LSD and similar substances. Psychedelics "helped me to escape—albeit momentarily—from the prison of my mind," Dick Alpert divulged. "They overrode the habit patterns of thought, and I was able to taste innocence again."[82]

Herein lies a basic tenet of the utopian idealism that fueled not only IFIF and the Pranksters but the psychedelic revolution as a whole. Psychedelics were seen as the ultimate revelatory street therapy. They were "keys to worlds that are already there,"[83] as Kesey told one interviewer, and they offered people new perspectives and new ways to think about reality and their place in it. "I was permanently rewired," insists John Perry Barlow, a friend and lyricist for the Grateful Dead's Bob Weir. "[M]y sense of the universe was forever changed." The value of a substance like acid—as its nickname implied—was that it seemed to somehow burn through the layers of a person's "hang-ups" and reveal a glimpse of their true humanity in all its naked innocence and fragile glory. Racism, sexism, war, conflict, greed, jealousy—the flotsam and jetsam of social conditioning—all would be exposed as relics of human prejudice and insecurity that served no function except to divide people and distort the reality of their commonality. Thus, though usually considered to be hallucinogenic, psychedelics were also thought to reveal a more authentic version of reality than what people usually experience in their normal, "unaltered" state. John Perry Barlow recognized this paradox the first time he took LSD. "I sensed the complete connectedness of everything," he recalled. "It was obvious to me that all of the separateness I ordinarily perceived was, in fact, an artifact of cultural conditioning, and was indeed less "real" than what I was supposedly hallucinating."[84] Kesey agreed: "This is what LSD taught us." He told an online interviewer that "there is another reality going on right now, in front of all of us—but it is a reality that doesn't have any physical form."[85]

The revelatory aspect of psychedelics had implications beyond the individual because it was thought that if sufficient numbers of people became conscious of this "other" reality, then their consciousness would be altered along with their lives, and society would be therefore be transformed for the better. "[W]e were trying to body forth a new consciousness, a completely new way to relate to your world," Kesey once explained of his intent.[86] Call it raising consciousness, re-imprinting, heightening awareness, enlightenment, or whatever you like, psychedelics were supposed to offer a life-changing experience like no other. "The real rebellion is approaching not only each other but also the Universe with another kind of consciousness . . . [in which] we are at one with what is going on."[87]

The utopian idealism of the psychedelic movement endured scathing attacks from all quarters. The mass media, intrigued at first, quickly moved on to mockery and scaremongering in equal measures. The authorities, frightened by something that was clearly beyond their control, decried psychedelic idealism as the rantings of dangerous and deranged individuals and responded with predictably heavy-handed prohibition. It did not help that this idealism was also oftentimes obscured by adherents' missteps and excesses, but nevertheless idealism remained at the heart of the psychedelic movement. For true believers, a commitment to their drug-fueled utopianism was the foundation upon which they built their personal and political philosophies. Pursuing the goal of "freeing the mind" and living an "authentic" life was felt to be far more meaningful, more personal, and ultimately more revolutionary than signing on to any tired old leftist ideology or marching in yet another dreary street protest. Who needed marxism and its conflict-driven analysis of historical change, when a single LSD trip might exorcise the "ghosts of the past" that Marx had famously said weighed down human progress. Forget social movements and collective action; this was a personal, individualistic revolution where everybody had the potential to "break on through to the other side," as the Doors' Jim Morrison put it.

At the very least, Kesey believed that the psychedelic experience might break down some of the conservative values of the 1950s, values that he viewed as a constraint on individual liberty and human possibility. From Kesey's perspective, LSD came at precisely the moment it was most needed. "I think at that time in our history there was a stiffness that went around the US like a tarter on the teeth," he told one interviewer in hindsight. "LSD was a way of going in there and getting the tarter loose so that the gums could be healthy again.[88] Musician David Crosby remembered feeling the same way. "We had a strong feeling about drugs, or rather, psychedelics and marijuana," he recalled. "We thought they would help us blast our generation loose from the fifties."[89] That they did, and more.

While Kesey and the Pranksters are remembered for their all-American pursuit of psychedelic merriment, there was also an idealistic aspect to their activities that often went unstated and, as a result, is often left unacknowledged. Kesey was always something of a joker, and so it should come as no surprise to find him viewing the psychedelic experience as a lot of fun. The rebellious side of him also appreciated that the drugs that were capable of inducing laughter *and* introspection were perhaps the most subversive drugs of all. That is not to say that Kesey and the Pranksters took these powerful substances lightly. Most of the Pranksters seem to have genuinely believed that these strange mind-altering substances had some sort of broader social or even cosmic significance, but that belief was rarely uniform, consistent, or well thought out. The sense that psychedelics were inherently meaningful and valuable remained a vague constant for most of them—even today—but the meanings and values that they might have prescribed to psychedelics varied over time and from person to person. Some of what they believed seems foolish, naïve, and even dangerous in hindsight, but we would do well to remember that Kesey and the Pranksters (and others like them) were true pioneers, exploring waters uncharted by the Cold War American society that they lived in. While this gave these early voyagers a brief moment in time when they could go about their adventures unhindered by too much legalistic prohibition and oversight, it also meant that they were, in essence, fumbling around in the dark in blissful ignorance, working with only limited knowledge about the nature of these drugs and the strange terrain that they uncovered.

Faye Kesey, née Norma Faye Faxby. Faye was raised in Springfield, Oregon, where she first encountered Kesey in junior high school. She attended Oregon State College, where she was Lane County representative, but later transferred to the University of Oregon to major in dietetics.

(Photo by Hank Kranzler; image courtesy Hank Kranzler estate)

Faye and Ken Kesey, early 1960s. Faye and Kesey married on May 20, 1956, at the First Congregational Church, Eugene, Oregon. They were together until Kesey's death in November 2001. They had three children, Zane, Jed, and Shannon. Jed Kesey died in an accident in 1984.

(Photo by Hank Kranzler; image courtesy Hank Kranzler estate)

Ken Kesey, author. This photo dates from 1963/64, before the June 1964 publication of *Sometimes a Great Notion* and the summer bus trip that was planned to coincide with its release. Kesey's first novel, *One Flew Over the Cuckoo's Nest* (1962), had established his reputation as one of America's most prominent young writers.

(Photo by Hank Kranzler; image courtesy Hank Kranzler estate)

Ken Kesey through the looking glass, doing his best to look like Marlon Brando. Kesey started writing *Sometimes a Great Notion* on Perry Lane, but he relocated to La Honda in the summer of 1963 after his cabin on the Lane was demolished. This photo was probably taken in the front room of Kesey's house on Perry Lane, shortly before its destruction.

(Photo by Hank Kranzler; image courtesy Hank Kranzler estate)

Kesey wrote virtually the entire *Notion* manuscript in longhand on yellow legal pads, cutting and pasting here and there, and then sending off his work to his publisher, Viking, where a secretary typed it up for his editor to read. *Notion* received mixed critical reviews at the time, but it is now recognized as Kesey's best book and acclaimed as a classic of American literature.

(Photo by Hank Kranzler; image courtesy Hank Kranzler estate)

Kesey working on a project at his writing desk, probably in the front room of his Perry Lane house. Most of the furniture, including the desk, the sofa, and the book shelves, was homemade from everyday construction materials. The large painting in the background was painted by Ann Murphy, one of Neal Cassady's girlfriends. This photo dates from early 1963.

(Photo by Hank Kranzler; image courtesy Hank Kranzler estate)

Kesey kept an elaborate chart on the wall of his writing room to help him keep track of the complicated structure of *Sometimes a Great Notion*. His effort to tell a compelling narrative from numerous points of view was very ambitious, and it was a draining experience that Kesey was unwilling to repeat.

(Photo by Hank Kranzler; image courtesy Hank Kranzler estate)

Kesey walking toward his house at La Honda. The house sat on the southern bank of the La Honda Creek, in a beautiful rural setting, surrounded by enormous redwood trees. The one-story house was built in 1942 by the Pepper family and originally named Wychward. La Honda was a fairly isolated village community, nestled on the westward slopes of the redwood hills that separate Palo Alto from the Pacific Ocean.

(Photo by Hank Kranzler; image courtesy Hank Kranzler estate)

Kesey and his Prankster friends often decorated the woods around his property in La Honda with useful or artistic objects. They hung speakers in the woods and a Ron Boise metal sculpture from a tree in the front yard. Sometimes they left bottles of soda in one of the cool running streams behind Kesey's house, for the refreshment of anyone who chanced upon them. Here, Kesey places a clay pipe on a redwood tree stump.

(Photo by Hank Kranzler; image courtesy Hank Kranzler estate)

Kesey decorating his property in La Honda with a skull that was probably a relic from his time as a magician and fortune teller (see p. 38), and from his days at the University of Oregon. Kesey's isolated home hosted many an interesting gathering. On one occasion, Kesey and the Pranksters staged a mock ritual for the benefit of their guests Kenneth Anger and Anton LaVey, both renowned Satanists. Kesey burned some of his books, and one of the Pranksters slaughtered a chicken that had been hidden in a golden cage suspended among the trees.

(Photo by Hank Kranzler; image courtesy Hank Kranzler estate)

6

Sometimes a Great Notion

Lieutenant Babbs

When Ken Babbs chose to enroll in the Navy ROTC program at Miami University of Ohio, he was driven by good old-fashioned fiscal logic as much as by a desire to serve his country. He figured that since he was probably going to get drafted for two years after college, he might as well sign up early and get the military to help pay his college expenses in exchange for an extra couple of years of service. The summer before he arrived at Stanford, Babbs had done some navy training aboard a ship and found that life on the ocean waves was not to his liking. A marine officer persuaded him that the marines might be a better option than the navy, and when Babbs finished his year at Stanford (1958–59), he and his new wife, Anita, headed off to the Marine Corps base at Quantico, Virginia, to take up his commission as a second lieutenant. Toward the end of his basic officer training, Babbs decided to try out for flight school. He passed the physical and all the required tests and was accepted into the program. So in April 1960, while Kesey was learning how to get high courtesy of the Menlo Park VA hospital, Babbs moved to Pensacola, Florida, to begin learning more conventional ways of getting off the ground.

Babbs was a good student, and eventually an excellent pilot, but as one might expect for a Prankster-to-be, he was not exactly a perfect fit for the military. As time went on, his mischievous nature got him tagged as a bit of a troublemaker, a role he was only too happy to play to make his time in the service more manageable.[1] Babbs's progressive politics also set him somewhat outside of the mainstream, particularly on questions of race. After a

fight broke out between some black marines and white marines in the barracks, all the black marines shaved their heads as a show of solidarity. Babbs
raised quite a few eyebrows when he decided to do likewise, boldly pro-
claiming his allegiance with the lower-ranked black marines on the base.[2]

By the spring of 1961 Babbs had earned wings and completed his
advanced flight training. He was offered the choice between flying jets
or helicopters. Much to the disgruntlement of his instructors—all hot-
shot jet pilots—Babbs chose the helicopter option. He learned to enjoy
helicopters, but initially he regretted the decision, finding the learning
curve difficult.[3] Toward the end of his flight school and helicopter training, Babbs requested a posting back to California, and in the early summer of 1961, he transferred to MCAF Santa Ana, part of the giant El Toro
marine base located about an hour south of Los Angeles.

Babbs and Anita (and their two young kids) moved into a place in San
Juan Capistrano. Babbs was happy to be back on the West Coast, close to
his friends. He drove up to Perry Lane whenever he got the chance. He
and his brother John also spent a week visiting the Keseys in Oregon,
one of the highlights of which was the Babbs brothers' first experience
with IT-290, courtesy of Kesey's favorite desk at the VA hospital. This was
during the period when Kesey and Faye were living in the rented house
close to the McKenzie River in Springfield while Kesey worked at the
creamery. Babbs and his brother swallowed the IT-290 and spent the day
playing alongside the river, simply having fun and enjoying the beautiful
summer weather. As evening approached, they came across some logging
equipment just off the path that led to Kesey's house. They picked up
some rocks and gleefully started banging them on a fearsome-looking
six-foot diameter circular blade. The blade rang like a bell and to their
delight they found that if they turned it they could alter its pitch in weird
and wonderful ways. Their musical experiment was interrupted by a stern
old man who told them in no uncertain terms to get off his property. The
two were happy to comply. A little further along the path Kesey appeared
out of the bushes, laughing as he told them that their racket was audi-
ble from a mile away and that he had come to warn them about the man
they had already encountered. The three made their way home, where they
celebrated the day's events with a barbecue and a trip to a bar where they
sat and smoked cigars while trading funny stories.[4] Babbs's introduction
to IT-290 was not exactly a mystical experience, but he still viewed it as a

profound moment in his life. For a while afterward, he even started dividing his life experiences into two categories: those that occurred before he had taken the drug, and those that took place after.

During a visit to Perry Lane during that same summer, Babbs arrived to find the place deserted. As the afternoon passed, he meandered around, grabbed a bite to eat, and rolled himself a joint. Stoned and content, he eventually settled on top of Vic Lovell's bed to read a little Henry Miller while he waited for people to come back from wherever they had gone. Sometime around five, a woman Babbs knew as Jane showed up with her two kids in tow. She was looking for a friend who lived on the Lane. Babbs fielded her questions and gave her a beer, and together they wandered outside. There, they met up with a short, wiry man hanging around Kesey's old place, temporarily sublet to Ron Bondoc and his wife, Gigi. The man was older than most of the Perry Lane regulars but he explained to Babbs that he often came over to Ron's on Saturday nights to watch sports on TV. This seemed like a steady arrangement and so, since residents rarely locked their doors on the Lane, Babbs, Jane, and Ron's friend opted to wait inside Ron's cabin.[5]

While Babbs turned on the TV, the stranger went into the kitchen and made some coffee. As they all talked, it slowly dawned on Babbs that the soft-spoken stranger was none other than Neal Cassady, the legendary soul and guiding light of the Beat movement. Vic and Ron had told Babbs that Cassady had been coming around the Lane, but it took awhile for Babbs to put two and two together. His first inkling came when the woman caught Cassady slipping some "medicine" into his coffee (it was methedrine). The second occurred when an excited Cassady started talking a mile a minute after he found out that Babbs was high and holding. Cassady was famous for this "coming on," for keeping up the sort of careering, frenetic stream-of-consciousness monologues that had inspired Jack Kerouac's stylistic retelling of the adventures that the two had shared together on the road in the late 1940s. Babbs was neither the first nor the last to be amazed by the spectacle that was Cassady. This was the man who had appeared as Hart Kennedy in John Clellon Holmes's first novel, *Go*; who had been celebrated as the "cocksman and Adonis of Denver;" and as "N.C." the "secret hero" in Allen Ginsberg's groundbreaking poem *Howl*; and, most famously, as the real-life Dean Moriarty, the "new American saint," in Jack Kerouac's *On the Road*. Far out.

Once Cassady had worked out that Babbs and the woman were not together, his attention shifted to her, much to the relief of Babbs. In his stoned state, he was having a little trouble keeping up with Cassady, and he welcomed the opportunity to sit back awhile and take it all in. At eleven that night—six hours later—a somewhat surprised Gigi Bondoc came home and broke up the show. Neal and the woman (and her kids) roared off to continue their partying elsewhere. Cassady had wanted to borrow Babbs's rental car, but Babbs politely declined, recalling that Dean Moriarty's driving in *On the Road* was as notoriously wild as his womanizing. Babbs crashed out at Vic's place and missed out on the final event of this particular adventure. At five the next morning, Gigi woke up to find Cassady sitting on her bed, horny, still high, and gibbering away about the healing powers of love. A frightened Gigi leapt out of bed, turned on all the lights, and ran to the living room, where she slept on the couch, leaving Cassady the bed. At nine, he emerged out of the bedroom, put a blanket over Gigi, and left.

Kesey's first encounter with Cassady had occurred when the Beat elder clattered unannounced into the Perry Lane courtyard in a Jeep with a blown transmission.[6] Hearing a commotion outside his front door, Kesey emerged to find Cassady stripping down the transmission and talking a mile a minute to the crowd that had gathered around him. "I watched him running around," Kesey recalled years later. "[T]his frenetic, crazed character speaking in a monologue that sounded like *Finnegan's Wake* played fast forward." Cassady had been a volunteer in the Menlo Park hospital drug experiments just as Kesey had, and Kesey remembered thinking, "Oh, my God, it could lead to this." Kesey perhaps realized that his own life was at some sort of crossroads, and that this rabid character before him represented one of the choices open to him, one pioneered by Kerouac, Burroughs, and Ginsberg, all of whom had also been influenced by Cassady, their friend. Cassady had been "a hero to all of us who followed that wild road, the hero who moved us all," Kesey concluded.[7]

FROM RAGS TO RICHES

Kesey and Faye had come back to live on Perry Lane early in 1962. Babbs and Anita drove up for a weekend in early February and, not surprisingly, a big party ensued. It was a grand celebration and a happy reunion; the

old Perry Lane crew was together again after a year or two of separa-
tion. Fueled by MP-14, the party went on for days.[8] They had good reason
to celebrate. *Cuckoo's Nest* had come out in January 1962 to mostly excellent reviews. The *New Yorker* condescendingly dismissed Kesey's writing style as "paste-pot colloquial," and a few other critics objected to some
of the ribald humor and "dirty" language in the book, but such reservations were few and far between. The *New York Times* glowingly described
Cuckoo's Nest as "a glittering parable of good and evil," while *Time* magazine proclaimed it to be a "brilliant first novel" that offered "a roar of
protest against middlebrow society's Rules and the invisible Rulers who
enforce them."[9] Kesey's literary name was made with his first publication.
Critical acclaim, however, did not immediately translate into best-seller
status. The book sold steadily and grew in popularity especially on college
campuses, where its message of heroic struggle and personal redemption
seemed to strike a particularly resonant chord with idealistic students. It
took awhile, however, for any money to start trickling in. At Kesey's first
autograph signing at Gill's Bookstore in Portland, for example, noted local
author and journalist Stewart Holbrook stopped by, sat with Kesey for
most of the long, slow afternoon, and ended up giving the young author
fifty dollars to help repair his broken-down car so he could get home.

Kesey's money woes took another turn for the worse when a woman
named Gwen Davis started legal proceedings against him. Davis had been
an occasional visitor to Perry Lane, and she had worked at the same VA
hospital as Kesey in Menlo Park. Her lawsuit claimed that Kesey had used
her as the basis for one of the minor characters in the book—a Red Cross
woman who briefly appeared in a couple of scenes—and that his portrayal
of her was defamatory. Kesey certainly did not pull any punches in his
portrayal: "The Red Cross Lady's underclothes are so tight it bloats her
face up when she laughs, makes it round and red as the sun," read one passage. "She's a Jew girl and tells lots of Jew jokes to show us it's okay we're
not Jews too. She's got funny blond hair and a brown mustache and no
eyebrows at all to speak of[;] . . . if you push her over she's weighted on the
bottom and straightaway rocks back upright." A later section gave the character a name: "I hear a silly prattle reminds me of someone familiar. . . .
It's the plump Red Cross woman, Gwen-doe-lin, with the blond hair the
patients are always arguing about."[10] Kesey and Viking eventually reached
a settlement with Davis. They agreed to pay her some compensation and

to remove the offending passages from all subsequent editions and re-prints of *Cuckoo's Nest*. Kesey simply replaced the Red Cross woman with an equally fat and derided "Public Relations" man.[11]

The settlement gobbled up most of the money that Kesey had made selling the movie and stage rights to *Cuckoo's Nest*. A number of people had recognized the performative potential of the book, and something of a scramble ensued to buy the rights. An agent named Hope Taylor had gotten hold of a copy in galley form. She read the book and liked it, and got in touch with an old friend, screenwriter and playwright Dale Wasserman. "I've just read the galleys of a new book," Taylor told him. "It's going to be important, and if there's a play in it, it should be written by you." Wasserman had a few reservations—he found parts of the book to be "blatantly misogynistic," and he thought that Kesey had indulged in "some gratuitous anti-Semitism"—but at the same time he was impressed by the vitality of Kesey's writing and appreciative of the antiauthoritar-ian sentiment that lay at the heart of the book. "[W]ithout question," he recalled, "the book had imagination, power, and most potent of all, a theme that was exquisitely timely."[12] Wasserman immediately contacted Kesey's agents to inquire after the theatrical rights to the novel, only to be told that "somebody else" had already expressed an interest, also implying that Wasserman's competition had more money and considerably more clout than he. That "somebody else" turned out to be a production com-pany called Joel Productions, owned by movie star Kirk Douglas.

On the advice of his producer friend Edward Lewis, Douglas had also read a copy of *Cuckoo's Nest* in galley form, and he was "crazy" about it, seeing it not only as a potentially great movie but also as a vehicle for his return to the stage, where he still felt he had something to prove. About a week before the book came out, Kesey traveled down to Los Angeles to meet with Douglas and thrash out the terms of the sale. The young author was naturally thrilled with this turn of events. Less than five years ear-lier, Kesey had left Tinseltown with his tail between his legs, and now here he was, vaulting over all the other wannabes at the invitation of one of the biggest Hollywood stars of the day. Kesey and Douglas got along well—Douglas's rags-to-riches life story and his tough-guy screen per-sona would have doubtless appealed to Kesey—and the young author agreed to sell both the stage and screen rights to his book outright. The deal was finalized about a week after *Cuckoo's Nest* was published. In later years, Kesey would bitterly regret having given up all and any royalties to the stage and screen adaptations of his novel—particularly when the 1975 movie version, starring Jack Nicholson, won five Academy Awards and went on to make millions—but at the time he was happy enough. He received a five-thousand-dollar option for the first year, plus the opportunity for much more—up to eighty-five thousand dollars—if everything came together successfully.[13]

Douglas was also happy with the deal. He quickly set about transforming the book into a play, turning ironically to Dale Wasserman to write the adaptation. The two already knew each other—Wasserman had worked on the screenplay for one of Douglas's biggest movies, *The Vikings*—and Douglas knew of Wasserman's failed attempt to buy the stage rights to Kesey's book. After some negotiation, Douglas offered to sign the theatrical rights over to Wasserman in exchange for him adapting *Cuckoo's Nest* for the stage. Douglas made it clear that he had every intention of bringing the play to Broadway in the fall of 1963 with himself in the starring role as Randle P. McMurphy. Wasserman eventually agreed to all of Douglas's terms, even though this deal offered him no money up front. Still, he had faith in the quality of Kesey's story and, more to the point, he thought Douglas was well suited to the role of McMurphy. It was probably one of the smartest decisions Wasserman ever made. Even though Douglas's Broadway production was actually a commercial flop, a later New York production ran for almost four years, and another in San Francisco ran for five years straight. The popularity of the play continues to this day. In 2001 Gary Sinise was nominated for a Best Actor Tony award for his portrayal of McMurphy in a revived Broadway production, and around the world there are approximately 150 productions of *Cuckoo's Nest* staged per year, performed in any of twenty-seven languages. Kesey viewed this success with mixed feelings. He earned no royalties from these productions, but their success—and the initial involvement of Kirk Douglas—raised the profile of the book and aided in its own eventual popularity. (*One Flew Over the Cuckoo's Nest* has so far been reprinted more than one hundred times in the United States alone.) Kesey was not ignorant of this fact. "Without the play," he once admitted, "the novel would have made a small bubble."[14]

While Kesey was enjoying the first fruits of his success, Babbs was facing a far different reality. The previous fall he had received word that he and his squadron would ship the following July to the Far East. Vietnam beckoned. Though he downplayed the potential danger, he was worried enough to write and tell his brother that he was making out a will.[15] On Monday, June 18, roughly a month before Babbs was due to ship out, Kesey arrived in San Juan Capistrano in plenty of time to prepare for a huge leaving party that Babbs had planned for later in the week. Kesey was accompanied by Gus Guthrie, the daughter of famous author A. B. Guthrie, who had written *The Way West* and *The Big Sky* (by chance one of Babbs's favorite books). Gus had worked at Viking Press when *Cuckoo's Nest* was in production, and when she moved to the West Coast in the spring of 1962, she looked Kesey up and joined his social circle. The trio headed off to Mexico for a one-day visit to Tijuana, then back over the border to Anaheim, for a trip to Disneyland. They spent Thursday driving around exploring Los Angeles, ending up at a jazz joint in Hermosa Beach, where they were treated to the delights of Howard Rumsey and his Lighthouse Allstars. Babbs's father flew in from Ohio late on Friday night, just in time for a long boozy party that started at Saturday lunchtime with a game of basketball in Babbs's swimming pool and only ended in the early hours of Sunday morning when the group got thrown out of a bar after one of their rowdier members threatened to let off a giant M-80 firecracker.

Kesey left a few days later with plans in place for Babbs to travel up to Oregon again in a week or so. On the way there, Babbs took a detour to see Mitch Strucinski. Mitch had landed himself in Vacaville Prison after stealing some rare manuscripts from Stanford in 1960, an act that was understandably the talk of the campus. It even earned a mention in *Time* magazine. After visiting Mitch, Babbs and his family drove up to Springfield to spend time with Kesey and his family. John Babbs was also along for the trip. After a couple of days hanging out in Oregon, Kesey, his brother Chuck, Babbs, John, and Kesey's old fraternity brother Mike Hagen loaded up a car and drove up to Seattle to sample the delights of the World's Fair. That sounds innocent enough, but unlike others passing through the gates, Kesey and his cronies were tripping out of their minds on some of Kesey's illicit supply of psychedelic drugs. Foreshadowing later efforts to capture their experiences on tape, the crew even made a recording of their adventures on Kesey's portable reel-to-reel. Everybody had such a good time that the episode became legendary in Prankster circles, not least because the bus trip of June 1964 was motivated in part by a desire to re-create the Seattle experiences at that year's World's Fair in New York.

Babbs returned to his unit to prepare for his departure, and Kesey went back to Perry Lane to continue chipping away at *Sometimes a Great Notion*, his new novel in progress. Parties were as much a feature of life on the Lane as they had ever been, and the fresh faces in the crowd quickly learned that they had better have a strong constitution if they wanted to get the most out of Kesey's pharmaceutical hospitality. Drugs now routinely greased the wheels of Kesey's social circle, and an affinity for them was certainly one qualification for inclusion, but it was by no means the only or even most important way to fit in. His scene was a reflection of his own personality and background: an odd mixture of family, jocks, fraternity brothers, gifted artists, and writers. Women were always welcome to join the party—for obvious reasons—but they had to have very strong personalities if they wanted to be treated anything like equals. Psychedelics may have transported people to all manner of unfamiliar realms, but whenever they came back they tended to return to the same old gender politics and gender roles they had left behind. Women on the scene were more sexually liberated than women in mainstream society, but they remained stuck with the same old domestic duties: cooking, cleaning, sewing, and child rearing. Vic Lovell's description of some of the younger women who used to hang around the lane—"cute, lively, and except for their sexual availability, which varied unpredictably, utterly useless"—should give us some insight into the gender sensibilities in play at the time.[16] Prankster Gretchen Douglas recalls the Merry Pranksters as little more than a "fraternity on wheels."[17]

Drugs were increasingly available on the Lane and around the Bay Area. Sally Demma and a few other regulars had started dealing pot by this point, and another couple, one of whom worked in a pharmaceutical manufacturing facility, was openly selling stolen prescription pills out of a case they kept in the trunk of their car. This married couple kept the Lane and others well supplied with drugs and made lots of money in the process, but they were far too cavalier about their little enterprise, risking the attention of the law.[18] In the end, it was Sally and her friends who got busted first. Sally ended up serving three months in the county jail in Redwood City for possession. A contingent from Perry Lane visited her every week.[19]

Dealing drugs—what Timothy Leary once called "an ancient and honorable human profession"—was a common way to finance the sort of fringe existence that many of these people were increasingly adopting.[20] Small-time operators like Sally and her friends were usually involved in the scenes that they served, and they usually made only relatively small amounts of money. Unrelated to the organized criminal set that began to move into the drug business later in the decade, these people were valued by their communities even as they were vilified by the authorities. Dealers actually played an important role in the history of the emerging psychedelic community, channeling news, gossip, and information among scattered groups of people and acting as important points of connection among the various scenes in and around the Bay Area. Cassady, for example, flitted from place to place selling various substances to subsidize his lifestyle and making connections as he went. Around the North Beach section of San Francisco, he was known as the Johnny Appleseed of pot. Phil Lesh first met him in 1963, when Cassady was selling pot and little vials of methedrine.[21] Chateau dweller Page Browning was also known to Kesey's scene as a small-time dealer. Browning would eventually become a full-fledged Prankster, and it was his friendship with Jerry Garcia, his former roommate, that led to the Grateful Dead being invited to visit La Honda and later play at the Acid Tests.

The Perry Lane scene was just one among many. The Haight-Ashbury district of San Francisco, "discovered" with such fanfare by the mainstream media in 1967, had actually been a scene for a good few years prior to that date. It was home to wannabe artists and poets, disaffected college students (many from the nearby San Francisco State University), and various beatniks and bohemians who had left the North Beach area of the city when it became overrun with tourists and topless bars in the late fifties and early sixties. Similar groups of people could be found in other parts of San Francisco, as well as in Berkeley, Sausalito, Palo Alto, San Jose, Santa Cruz, and lots of places in between. Their earliest public meeting places were the coffee houses that popped up in various locations— the Cabale in Berkeley, the Top of the Tangent in Palo Alto, the Offstage in San Jose—all of which offered a place to hang out, look cool, and listen to local folk musicians and poets. Parties were important gathering places too, serving as meeting places for individuals from across the various scenes. When Chet Helms first started promoting shows in San Francisco

in late 1965 and early 1966, he would drum up a crowd simply by calling up the two or three hundred people that he knew from the local party
scene. "We had been part of a big party circuit," he recalled years later,
"and that was sort of how we would organize the parties."[22]

Differences existed within and across the various scenes, but they were
joined together by a common desire to explore beyond what they perceived as the constraining social norms of the era. People who were a part
of these groups gradually developed a sense of commonality with one
another, an identity perhaps, based on a set of shared interests and attitudes toward art, politics, music, personal freedom, and drugs. Drugs were
especially important to this sense of connection. A shared appreciation
for their properties gave people what felt like membership in a special
club where they were exclusively privy to experiences and pleasures that
the rest of the "straight" world had yet to understand or embrace. The illegality of these drugs only served to strengthen the bond among enthusi-
asts, transforming disparate groups of people into something resembling
a community. "[E]verybody took drugs, different kinds of drugs, whatever kind of drugs they could find," remembered the Berkeley-based musician Country Joe McDonald. "Mostly it was marijuana, mushrooms and
psychedelics. . . . None of this stuff was happening with any sense of danger because something magical was going on that was hard to explain
then, and is still hard to explain now. An innocence, I guess . . . a sense
of community, of communication. We developed family roots that were
just wonderful . . . It was a rare moment for those of us who made music,
being in this really happy environment full of really intelligent people
who were all doing some very heady stuff."[23]

The Perry Lane scene maintained a strong connection to Stanford and
Stegner's writing program, even though Kesey had long since stopped
attending the Jones Room seminars himself. A writer by the name of Ed
McClanahan, one of the recipients of a Stegner fellowship that 1962–63
academic year, became a regular on the Lane and a lifelong friend of the
Kesey family. McClanahan had been a participant in Stegner's program
back in the midfifties, and he already knew a few Perry Lane people, including Vic Lovell, Jim Wolpman, and fellow Kentuckians Wendell Berry,
James Hall, and Gurney Norman. He also knew Kesey, having paid him a
visit the previous year in Oregon, where Kesey was researching *Sometimes
a Great Notion* and McClanahan was closing out a stint as an English

instructor at Oregon State College (now University) in Corvallis. When McClanahan moved down to California to begin his studies at Stanford, he sought out his friends and rented a house on Alpine Road, a few blocks from Perry Lane.[24]

McClanahan became an active participant in the Thursday night reading sessions that were held on the Lane and occasionally at his house. "Originally it was Kesey and I and Vic Lovell and whoever happened to be around," McClanahan recalled. "The others didn't have to be writers, but they wanted to hear us read our stuff."[25] Kesey was very excited about these events, and it is clear from the way that he encouraged a deliberately open-ended, informal setting that they were in some ways literary precursors to the Acid Tests. McClanahan found the atmosphere at these events to be liberating. "We were all learning how to smoke dope, and we would read our work to each other," he told interviewer Todd Bauer. "What was really nice was that it was an opportunity to try stuff out on an audience before you went into the more formal atmosphere of the seminar."[26]

Drugs were around at these parties, but they were secondary to whatever else was going on. "These parties were full of life and laughter," remembered Gurney Norman. "It is hard to see anything in the least bit decadent about them. They were very sweet and dear and above all, extremely literary. . . . I'm in no way envious of Paris in the twenties because we had Palo Alto in the sixties."[27] Kesey was undeniably fascinated with psychedelic drugs at this point in his life, but he defined himself through his writing, not through drugs. At the *Cuckoo's Nest* release party in February 1962, for example, Kesey took time out from all the craziness and drunken dancing to take Norman outside to his writing shed. There, he handed him the first fifty pages of *Sometimes a Great Notion* and asked for comments. "So there in the middle of this party, Ken wanted to talk about fiction," Norman recounted. "Drugs were a spice in the cake for Kesey. He'd rather talk about Melville and Moby Dick than about drugs."[28] When Kesey showed Ed McClanahan a rough draft of the first part of *Notion*, McClanahan thought it was terrific, but he had one burning question: whose amputated arm was hanging over the river in the opening scene? Kesey's answer was typically quixotic: "Shit, I don't know whose arm it is," he told his friend. "[T]hat's what I'm writing the book for, to find out." McClanahan was amazed by this impulsive, unstructured approach to writing. "I think it's true," he insisted years later. "[H]e really didn't know what he was writing about until he wrote."[29] Whatever his writing process entailed, Kesey was well aware that he was under pressure to match the success of *Cuckoo's Nest*, believing that an author's reputation could be made or broken by the second novel, not the first.

Despite these misgivings, or perhaps because of them, *Sometimes a Great Notion* was a remarkably ambitious book. The narrative describes a feud between the Stamper clan and the local union. The story made for an enjoyable, dramatic yarn, but it also allowed Kesey the opportunity to explore much larger themes about the nature and the place of the individual in modern society. As if that were not aspiration enough, Kesey also chose to tell the story from the perspectives of many of its major characters at the same time, or at least as many as was technically possible. This time Kesey set out to try to capture reality in all its multiperspectival complexity. This was an ambition of staggering proportions, and Kesey deserves great credit for the extent to which he eventually succeeded—even if not perfectly—in attaining such lofty heights. By employing such an unusual narrative technique, Kesey was trying to build on the success he had achieved with *Cuckoo's Nest* where, to much acclaim, he had told his story from the peculiar perspective of Chief Bromden. The fractured reality of the psychedelic drug experience also inspired Kesey to write a book that presents reality as a matter of perspective. When an interviewer asked him about the drug experiments at the VA hospital, Kesey struggled to answer. "It's very difficult to explain," he said. "In fact it's taken me eight hundred pages to do it in [*Sometimes a Great Notion*]. . . . I'm fooling around with reality and what reality can be."[30] In a later interview, Kesey explained further that he was "just trying to take what is in front of us and change it around to get another way of looking at it, to see what it's about."[31]

Kesey read from some early drafts of *Notion* at those Thursday night get-togethers, but he was not the only one contributing something worthy of note. Though not a regular on the Lane, Larry McMurtry would also occasionally attend these sessions, reading chapters from what would become his 1963 novel, *Leaving Cheyenne*. McMurtry, who lived in San Francisco and commuted twice a week to Stanford, was far more straight-laced than most of the people on the Lane, yet he and Kesey enjoyed a close friendship. The two had first encountered each other in the Jones

Room back in September 1960 when Malcolm Cowley had asked Kesey, the class veteran, to read what would turn out to be the first few chapters of *Cuckoo's Nest*. Like the others in the room that day—the list included Gurney Norman, James Baker Hall, Christopher Koch, Peter Beagle, Joanna Ostrow, Dave Godfrey, and Robin Macdonald—McMurtry faced a choice: either you could decide to like this Paul Bunyan–esque character and his alpha male personality, or you could let him irritate the hell out of you. "Ken cleared his throat," McMurtry recalled of that first reading. "[W]e bristled, and then relaxed and decided to be bemused rather than annoyed. Why? Because Ken Kesey was a very winning man, and he won us. . . . he wanted to be the [center of attention] so badly; so we let him get away with it."[32] McMurtry enjoyed Kesey's company, but preferred him in isolation, away from what he called the "court" that Kesey always seemed to attract. "To enjoy the strength of Ken's friendship," McMurtry once wrote, "it was necessary to separate him, for a time, from the court, because if the court was sitting he would play to it, meddle with it, charm it, vex it."[33] Kesey and McMurtry kept in touch after the latter left San Francisco and got a job teaching at Rice University in Houston, Texas (his home state). However, apart from an occasional visit—including a memorable stopover on the 1964 bus trip—theirs was mostly a long-distance friendship.

While McMurtry kept his distance from the Perry Lane scene, others were happy to join the fray. Ed McClanahan introduced a new face to the reading group, a talented New York writer called Robert Stone. Stone had lived quite a colorful life before finding his way to Stanford. As a teenage high school dropout who was "more or less permanently in the grip of romantic adolescent impulses,"[34] he had joined the navy and volunteered for a year-long expedition that circumnavigated the globe and included a rare stop at a U.S. base in Antarctica. He got out of the Navy in 1958 and went back to New York, where he briefly attended New York University and moonlighted at the *New York Daily News*. Stone then moved to New Orleans for a while, holding down a variety of jobs and starting on what would eventually become his first published novel, *Hall of Mirrors*, in his spare time. A chance encounter with a former professor from NYU led to Stone applying to Stanford. He was accepted and offered a fellowship for the 1962–63 academic year. His first day in the Jones Room was memorable. "I turned up for class that first day and I found myself sitting across the table from this guy wearing blue suede shoes and a two-toned country-and-western jacket and wrap around shades and a pompadour," Stone remembered. "Being a New York boy, and thinking I was sharp, I couldn't figure out what this hick was doing there."[35] This "hick" was Ed McClanahan, and despite Stone's early misgivings about the Kentuckian's unique sense of style, the two quickly became firm friends.

Stone's first party on the Lane was equally memorable. He arrived to find Kesey leading a stoned reenactment of the epic thirteenth-century battle between a Russian peasant army—led by Alexander Nevsky—and an invading band of Teutonic knights. Brooms passed for lances, saucepans as armor, with Kesey taking the part of—who else—the heroic Nevsky. Despite Stone's willingness to join in such folly—for the record, Stone was a knight—Kesey initially had his doubts about the New Yorker. He told McClanahan that he did not trust Stone and that he thought he was a communist (which should give us some insight into the young Kesey's Cold War politics). Kesey even indicated that he did not really want Stone coming to the reading group. McClanahan persuaded Kesey that he was wrong, and soon enough Stone was a regular on the Perry Lane scene, and he became a good friend to the Keseys. Stone's passage into the group was probably eased by his writing talent, which was equal to anybody's. Lacking confidence, he was too intimidated to read from his work at the creative writing seminars—Scowcroft read it for him—but when Stone read on the Lane, his literary ability was good enough to silence a notoriously rowdy crowd. "The room was packed," Jane Burton, a close friend of Stone, recalled of one particular reading, "and you could hear a pin drop."[36]

Stone was no stranger to the world of psychedelics, and he was eager to learn more. He soon realized that getting high with the Perry Lane crowd was not something to be taken lightly. "They got a bunch of peyote and dried it out in somebody's stove," he recalled of one occasion in 1963. "I thought I knew about this stuff from my New York experiences, so I took twelve capsules, which turned out to be kind of a mistake."[37] Everybody piled into some vehicles and headed up to San Francisco to see John Coltrane perform at the Jazz Workshop. It was an intense evening for Stone, who enjoyed (or perhaps endured) his first synesthetic experience. "After sixty seconds of 'Trane, the percussion was undulating in great white waves of jagged frost, the serrated edges as symmetrical as if they had been drawn by an artist's hand," Stone recounted years later, the memory still vivid in his mind. "The brass erupted in bands of bright color, streaming out of the brazen instruments like a magician's silk." It was too much for Stone and so he got up and left the club with his wife. While the others went on to see Lenny Bruce, Stone and his wife wandered the streets of San Francisco, waiting to come down and wondering just what sort of turn their lives had taken. Like McMurtry before him, Stone would never live on Perry Lane or sign on as a fully committed member of Kesey's court, but he has written fondly of the period, describing it as the happiest time of his life. His broader assessment of the import of the moment is more circumspect, tinged by a warm but characteristically hard-headed skepticism: "Kesey was, more than anyone I knew, in the grip of all that the sixties seemed to promise," Stone wrote in 2004. "Those who cared most deeply about the changes, those who gave their lives to them, were, I think, the most deceived."[38]

Gurney Norman had been a regular on the scene since his arrival at Stanford in the fall of 1960 (he would eventually marry Chloe Scott.) He was still around in 1962 and 1963, mostly only on the weekends, during the period when Kesey was writing *Sometimes a Great Notion*. Like Babbs before him, Norman had paid his way through college with the help of the ROTC, and in June 1961 it came time for him to fulfill his military obligation. Six months of basic training later, the U.S. Army posted the newly minted Lieutenant Gurney Norman to Ford Ord in Monterey, just a few hours' drive south of Palo Alto. Norman spent his weekdays in charge of training new infantry recruits and then, come Saturday afternoon, he would shed his military uniform and head up to Perry Lane to resume his weekend bohemian existence. He was a popular figure, a fun person to have at a party, likely to suggest some crazy game or other, or to gather people into a circle and have them sing "May the Circle Be Unbroken." On his birthday, the Perry Laners hung a sign in the courtyard oak tree that read, "Gurney Norman: A Force for Good."

It was Norman who introduced future Prankster Ron Bevirt to the Perry Lane scene. A native of Saint Louis and a literature graduate of that city's Washington University, Bevirt had also signed on with the ROTC. He had no interest in a career in the military; he simply figured that since military service was inevitable, it was better to be an officer than not. After he had completed his six months of basic infantry training at Fort Benning in Georgia, Bevirt requested a transfer to California, and the army sent him to Fort Ord. He was a year or so behind Norman, but the two found themselves living in the same bachelor's quarters on the base. Norman was fond of serenading his fellow officers with the occasional ditty—"I never will marry, I'll be no man's wife, I expect to live single all the days of my life," was one that Bevirt still remembers—and such behavior set Norman somewhat apart from the others around him. While the macho types spent their spare time waxing their muscle cars, Norman and Bevirt would sit and talk about literature and writing. Not surprisingly, Norman told his new friend all about Perry Lane and Kesey, whom Bevirt had already read about in *Time* magazine's review of *Cuckoo's Nest*. It was just a matter of time before the two army buddies found themselves heading north one weekend to go to a party on the Lane. Kesey was there, as were Chloe Scott, Roy Sebern, Ed McClanahan, and Jim Wolpman. Bevirt enjoyed the pot and red wine that lubricated the learned discussions that night, but more important, he felt a connection to the people that he met. He went back to the Lane a number of times after that first party, sometimes with Norman, but increasingly on his own. Norman had decided to start cutting back on the visits and the parties, wanting to concentrate on his writing.[39] Bevirt had few such concerns at this stage in his life. He found that hanging around Kesey and his friends was both intellectually stimulating and a great deal of fun. "As soon as I laid eyes on the Perry Lane people," Bevirt recalled, in a sentiment echoed by many others in this story, "[I had] a feeling of, these are my people, this is what I've been looking for all my life."[40]

THE RIDGE RUNNERS

On Monday, July 16, 1962, Lieutenant Ken Babbs made his way to Travis Air Force Base to begin his journey to Okinawa, Japan, home of the Third Marine Division in the Far East. Waiting at the airport for his noon flight, Babbs hid behind a newspaper, took out a small vial of pot, and rolled three joints, smoking one of them right there and then as he contemplated what lay before him. The flight took seventeen hours in all, with brief stopovers in Honolulu and Wake Island along the way. Within a matter of weeks, Babbs's squadron—Squadron 163, known as the Ridge Runners—was transferred to a base at Soc Trang, on the southern coast of Vietnam, just west of the Mekong Delta. This was August 1962, a time when direct U.S. military involvement in Vietnam was relatively new. The previous year, President Ngo Dinh Diem of the Republic of South Vietnam had formally asked President Kennedy for assistance in his fight against the Viet Cong (VC), an insurgent guerrilla force backed by the communist government of North Vietnam, which was fighting to unify the divided country. During an official visit to Saigon in 1961, Vice President Lyndon Johnson assured Diem—whom he called "the Churchill of Asia"—that maintaining the independence of South Vietnam was crucial to U.S. interests in the region. Kennedy responded to Diem's request by sending an American "advisory" mission to train and bolster the South's army: the Army of the Republic of Vietnam (ARVN). Babbs's helicopter squadron was one of the first complete units to arrive in the country.

The Ridge Runner flew missions every day out of Soc Trang from dawn 'til dusk, with some pilots logging over a hundred hours of flight time in August alone. Most of the time they were flying daily troop-carrying missions for the ARVN, but they also flew more than fifty combat missions, dropping ARVN forces into battle and removing the injured. Occasionally they would evacuate South Vietnamese civilians from villages that Diem's government had decided were no longer tenable.

Even though U.S. forces were not meant to be involved in the fighting— U.S. military forces were there only to "advise" the ARVN—nobody seemed to have told this to the Vietcong. "At first, the VC were afraid of the helicopters," Babbs told one interviewer. "They didn't know how powerful they were. Eventually they learned you could put one out with a single bullet. The longer we were there, the worse it got."[41] On one occasion, bullets splattered the water of the rice paddy where Babbs was coming in to land. With a full load of troops and receiving fire, Babbs touched down hard in the water, water splashing up from the wheels. Facing a hail of bullets, Babbs was forced to take evasive action. He gunned the powerful motor, lifting the helicopter back into the air again in an effort to find a safer landing zone. Babbs put down again thirty feet away and hurried to unload his human cargo. Back at the base, the crew inspected the helicopter and stuck their fingers through three bullet holes in the tail cone.

Babbs's closest shave came when some VC shot at him with a rifle grenade while he was transporting a load of ARVN troops. Somehow the grenade passed right through the blades of the helicopter. "How that thing went through and never hit one of those rotor blades, man, I'll never know," remembered Babbs. "That was the most scared I ever was."[42] Babbs was piloting a UH-34 D chopper—known to all as the "Hussy"—which was primarily a troop transport vehicle. It was armed, but it was not an attack helicopter; pilots had to rely on its power and speed to keep them out of trouble. "Only two kinds of pilots over here," Babbs reported in an article he published in the *Marine Corps Gazette*: "the quick and the dead."[43]

In September the Ridge Riders left Soc Trang for Da Nang, on the east coast of Vietnam, not too many miles from the Demilitarized Zone that divided North and South Vietnam along the 17th parallel. The climate was very different in and around Da Nang—more rain, more cloud cover coming off the mountains—which grounded the helicopter crews for a lot of the time. The mountainous terrain also made for much more difficult flying, with maneuverability particularly tight in the hilly areas where Babbs's squadron was operating. This made landings far trickier. "Our approaches into the landing sites were fast, plunging descents, followed by a flare to kill off the airspeed, then a no hover touchdown," Babbs wrote in the *Marine Corps Gazette*. "With our main gear barely resting on the deck, the plane dancing on its struts, we were ready to leap off again as soon as the crew signaled we were unloaded."[44] Resupply missions continued to be the most typical assignment for Babbs's squadron, though they also carried out enough combat troop lifts into unsecured landing zones to keep things interesting. As one of the first units to practice this type of "heliborne assault," Babbs's squadron pioneered tactics that would be used throughout the long conflict in Vietnam.

Such caution was a necessity. In Soc Trang, Babbs's squadron had never fired on anyone unless they were taking fire. By comparison, most of the areas that the squadron flew into during their time at Da Nang had been classified as "free kill areas," which meant a pilot or gunner did not have to wait until someone shot at him before he could shoot at them. Also, every strike mission the Ridge Runners flew out of Da Nang was accompanied by some sort of aerial bombardment. Eventually, most helicopters in the squadron had an M-60 mounted underneath to boost their firepower. If this was "advising," as the United States still claimed, it was certainly of the "hands on" variety.

Babbs's squadron left Vietnam on January 7, 1963. It was not soon enough for Babbs, who had been counting down the days ever since he got there. In all, he spent about five months in the country. Any idealism he might have once had about America's mission in Vietnam had evaporated once he had witnessed the conflict for himself. "You didn't have to be there for ten minutes to realize that it was a bunch of bullshit," he told an interviewer many years later.[45] His squadron took up a posting at MCAF Futema for a couple of months, flying daily search-and-rescue missions in support of the marine division and the army and air force units stationed on Okinawa. Babbs never saw any more combat, but danger still lurked. His friend and sometime copilot Gordon Gunter—who had visited Perry Lane with Babbs—was badly burned when his helicopter crashed, injuring the other pilot and killing the entire Navy gunfire spotting team on board.[46] Babbs had more than had enough.

THE END OF PERRY LANE

By the summer of 1963 the Keseys' financial situation had started to improve. "Life is much nicer now. We eat better and we get the car fixed when it gives us trouble," Kesey told a reporter from the *Eugene Register-Guard*. "[*Cuckoo's Nest* has] been picked up on a lot of campuses as a textbook. They're using it at Harvard for a psychology course. And it's being used as a text in a number of contemporary writing courses on campuses in the Bay area."[47] The additional money came in handy, not least because the Kesey family, including adopted daughter Shannon and firstborn son Zane, were about to be made homeless.

As early as the summer of 1959, word had reached the people living on the Lane that part of it—the courtyard section that housed the Keseys and Vik Lovell et al.—might be coming up for sale. Alarmed, Kesey and the others tried to buy it, believing that the owners would look kindly upon a low offer from them rather than accept an inflated offer from some hardhearted developer. Unfortunately, financial reality triumphed over sentimentality, and in 1963 the Johnsons eventually agreed to sell their holdings on Perry Lane to a Menlo Park realtor, J. C. Britton, for fifty thousand dollars. "They didn't want to sell," Britton told a reporter from the *Palo Alto Times*, "but they needed the money for retirement."[48] A local company, named Campodonico and Murphy, drew up plans to replace the four old wooden cabins around the courtyard with six one-story homes that Britton planned to put on the market for thirty-six thousand dollars apiece. The Keseys received an eviction notice, as did Lee Anderson, Jane Burton, and Vik Lovell. The first phase of the demolition—Lee's place and Vic's place—was set to begin on Monday, July 22, but since Faye had just given birth to son Jed, the Kesey family was allowed to stay on a little longer, until the beginning of August.

Emotions among the residents on the Lane ran high. "We had thought of demolishing the houses ourselves to spare them from the brutality of the bulldozers," Kesey told a reporter. "We also considered hanging the contractor's effigy. . . . [We] may even fill the trees with effigies." They did no such thing. Instead, they did what they had done so many times before: they held a big party. It began at dusk on the Friday before demolition day with residents and close friends feasting on cup after cup of Kesey's venison chili. As the evening progressed, more and more people turned up—lots of them former residents of the Lane—until the crowd numbered around a hundred. It was a wild affair, a fitting wake for a time and a place that had meant so much to them. The tree in the middle of the lane was festooned with colored ribbons and lit by a bright floodlight. On one of the branches sat a large doll holding a circular card that simply read, "YES." "'It expresses the affirmative position," one of the party-goers, San Francisco poet Jack Gilbert, explained to a puzzled reporter. "It's better than 'No.'"[49]

Gurney Norman organized a giant game of human cat's cradle. "We were all stoned on acid and trying to keep track of where everyone was at the same time," recalled one of the participants, Robert Stone. "I remember Gurney yelling, 'All the thumbs raise their hands.'"[50] At the height of the party, some of the men dragged an old piano from one of the houses into the middle of the street, and everybody proceeded to smash it to bits using whatever they could lay their hands on. Press photos of the event showed a man and a woman hitting the old piano with axes while flames and sparks flew out of its back. "It is the oldest living thing on Perry Lane," Kesey proclaimed absurdly to the press. "Its annihilation is symbolic."[51] He later regretted the destruction of the piano, in part for the piano's sake, but also because the act upset the children that witnessed it. As dawn broke, the last of the partiers drifted away like the smoke from the still-smoldering piano. A few people took the opportunity to fall asleep under the shelter of the giant oak tree for one last time.

On Monday, demolition day, a small crowd of residents and children gathered to watch the destruction of the first two cottages. Bits of furniture, clothing, paintings, and art supplies littered the site, most of it hurriedly removed from the condemned properties at the last minute, some of it debris left over from the party. It was a busy scene. Mrs. Sims, the lady who lived in the house that backed onto the courtyard, was still trying to clear stuff out of Lee Anderson's place to take to the Goodwill store. As she carried away the discarded junk, she tried to calm an angry Jane Burton, who was vowing revenge to anyone who would listen. Kesey wandered around talking into a portable tape deck, recording his impressions of the day for posterity and making notes for his novel-in-progress about the Lane.[52] He watched the demolition crew go from plot to plot, listening as some of the gathered residents berated the bulldozer operators, venting their frustration but achieving little else. Others held their emotions in check. Roy Sebern found a patch of grass and sat impassively with his friend Ann Moore, observing the scene, his elbows on his knees, his familiar horn-rimmed glasses perched on his nose and a straw hat protecting his head from the hot July sun. Another woman knelt quietly beside a tree, holding on to the roots as if for moral support as the scene unfolded before her.

Kesey watched the bulldozer rumble toward Vic Lovell's cottage. Vic, his chin resting on his clenched fist, was lying on a pile of trash that had been cleared out of Jim and Anita Wolpman's place. He watched as the bulldozers efficiently tore up some shrubs and bushes that had taken him years to cultivate. Next to go was the pepper tree over by his house, the one where he and Kesey hid their first stash of drugs in a hole in its trunk. Finally, the bulldozers flattened the two cottages, and it was done: the heart of Perry Lane was gone. "Only the devil, I thought, could have the power to destroy something which had existed so long," Lovell wrote a few years later. "The Lane was a delicate balance of forces, and it never recovered. . . . I cannot write of it now without weeping."[53]

7

A New Prometheus

THE MAVERICKS OF LA HONDA

The Keseys' new home in La Honda was only fifteen miles or so from
Perry Lane, but the two places could not have been more different. La
Honda was a fairly isolated village community, nestled on the westward
slopes of the redwood hills that separated Palo Alto from the Pacific
Ocean. The location looked and felt more like Oregon than California,
possessed of a rainy climate and an earthy character that even Hank Stamper would have found familiar. In the mid-nineteenth century the place
was not much more than a few lumber mills and a stagecoach stop, but
it grew as its industry expanded. A schoolhouse was built in 1870, and
local legend had it that in 1877 some members of the infamous Younger
Brothers gang settled in the area and built the old Pioneer Mercantile
Store in what was then the center of La Honda. By the turn of the century,
the commercial and residential heart of La Honda had moved about three
quarters of a mile up the road from the Pioneer Mercantile Store to its
present-day location. It had a saloon, a dance hall, a new schoolhouse, a
post office, a hotel, a blacksmith, and a burgeoning tourist industry that
attracted hundreds of visitors from San Francisco and elsewhere on the
peninsula. To meet the growing demand, La Honda soon boasted four
hotels and seven bars, one of which was famous for hosting frog-shooting
competitions and musical entertainment by a group with the unlikely
name of the Tapioca Band. On summer weekends, up to three hundred
campers would pitch their tents all over La Honda, especially down by
La Honda Creek, which was renowned for its bountiful supply of trout.

La Honda's heyday did not last long. When its virgin timber ran out in 1910, its logging industry rapidly declined. And with the advent of the automobile, vacationers from the city started venturing farther south to Santa Cruz or Monterey. The final nail in the coffin came with the stock market crash of 1929, which collapsed real estate values and put an end to any large-scale residential development in the area for the next thirty-five years. Its economy in tatters, La Honda become something of a forgotten backwater, home to mavericks and a few old-timers; all possessed of "a spark of pioneer in their blood that makes them want to venture out where conformity has never yet been witnessed," as one newspaper reported.[1] By the early 1960s La Honda was starting to recover, in part because it was turning into the peninsula's version of Big Sur; increasingly it was home to all manner of artists, writers, naturists, and people who just wanted to get away from it all. Robert Stone described it as a place that "had the quality of a raw Northwestern logging town, transported to suburban San Francisco."[2] No wonder Kesey loved it. In August 1963 he, Faye, and the kids, including the new one, Jed, became the latest and most famous mavericks on La Honda's block.

It was Kesey's father, Fred, who first spotted the log house for sale at 7940 La Honda Road, about half a mile from the Boots and Saddle tavern on the outskirts of what remained of La Honda central. The one-story house, built in 1942 by the Pepper family and named Wychward, was a modest place, less than sixty feet long and only about thirty-five feet deep at best. One master bedroom and two smaller bedrooms took up most of one side of the house. A tiny kitchen and an equally small bathroom were tucked away at the back. The kitchen looked out onto a small, elevated clearing that looked like a fairy circle among the trees. The biggest room by far was the living room—about thirty feet by fifteen—which had a tall, vaulted ceiling paneled with thirteen-inch-wide redwood boards that had most likely been milled on site. The high ceiling's pine and fir beams gave the place the feel of an old Viking lodge. A stone fireplace settled in one corner, a woodstove stood against the back wall, and French windows ran along the entire length of the house's frontage.[3] The house sat on the southern bank of the La Honda Creek. This often misty, sometimes raging stream ran along the line of the property and separated it from the road out front. A small, gated bridge across the creek was the only way to access the property from the road. From the bridge to the front door was about a hundred feet.

Behind the dwelling, the ground rose steeply up a hill that was covered in towering redwoods. At the top was a clearing that came to be dubbed Barking Bug Meadow after Zane once exclaimed on a walk up there that "them damn bugs are all the time barking."[4] Roughly a thousand acres of forest encircled the house, much of it part of what is now Sam McDonald State Park. One could neither see nor hear any neighbors from the house, but it was plainly visible from the road that ran along the length of its property. Some of the trees in the forest were hundreds of years old, but most of them were second growth, born in the twentieth century after the logging declined. Lots of huge redwood stumps could be found scattered among the trees, all that remained of the ancient forest that once covered these slopes. But new growth, old growth, it did not really matter; the place was spectacularly beautiful, the house an organic part of the woodlands that engulfed it. Yes, it could be dark and dank—especially in the winter when the sun shone through the front windows for little more than an hour during the day—but it was just about as close as a person could get to living in nature without having to get cold and wet.

Kesey rapidly set about making the place his own. He began by fixing three large speakers to the roof of the house, out of which he would blare loud Sousa marches or stirring Beethoven quartets. Later, he and his friends would hoist additional speakers into the redwoods high up above, along with strings of colored lights. The woods became an improvised art gallery with weird mobiles hung from branches and paintings of brightly streaked colors nailed to tree trunks. Kesey took to hiding objects around the place, here a tiny tin toy horse lodged in the hollowed-out base of a huge pine tree, there a small skull resting on the branch of another. Later, Ron Boise, a Santa Cruz artist of some repute, would add some of his metal sculptures to Kesey's house at La Honda, including a full-size figure of a man that hung from one of the tall trees in the yard. Bottles of Kool-Aid sat cooling in a small stream that ran down the hill, held secure by rocks until someone was passing and thirsty. Morning glory vines grew everywhere, a product of Kesey's recent discovery that the seeds possessed psychedelic properties.[5] He had taken to filling the magazine of his shotgun with the seeds and then blasting them across the highway into its far bank to facilitate their widespread distribution.

A small building, no bigger than a medium-size garden shed, stood apart from the house, close to the creek. Kesey made this his writing room and den, sharing it at one point with a litter of dachshund pups who lived beneath its floor. The building was referred to by all as "the back house," and it was there that Kesey put the finishing touches to *Sometimes a Great Notion* during his first couple of months in La Honda. *Notion* is set in Oregon, but one cannot help but wonder whether Kesey's La Honda surroundings were not also inspiring him as he wrote. The opening passage of the book, for example, beautifully describes the flashing tributaries of Oregon's Waconda Auga River, but it was the La Honda Creek that Kesey heard as he worked on that passage.

Kesey wrote virtually the entire *Notion* manuscript in longhand on yellow legal pads, cutting and pasting here and there, amassing piles of paper fragments, each bearing a phrase or a sentence or two that Kesey hoped to use somewhere in the mix. He kept an elaborate chart on the wall of his writing room to help him "keep tabs on who's where and how and who's telling you so," as he explained to one interviewer.[6] Chapter by chapter, he assembled the passages together, using italics, capitals, and parentheses to distinguish the multiple perspectives, oftentimes within the same paragraph, and sometimes even within one sentence. Amazingly, it took him little more than a year to write the first draft of a book that was, by any measure, big, bold, and unique. When one considers that Kesey wrote the bulk of it on Perry Lane with all of its pleasurable distractions, his efforts seem all the more remarkable. By March 1963 he had sent his handwritten manuscript to Viking, where some poor secretary had to type up the assembled papers into a coherent document. Kesey had high hopes, but he also knew that the scale of his ambition could be his undoing. The writing of *Sometimes a Great Notion* had certainly taught him a lot about writing, but the process had been exceedingly laborious. He determined never to try and write anything so structurally cumbersome again.[7]

Kesey's editor at Viking sent him a six-page letter full of suggestions for revisions and improvements. He worked hard to accommodate her wishes but found her request to make Lee Stamper more likable particularly difficult, since the character was so much a part of his own personality.[8] He sent a copy of the manuscript to Babbs for comment, in part because he trusted his old classmate's opinion more than that of his editor. Babbs responded full of praise and enthusiasm. He particularly liked the Hank Stamper character, who, despite his rough exterior, seemed wiser than his overeducated brother Lee. Babbs was impressed enough to write to his brother, telling him about Kesey's progress. "His book is a knockout," he wrote in July 1963. "[F]rom what I read he won't have a best seller, but a work that will put him right up with the big boys of the day, Mailer, Jones, Updike, Roth—none of them have tried anything as tough as what he has done in the way of construction."[9]

Viking had made it clear that Kesey would receive the second half of his five-thousand-dollar advance only after he had completed a second draft. Kesey, though, was loath to embark upon the wearisome task of revision. By late spring he had still not read all the way through the typed manuscript that Viking had sent him. He finally got down to business over the summer, though he found it no easy task. The work took its toll, draining Kesey's enthusiasm for writing and fostering a hatred for his poor old typewriter. He jokingly told Larry McMurtry that he was thinking about drawing his novels in the future.[10] It was a throwaway comment, but it was the first hint that in the year to follow, Kesey would announce that he was giving up writing.

By the fall of 1963 Kesey was done with his revisions but the effort had left him exhausted and uncharacteristically modest, unsure whether he had produced a masterpiece or a dud.[11] Kesey's lack of confidence was misplaced. The book was certainly overly ambitious and demanding of its readers—how could it not be given the scope of Kesey's aspirations?—but it was also a tale so beautifully written and so powerfully told that most readers would surely choose to have forgiven the author his youthful conceit. *Sometimes a Great Notion* would turn out to be a breathtaking accomplishment, a genuine classic of twentieth-century American literature.

Cuckoo on Broadway

The Boston run of *Cuckoo's Nest* ended on November 9, 1963. The plans to stage additional warm-up shows in Buffalo were scrapped and the cast headed straight to New York City to prepare for their Broadway debut. Opening night—November 13—at the Cort Theatre was a sellout. Kesey, Faye, Grandma Smith, Chuck, and his wife, Sue, flew in as Kirk Douglas's personal guests. Dorothy Fadiman, a friend of Kesey's from Palo Alto, was there, as was Carl Lehmann-Haupt, Kesey's one-time neighbor on the Lane. George Walker had driven cross-country to attend what turned out to be quite a star-studded occasion. Attendees included two of President Kennedy's sisters, Jean Kennedy Smith and Patricia Kennedy Lawford;

George Plimpton, journalist, sometime actor, and founder-editor of the literary magazine *The Paris Review*; pop singer Tony Martin and his actress/dancer wife, Cyd Charisse; and Tony Award–winning songwriter Jule Stynes. After the performance, a tuxedo-wearing Kesey mingled with the guests at a postproduction party at the Four Seasons Hotel, and then sat with Kirk Douglas in Schraffts, a nearby restaurant, waiting for the newspaper reviews to come out. Kesey thought the play was great. "Marvelous, it was absolutely marvelous," he recalled years later.[12] "Kirk Douglas was so good it was like I had written it for him."[13]

A few of the reviewers felt the same way. The *New York Daily News* lauded it as "a most enjoyable and exciting play," and the influential Norman Nadel of the *New York World Telegram and Sun* called it "a wacking good play, beautifully cast, directed and staged." Unfortunately, a good two-thirds of the reviewers felt differently, often vehemently. Howard Taugman of the *New York Times*, for example, called it "a crazy quilt of wisecracks, cavortings, violence and histrionic villainy." The *Village Voice* dismissed it as "a very bad play for very good reasons . . . bathroom humor played for its own sake." One concerned critic even questioned whether such a play was in the public interest. By far the most damning review came from Walter Kerr at the *New York Herald Tribune*. "'One Flew Over the Cuckoo's Nest' is so preposterous a proposition for the theatre that it could be dismissed very briefly if it weren't for the extraordinary tastelessness with which it has been conceived," Kerr began his piece. "I'd like to make it plain at once that when I speak of the evening's essential cheapness I am not in the least thinking of its deep and abiding fondness for the scatological; of its interest in whores who are therapeutic for male virgins, of the whooping and hollering that goes on over a toilet flush, of the vodka that is served out of enema bags, of the 'Frig 'em all' that is intoned like a litany."[14] Kerr concluded by suggesting that Kesey was an "unlucky man" for having had his novel adapted so poorly for the stage (even though it seems clear that Kerr had not read the book).

Douglas and his supporting cast escaped relatively unscathed in this barrage of damnation. Even the worst of the reviews respectfully praised the Hollywood star's performance, and one of them went so far as to offer him some sympathy for having to carry the heavy "load" of a play of such "cheap" and unconvincing quality. It was the substance of the play itself that the critics objected to, and so, not surprisingly, they reserved their sharpest invective for its creator, Dale Wasserman. He was an easy target, devoid of the protective armor carried by movie stars and wealthy producers. Some of the comments directed at Wasserman were just brutal. "It would take a knowing, compassionate, perceptive, ironic, and enormously skillful playwright to make this germ sprout," wrote John McCarten in the *New Yorker*. "[A]nd it is unfortunate that Dale Wasserman . . . has none of the necessary attributes."[15] Wasserman was not around to hear such remarks. He had skipped out before the play even opened on Broadway. "It was not my play," he explained in 2003. "It was dramatic goulash cooked by Hollywood chefs. . . . [I chose] to save my sanity by decamping to California.[16] There, he wrote his own tale of mad men and heroes: *Man of La Mancha*, his masterful stage adaptation of Don Quixote.

The poor reviews killed whatever chances the Broadway production had of being a success. Norman Nadel conceded as much. "It was a good play. It was interesting, it had vitality and very lofty moments," he recalled a couple of years later. "I'd say this is a case where with a better press, that play could have made it."[17] Kirk Douglas kept the production limping along for a few more months, in part by not paying himself a salary for his acting duties. When he asked the cast to take a pay cut to help keep the operation afloat, they refused and Kirk pulled the plug. The last of Cort Theatre's eighty-two performances took place on January 25, 1964. Douglas was crushed. "I crawled back home to Los Angeles like a wounded animal, defeated in my last battle to become a star on Broadway," he wrote in his autobiography. "I gave New York a classic and they don't even realize it."[18]

The World's Fair and the Day Time Stopped

Kesey was as disappointed as everyone else with the poor reviews. He found Walter Kerr's diatribe so offensive that he was driven to write and tell the critic that he had personally enjoyed the performance and Wasserman's stage play. Haughtily, Kesey also told Kerr that he did not appreciate being called an "unlucky man" by someone whom he had never even met.[19] Faye and the rest of the Kesey family were booked to fly home from New York, but not before everybody had a chance to enjoy a few more fun days of sightseeing in and around New York. They camped out at Carl Lehmann-Haupt's third-floor walk-up apartment on the Lower East Side.

Carl and his younger brother, Sandy, spent the next few days showing their friends around New York, visiting museums and driving around in the old Chevy station wagon that George had driven from California for the occasion. A big mustard squeeze-bottle full of boiled peyote that George had brought with him helped to keep things interesting.

One of the places they went to see was the New York World's Fair, then being built on a site on Long Island in preparation for its opening the following summer. The sight generated much excitement within the group. Kesey had often talked about the great time that he, Mike Hagan, Babbs, and several others had all enjoyed at the Seattle World's Fair the previous year. Kesey and his pals decided that they would come back the following summer to visit the fair. "We decided well we're going to want to have to go to this fair," remembered George Walker. "And that kind of just got into the back of our minds."[20]

Kesey, George, and the Lehmann-Haupts spent about a week tripping around New York. When it came time to leave, Kesey decided that instead of flying he would drive home with George. At Carl's prompting, Kesey had also asked Sandy to go along with them, inviting the young man—he was just twenty-two—to come and stay with him in California for a while. Sandy—born Hellmut Alexander—was the youngest child of author and bibliographer Hellmut Lehmann-Haupt. Born and raised in New York, Sandy had had something of a difficult childhood, at least according to his brothers.[21] "He had a hard life," Carl wrote after Sandy died in October 2001. "[He] was in trouble long before he met Kesey."[22] Sandy's mental health problems had caused him to drop out of New York University after only six months of study. He used his interest in electronics and audio equipment to get a job as a sound engineer, but his health remained a challenge. At one point he tried to commit himself to a psychiatric ward, but Carl talked him out of it. Carl thought that getting Sandy out of New York, away from his family and his bad habits, might be just the thing his brother needed. The trip with Kesey out West was supposed to be recuperative, an opportunity for Sandy to get his head together and start anew. Unfortunately for Sandy, it did not quite work out that way.

Making the most of what New York had to offer, Kesey, George, and Sandy spent their last night in the city going to Loews downtown movie theater, where they caught a late showing of a Western, *How the West Was Won*. Then, to round the evening off, they paid a visit to Ripley's famous

Broadway *Believe It or Not!* exhibition. Of course, they were all high courtesy of Walker's mustard bottle. By the time our three amigos were ready
to leave the city, dawn had already broken on a new morning: November
22, a memorable date.

Kesey and George sat up front sharing driving duties. Sandy was
crammed in the back with the luggage, the sleeping bags, and a set of tri-
angular drums that someone had made for him. They drove out of the
city and headed west across the state of New York and into Pennsylvania.
The occasional slug of peyote made the colors and the early morning mist
radiant in their beauty. "It makes the driving interesting," Kesey casually explained, "especially the late fall in that northern part of America."[23]
Conversation ebbed and flowed, as it does on long road trips, but a steady
diet of teenage rock and roll on the Chevy's radio kept the mood light.
Kesey was at the wheel looking for a Howard Johnson's restaurant for
some pie and coffee when an urgent news bulletin interrupted the blar-
ing radio to report that President Kennedy had been shot in downtown
Dallas. The car went quiet and stayed that way as the radio devoted its
coverage to the unfolding events. An hour or so later, word came that the
president was dead. Kesey and his friends could not believe what they
were hearing.[24] Kennedy's administration had seen some trying times over
the previous three years—the Bay of Pigs fiasco, the mounting civil rights
struggle, the Cuban Missile Crisis—but no one had seriously predicted
that he would be cut down by an assassin's bullet, the first president since
William McKinley in 1901 to suffer such a fate. News of Kennedy's assassination filled the airwaves for mile after Midwest mile, but it was still
difficult to believe that the reports of his death were true. Kesey was still
in a state of shock even as they approached Chicago. He had never much
cared for party politics or politicians, but as for so many others of his
generation, there was something about the youthful, energetic Kennedy
that inspired him with hope and optimism. Writing about the event
twenty years later, Kesey remembered finding solace in the communal
grief the country experienced in the wake of the tragedy. "As we drove
we saw this look in people's faces," he wrote. "[A]nd they would look at
us, and there was an energy to it. It was a good energy and we liked it.
We liked the feeling of the country and the look of the country and the
look of the people. It was like a light was shining and everything else
was foggy."[25]

The three weary road warriors bedded down somewhere beyond Chicago, abandoning plans to sample that city's Friday night delights. George spread out across the wide front seat, and Kesey and Sandy settled into their sleeping bags in the back. Kesey had not slept in almost forty-eight hours, but the events of the day left him sleepless still. He lay quietly and reflected on Kennedy's presidency: the speeches, the images, the Democratic convention of 1960 that Norman Mailer had described so unforgettably in his *Esquire* article, "Superman Comes to the Supermarket." It was a long night.

The next day, the weather became progressively worse the further west they drove. The radio continued to broadcast and analyze every detail of the tragedy; the hospital reports, the open window on the sixth floor of the Texas School Book Depository, the shooting of Officer Tippet (the policeman allegedly slain by Lee Harvey Oswald), the ascension of Lyndon Baines Johnson to the presidency, the capture of Oswald, and on and on and on. Kesey quickly grew sick of the endless punditry, but he could not bring himself to turn off the radio. By the third day, they had reached Jackson Hole, Wyoming, and the snowfall that had accompanied them across the state had grown into a blizzard. As the roads worsened, our not-so-merry band of travelers were eventually forced to pull off the road onto the forecourt of a closed-down Chevron gas station and wait for the blizzard to stop, or at least to slow down a little. Kesey was exhausted and emotional, worn down by "three days on peyote and national grief." He looked up to watch the snow-filled sky form a backdrop to the big red, white, and blue Chevron sign that stood high above the gas station. His eyes started to fill with tears. "I began to cry," he remembered. "[N]ot so much for the president as for something American that was innocent and bright-eyed and capable. . . . [W]e lost the last person I can think of that we could believe in."[26]

Something else happened on that trip, something that both Walker and Kesey have suggested propelled them back to New York the following summer. Tragedy brings people closer together. It focuses their attention on one particular thing, causing a commonality of consciousness that is rare in our modern world. Our three travelers picked up on that feeling; it felt new and exciting, and worth exploring. "[W]e realized that there was something about traveling across the country with everybody's mind at this certain place that had a kind of power, a kind of magic to it." Walker recalled. "We got to thinking more about this trip that we were making next summer, started adding up all the people that were going to want to go. . . . [It] galvanized our consciousness about this trip."[27] Kesey credited the moment with even broader historical significance: the bus trip "spun off this feeling of seeing the landscape of the American people in this new way. I think the whole hippie movement, this love-everybody feeling for each other was born of that feeling. It was born of the death [of Kennedy]. . . . When God wants to really wake up a nation, he has to use somebody that counts."[28]

PROMETHEUS REBORN

Back at La Honda, it was time for Kesey to decide what he wanted to do next. Fame had certainly started to come his way, and it was clear he was starting to garner a reputation and a following among a certain set of readers who appreciated his ideological message as well as his writing. In June he had been featured on the cover of a well-respected writers' trade journal, *Author and Journalist*, which heralded an "underground of avid admirers" who saw in his work the "tentative beginnings of a new kind of fiction writing, a relatively new approach to charting the heart of man."[29]

In the fall, Kesey was also featured, or rather celebrated, in *Genesis West*, a small literary magazine that was published in San Francisco by its editor and creator, Gordon Lish. *Genesis West* contained an excerpt from *Sometimes a Great Notion* and a lengthy interview with Kesey that provides a rare glimpse into the mind of the twenty-seven-year-old author. Lish, the interviewer, was clearly blown away by the young Oregonian, and his reverential approach to his subject offers a useful illustration of the effect that Kesey could have on others. So entranced was Lish by the sound of Kesey's voice that he forgot to turn on his tape recorder for the first three hours of their conversation. He had only known Kesey for a relatively short amount of time, yet he felt driven to describe him as one of the most influential figures in his life: one of those "few persons we meet whose effect upon us spiritually, emotionally, or intellectually threatens to achieve such massive influence that we suppose flight from them the only means toward preserving what we have been, what we long ago had convinced ourselves to remain."[30] Kesey had always been charismatic, but now he was becoming charismatic *and* famous, and that gave him something new: power. At this point in his life, one can almost sense him struggling with what to do with it.

For now, Kesey was still devoting a lot of his energy to writing. He was pretty worn out after finishing *Sometimes a Great Notion*, but he had no intention of resting on his laurels. Once back in La Honda after the Broadway trip, Kesey lined up his typewriter and started outlining a new project about "a place, and a lot of people that I love," as he told Gordon Lish. Kesey was planning to write a book about Perry Lane. This was not a new idea. He had been thinking about it for a while, but he felt that he needed to distance himself from Perry Lane before he could fictional-ize it. "[T]he scene here is so overpowering that to write about it while being in it is somewhat like a drowning man in a hideous maelstrom of broken limbs and shambled lives and mashed egos," he told Babbs. "Too much love and too much hurt, all at the same time, constantly—with people who are gigantic in character and goodness that is strange to them and cruelty that is not—and I've got to get away to see it bet-ter."[31] Moving to La Honda gave him the distance he was looking for, and in the last months of 1963 Kesey finally got around to working on his new baby, tentatively named "One Lane." He completed at least one draft chapter, but more important, he wrote an eighty-page outline of the complete book.[32]

Kesey had told a few interviewers that he intended to write something from the perspective of a young disc jockey or an artist, but he eventu-ally settled on telling the story through the eyes of a young Connecticut innocent named Matthew Murphy, a student at Stanford University Law School. His father has arranged for him to stay with friends on the Lane while he goes to school, and as the plot unfolds, events conspire to change Murphy and those around him in unexpected ways. We follow the story mostly from Murphy's perspective, but Kesey also planned to allow him-self an all-knowing author's voice as well. Most of the action took place in 1959–60, but Kesey intended to begin the book with a chapter that described the Lane's early history and significance.

Shortly after World War I, so Kesey's story goes, a disgruntled student—Mr. Johnson—tricks the U.S. Army into selling him a plot of land on the outskirts of the Stanford University campus. Johnson sets about trans-forming the lane of barracks that comes with the land into dwellings for his friends, all of whom share his hedonistic spirit and rebellious nature. As a result of his efforts, a small bohemian community is born on what becomes the Lane, much to the disgruntlement of the local authorities who struggle to control it and resent its independence.

Johnson is portrayed as a Prometheus-like figure, responsible for bringing the fire of rebellion and enlightenment to the people on the Lane. He leaves the area in 1930, somewhat against his will, but he retains the ownership of the land and its properties. He eventually returns five years later to find the place empty of all the people that he had once known and loved. At first, he is disappointed, but soon he realizes that the rebellious spirit of the place lives on in the new tenants, different though they may be from the originals. He is happy in the knowledge that the Lane is still an important crucible of revolution and change.

History lesson over, Kesey intended the story proper to begin in the fall of 1959. We follow Matthew Murphy as he arrives on the Lane to find himself right in the middle of a huge street party. The wildness of the event is an eye-opener for the young student. Wandering around, suitcase in hand, he encounters lots of drunken debauchery and lewd behavior as he tries to locate his father's friend's house. At the end of the party, a big fight breaks out between a group of frat boys and some of the Lane's inhabitants. The police arrive and try to arrest everybody involved in the fighting. They cart away a large number of people, but when they get to the station they realize they had not arrested any residents of the Lane, only a bunch of guys from the same fraternity, all of them sons of the well connected. Frustrated, the police chief resolves to do something about the Lane once and for all. It has long been a thorn in his side.

The chapters that follow introduce us to the major characters on the Lane. We learn of their troubles and their stories, and we witness their unconventional morals and manners. We find that the Lane is under threat from all directions. It is targeted by the police who distrust its liberalisms, and hounded by the local authorities who object to its unincorporated freedoms. The Lane residents also find themselves at odds with the local frat boys who crash the parties and invariably provoke fights. The neighbors nearby also oppose the Lane's rowdy existence, and even its allies, the rebel beatniks from the city, pressure the people on the Lane to conform to their ways, which the Lane residents see as a rather staid brand of hipster nihilism. In the story, personalities and relationships on the Lane are complicated and convoluted, sometimes even caustic enough to contribute to its eventual decline. After a series of complaints and charges, the local authorities seize the place and evict everybody, despite the last-minute efforts of a very old and very sick Mr. Johnson. At the end of the story, one of the former residents of the Lane sets fire to its empty buildings, burning all the homes to the ground. At first, Johnson is distraught but then realizes that the flames are not destroying the rebellious spirit that the Lane had nurtured over the years; rather they are merely serving to spread its influence like sparks on the wind. The End.

Kesey's "One Lane" plot was obviously a barely fictionalized account of the rise and recent fall of Perry Lane. The story is full of familiar events and situations, from the pig-roast party at the beginning of the book to the destruction of the Lane at its end, and its cast of characters was clearly born of the people that Kesey had lived with there. Anyone familiar with his circle of friends would have been able to easily identify them in the narrative. Some of Kesey's characterizations were flattering, but certainly not all of them, and it is doubtful whether many of his old friends and neighbors would have been pleased with the way they were depicted in his novelization of their recent past. Not that Kesey made an inflated hero of his own fictional namesake. Far from it. Even though he depicted himself as the leader of the bohemian set on the Lane, he chose to show himself as something of a fake, someone who was more than capable of abusing and manipulating his status for his own selfish ends. In this, Kesey may have been exploring the darker side of his personality or struggling with the burden of leadership that he had enjoyed (and endured) as long as he could remember. Either way, he came across in the narrative as a character possessed of far more flaws than virtues.

Kesey's mythical retelling of his own recent history makes for fascinating reading, in large part because it gives us some idea of his state of mind in late 1963 and early 1964. One needs to be careful reading too much into a work of fiction—and an unfinished work at that—but Kesey's not-so-subtle Promethean message in "One Lane" seems clear: he thinks a revolution is coming, and he does not think it can be stopped. He thinks that Perry Lane and its occupants were early participants in that revolution, even though only a few of them may have realized it at the time. Theirs was not a revolution of guns and glory. It was a new type of revolution:

one of morals, of manners, and of the mind. Its goal was not to bring about a regime change or anything as mundane as that. Politics—how passé. No, this was a revolution that would affect the way people thought and behaved: it was a revolution of consciousness. Perry Lane lived out that revolution in its own little way, breaking social and sexual conventions, experimenting with all manner of mind-altering psychedelic drugs, and daring to imagine that things and people could be different. The end of "One Lane" is clearly intended to be prophetic: the revolution is upon us, born of Perry Lane and other bohemian enclaves like it. Kesey's background and his politics were anything but radical, but here he was writing about revolution in 1963, a good few years before such talk became all the rage. "He noticed something that I didn't, that a revolution was in progress," Robert Stone admitted later. "Ken saw the revolution coming and felt that he had a social mission. He was going to use the power of his personality to do something special."[33] It was time for a real-life Prometheus to spread the fire to the masses and Kesey was the ideal man for the job.

Kesey was already making public pronouncements about revolution. In an interview in the spring of 1963, he claimed to be part of something he called the "Neon Renaissance."[34] The interviewer took this to be a reference to some sort of literary movement of young writers, but it is clear from Kesey's later comments to Gordon Lish that he understood it as something far greater than that. "It's a name I hooked onto a thing I feel is happening nowadays," Kesey explained. "What this is I cannot say exactly, except that it's a need to find a new way to look at the world, an attempt to locate a better reality, now that the old reality is riddled with radioactive poison." He claimed that he was not the only one searching for this new reality. He listed Ornette Colman in jazz, Ann Halprin in dance, the New Wave in movies, Lenny Bruce in comedy, and Wally Hendrix in art as like-minded explorers, all striving "to find out *what* is happening, *why*, and what can be *done* with it."[35]

These were the questions that Kesey had been asking himself. He could sense that change was coming, that a revolution of some sort was in the air, but he was still struggling to make sense of these feelings. Whatever was happening, it already felt special. "I can't imagine another scene, another period that I'd rather be living in," Kesey told Lish. "I think we're living in a wild and woolly time, a time that history students will one day view in retrospect and say, 'Wow! That 20th Century! Wouldn't that have been something to make!'"[36] Kesey was also starting to realize that he had somehow found himself in a unique position to do something meaningful, if not Promethean, in the "wild and woolly" time. "We're on the verge of something very fantastic," he explained in early 1963. "[A]nd I believe our generation will be the one to pull it off."[37]

By the end of May 1964, Babbs was out of the military for good and looking to reconnect with Kesey and his friends. In New York, Viking Press, Kesey's publisher, was preparing a big launch event for his second book, *Sometimes a Great Notion*, in July, which Kesey and his friends had plans to attend to coincide with a much talked about visit to the New York World's Fair. As Kesey counted the people who wanted to go along on the trip, it soon became clear that there was not going to be room for everyone in Babbs's big truck. "Hey," said George Walker, "maybe we should buy a bus?"

Notes

Introduction

1. Editorial, "The Prankster's Death," *New York Times*, November 13, 2001.

2. Ken Kesey, dedication to *Demon Box* (New York: Viking, 1986).

3. Jed and Lorenzo were members of the University of Oregon wrestling squad. On January 23, 1984, they were on their way to a wrestling meet in eastern Washington. Going over a pass in the Cascade Mountains, their van skidded on an icy road in white-out conditions and fell over a cliff. Jed and Lorenzo died from their injuries. Ken Kesey sued the university for negligence and won. He used the settlement to buy a new, larger bus for the wrestling team that was fitted with seat belts, unlike the one in which his son died.

4. The correct spelling of the name of the bus is a matter of some contention for those who care. Roy Sebern, the artist and friend of Kesey who came up with the name and first painted it onto the destination board, told me that he accidentally spelled the word "Furthur" the first time he wrote it in on the bus just days before it left on its famous 1964 bus trip to New York. The bus was repainted continually on the trip, and the spelling of its name was corrected within a matter of days. A close viewing of the film footage from the trip will confirm this fact (see Alex Gibney and Alison Ellwood, dirs., *Magic Trip*, DVD [New York: Jigsaw Productions, 2011]). Still, some people import great meaning to its original, misspelled name. Stanley "Bear" Owsley, the most famous amateur LSD chemist of the sixties, felt very strongly about the issue. "The name has power as it was, but loses that power when spelled in the ordinary way," he chided me in a December 31, 2002, e-mail. "You have a lot to learn about the power of naming. Calling the bus 'Further' is like calling that British band the Beetles."

5. Tom Wolfe, *The Electric Kool-Aid Acid Test* (New York: Bantam Books, 1969), 254.

6. Todd Brendan Fahey, "Comes Spake the Cuckoo. Ken Kesey: The *Far Gone* Interview," September 13, 1992, http://www.fargonebooks.com/kesey.html (accessed August 7, 2012).

7. Thomas Frank, *The Conquest of Cool: Business Culture, Counterculture, and the Rise of Hip Consumerism* (Chicago: University of Chicago Press, 1998).

Chapter 1. Sparks Fly Upward

1. Ken Kesey, "My Oregon Trail," *Vis a Vis*, March 1989, 66–70. Most of the information in this section about Kesey's early life in Colorado and Oregon comes from published sources, but I also draw some facts and details from entries in Ken Kesey's 1950s journal (Ken Kesey, "Journal," 1954–1962, Kesey family archives, Pleasant Hill, Oregon [hereafter "Kesey Journal"]).

2. Ken Kesey, "I Have My Fling at the Sport of Kings," *Oregon Daily Emerald*, January 17, 1956.

3. Quoted in Kesey, "My Oregon Trail," 66.

4. Ibid., 68.

5. Ibid., 70.

6. Allan Balliett, "Ken Kesey Goes Further," *Beat Scene*, January 1999, 24.

7. Quoted in Kesey, "My Oregon Trail," 70.

8. Ken Kesey and Paul Krassner, *The Last Supplement to the Whole Earth Catalog* (Menlo Park, CA: Portola Institute, 1971), 5. Most of the information in this section about Kesey's early life in Springfield comes from published sources, but I also draw some facts and details from entries in Kesey Journal.

9. Chuck Kesey went on to study dairy science at Oregon State University and to work with his father in the business. In 1969, he and his wife, Sue, established Nancy's Yogurt, one of the first U.S.-based companies to produce yogurt that incorporated acidophilus, a live culture that aids in digestion.

10. Ken Kesey, "Tranny Man," *Spit in the Ocean*, no. 1 (1974): 51.

11. Kesey, *Demon Box*, 32.

12. Kesey Journal.

13. Gordon Lish, "Ken Kesey: A Celebration of Excellence," *Genesis West* 2, no. 5 (1963): 40.

14. "Ken Kesey Is Still His Mom's Boy," *Eugene (OR) Register-Guard*, November 6, 2011, B1.

15. Ibid.

16. *CBS Sunday Morning Show* (1990), television.

17. Ken Kesey, "The Earth Is Your Canvas and You Are the Artist," 1950s, Ken Kesey Papers 1960–1973, Special Collections, University of Oregon, Eugene, Oregon (hereafter "Kesey Papers").

18. David Riesman and Nathan Glazer coined the terms "inner-directed" and "outer-directed" in their classic analysis of modern American society, *The Lonely Crowd: A Study of the Changing American Character* (1950). They were joined in their concerns by C. Wright Mills, *White Collar: The American Middle-Classes* (1952); and William H. Whyte, *Organizational Man* (1957).

19. "Truth Must Motivate Writer, Says Faulkner," *Oregon Daily Emerald*, April 15, 1955.

20. Lish, "Ken Kesey," 26–27.

21. Ken Kesey, *Sometimes a Great Notion* (New York: Viking, 1965), 20.

22. Lish, "Ken Kesey," 26, 29.

23. Dick Gaik, "Inching Back into Action," *Good Times*, February 5, 1970, 6.

24. Ken Kesey, interview by Bob Costas, *Later . . . with Bob Costas* (NBC, 1992).

25. Mark Christensen, *Acid Christ: Ken Kesey, LSD and the Politics of Ecstasy* (Tucson: Schaffner Press, 2010), 46.

26. Paul Pintarich, "Still Kesey after All These Years," *Oregonian*, August 24, 1986, C1.

27. Balliett, "Ken Kesey Goes Further," 24. Much of the information in this section about Kesey's early theatrical career comes from published sources, but I also draw some facts and details from entries in Kesey Journal.

28. "Ken Kesey Is Still His Mom's Boy," B1.

29. "Miller Students Display Talent in Assembly," April 27, 1951, in private clippings collection of Geneva Kesey.

30. *Miller's Log* 1952, Springfield High School Yearbook, Springfield, OR, 1952.

31. At the time of writing, this particular inscribed 1952 yearbook was offered for sale by Ken Lopez Bookseller, of Hadley, MA.

32. *Miller's Log* 1953, Springfield High School Yearbook, Springfield, OR, 1953.

33. Jack Wilson, "Ken Kesey Can Turn to Other Endeavors," *Eugene (OR) Register-Guard*, February 27, 1957.

34. Christensen, *Acid Christ*, 42.

35. Brian Booth, quoted in Jeff Baker, "All Times a Great Artist, Ken Kesey Is Dead at Age 66," *Oregonian*, November 11, 2001.

36. *Oregona* (Eugene: Student Publication Board, University of Oregon, 1955), 132.

37. Bob Sipchen, "Kesey and Co.," *Los Angeles Times*, February 11, 1990, 5.

38. Ken Kesey, interview by Kun, *Sputnik*, n.d., http://www.sputnik.ac/interview%20page/trip.html.

39. Robert Faggen, "Ken Kesey: The Art of Fiction CXXVI," *Paris Review* 35, no. 130 (1994): 88.

40. Ibid., 86.

41. Sipchen, "Kesey and Co.," 5.

42. Press clipping in the possession of Geneva Kesey, source unknown. Most of the information in this section about Kesey's early theatrical career comes from press clippings, programs, and other published sources; I also draw some facts and details from entries in Kesey Journal.

43. "Football Spirit Proves Good Enough for Basketball Season," December 10, 1952, press clipping in the possession of Geneva Kesey, source unknown.

44. Len Calvert, "Krempel's Directing Debut 'Impressive,'" *Oregon Daily Emerald*, February 1, 1954.

45. "Over 1200 High School Seniors Sign for Duck Preview Weekend," *Oregon Daily Emerald*, April 25, 1955.

46. The movie *Animal House* was shot in 1977 in the Beta house and in other locations around Eugene. The house was torn down in 1986.

47. Jeffrey Jane Flowers, ed., *Pioneers, Scholars and Rogues: A Spirited History of the University of Oregon* (Eugene: University of Oregon Press, 2002), 64, 65.

48. Nicholas L. Syrett, *The Company He Keeps: A History of White College Fraternities* (Chapel Hill: University of North Carolina Press, 2009), 237. Some progressive colleges had already moved to abolish Greek life on their campuses, arguing that their conservative inclinations undermined critical thought. When Amherst College made such a move in 1945, it argued that "fraternities represent an entrenchment of the world without inside the college community. They are the center of a kind of social education that reinforces conventional values of our society" (235).

49. Ibid., 247.

50. "Prankster Rings Alarm at Dance," *Oregon Daily Emerald*, November 17, 1954, 1.

51. "Three Panty-Raiders May be 'Going Home,'" *Oregon Daily Emerald*, October 28, 1955, 1.

52. "Giant Sling Too Effective, Students Find," May 24, 1955, clipping in Kesey Journal.

53. Syrett, *The Company He Keeps*, 8.

54. Larry McMurtry, "On the Road," *New York Review of Books*, December 5, 2002, 48.

55. Syrett, *The Company He Keeps*, 241.

56. Bob Keefer and Susan Palmer, "Oregon Loses a Legend," *Eugene (OR) Register-Guard*, November 11, 2001.

57. Robert Clark, interview by author, tape, Eugene, Oregon, November 18, 2003.

Chapter 2. From Hollywood to the Written Word

1. Kesey Journal. The following account of Kesey's time in Hollywood draws information and details from Ken Kesey's 1950s journal, with additional information gathered from various interviews and published sources.

2. Kesey claimed to have met Marlon Brando at the May 1960 San Quentin vigil for Caryl Chessman, a famous death row inmate who was executed on May 2, 1960.

3. As quoted in Gibney and Alison Ellwood, *Magic Trip*.

4. Sam Kashner and Jennifer MacNair, *The Bad and the Beautiful: Hollywood in the Fifties* (New York: W. W. Norton, 2002), 13.

5. Barbara Moore, Marvin R. Bensman, and Jim Van Dyke, *Prime-time Television: A Concise History* (New York: Praeger, 2006), 79.

6. Kashner and MacNair, *The Bad and the Beautiful*, 13.

7. The phrase "Live fast, die young [and have a good corpse]" was first uttered by a character in a 1947 novel—William Motely's *Knock on Any Door*—and then in a 1949 movie version of the book with Humphrey Bogart uttering the famous line.

8. Jack Kerouac, *On the Road* (New York: Viking, 1957), 8.

9. Christensen, *Acid Christ*, 42.

10. Nigel Cawthorne, *Sex Lives of the Hollywood Goddesses* (London: Prion, 1997), 171.

11. Kashner and MacNair, *The Bad and the Beautiful*, 14.

12. Robert Hofler, *The Man Who Invented Rock Hudson: The Pretty Boys and Dirty Deals of Henry Willson* (New York: Carroll and Graf, 2005).

13. Mary Desjardins, "Systematizing Scandal: Confidential Magazine, Stardom, and the State of California," in *Headline Hollywood: A Century of Film Scandals*, ed. Adrienne L. McLean and David A. Cook (New Brunswick, NJ: Rutgers University Press, 2001), 228n19.

14. Ken Kesey, letter to Faye, August 9, 1955, collection of Geneva Kesey.

15. Chip Brown, "Ken Kesey Kisses No Ass," *Esquire*, September 1992, 208.

16. Christensen, *Acid Christ*, 44.

17. These accounts of Kesey's activities at the University of Oregon are drawn from various interviews, archival printed and microfilmed sources, and Kesey Journal.

18. Program for *Fall Term*, University of Oregon, Eugene.

19. Ken Kesey, "Fall Term Script," 1955, Kesey Papers.

20. "Group Approves Assembly," *Oregon Daily Emerald*, February 17, 1956.

21. Ken Kesey, "Portland High Principals Refuse Opportunity for Review of Show," *Oregon Daily Emerald*, February 7, 1956.

22. Christensen, *Acid Christ*, 45.

23. *Oregona*, 183.

24. Census data indicates that in 2011, the median age for a man to get married was around twenty-eight years old, and for women, twenty-six. In 1956 men typically married by the time they were twenty-three, and women by the time they were twenty. See the U.S. Census Bureau's America's Families and Living Arrangements historical series Table MS-2, http://www.census.gov/population/socdemo/hh-fam/ms2.xls.

25. Ken Kesey, interview by author, tape, Pleasant Hill, Oregon, July 2001.

26. "Double Ring Rites Wed Miss Haxby, Ken Kesey," *Eugene (OR) Register-Guard*, May 27, 1956, 5D.

27. Much later in his career Arnold directed a number of movies, including *Blood Sport* (1989), starring Jean Claude Van Damme; *Alan Quartermain and the Lost City of Gold* (1987); and *Hands of a Stranger* (1987).

28. Faggen, "Ken Kesey," 73, 74.

29. Ken Kesey, "Sunset at Celilo," 1956, Kesey Papers.

30. Lish, "Ken Kesey," 20.

31. Billie Reynolds, "Emerald Artistry," *Emerald Empire News*, 1962, 12, press clipping in the possession of Geneva Kesey.

32. Ken Kesey, "Eugene Businessman Lauds Campus Action," *Oregon Daily Emerald*, January 31, 1956, 2.

33. Ken Kesey, "Senate Action Lauded by City Influential," *Oregon Daily Emerald*, October 23, 1956, 2.

34. Ken Kesey, "Southerners Oppose New Cottonpicker," *Oregon Daily Emerald*, February 14, 1956, 2.

35. In 1971 Marcia Falk, a teacher of literature and writing at Stanford, published a letter in the *New York Times* famously accusing Kesey (and Dale Wasserman, the

playwright responsible for converting the book into a play) of being racist and sexist in their depiction of characters in *One Flew Over the Cuckoo's Nest*. A number of scholars have echoed these sentiments in various journal articles; see, for example, Joseph Flora, "Westering and Women: A Thematic Study of Kesey's *One Flew Over the Cuckoo's Nest* and Fisher's *Mountain Man*," *Heritage of Kansas* 10 (1977): 3–14; Madelon Heatherington, "Romance without Women: The Sterile Fiction of the American West," *Georgia Review* 33, no. 3 (1979): 643–56; and Leslie Horst, "Bitches, Twitches, and Eunuchs: Sex-Role Failure and Caricature," *Lex et Scientia: The International Journal of Law and Science* 13, no. 1–2 (1977): 14–17. Others have leapt to Kesey's defense; see Janet R. Sutherland, "A Defense of Ken Kesey's *One Flew Over the Cuckoo's Nest*," *English Journal* 61, no. 1 (1972): 28–31.

36. Ken Kesey, "Oil and Water and Blood," early 1950s, Kesey Papers.

37. J. Sebastian Sinisi, "You Don't Need to Dial 911 If You Want the PC Police," *Denver Post*, July 24, 1994.

38. Wilson, "Ken Kesey Can Turn to Other Endeavors."

39. Ken Kesey, "Earthshoes and Other Remarks," *The CoEvolution Quarterly*, Fall 1976, 110.

40. Ernest Hemingway, "Soldier's Home," in *The Complete Short Stories of Ernest Hemingway*, ed. Finca Vigía (New York: Scribner's, 1987), 115.

41. Tom Clark and Ted Berrigan, "A Little Bit of Magic: Ken Kesey on Writing," *Beat Scene*, Autumn 2004, 43.

42. Kesey, "Earthshoes and Other Remarks," 111.

43. Clark and Berrigan, "A Little Bit of Magic," 43.

44. Wilson, "Ken Kesey Can Turn to Other Endeavors."

45. Kesey, interview by Kun.

46. Wilson, "Ken Kesey Can Turn to Other Endeavors."

47. Clark and Berrigan, "A Little Bit of Magic," 44.

48. Brown, "Ken Kesey Kisses No Ass," 208.

CHAPTER 3. SIN HOLLOW

1. Cathy Henkel, "He's Wrestled with Life All Along," *Eugene (OR) Register-Guard*, April 28, 1982.

2. Wilson, "Ken Kesey Can Turn to Other Endeavors."

3. *Miller's Log* 1953, Springfield High School Yearbook, Springfield, OR, 1953.

4. Tom Howser, "Wrestlers Encounter Agricultural Group," *Oregon Daily Emerald*, February 8, 1957, 4.

5. Wilson, "Ken Kesey Can Turn to Other Endeavors."

6. Lish, "Ken Kesey," 21–22.

7. In a bizarre twist to this story, Kesey wrestled Geister again in 1982 at an age-group wrestling tournament at Milwaukee's Rex Putnam High School. It was Kesey's first competitive match in twenty-two years. Kit Kesey, Ken's nephew, described the match kindly as "a lot of stalling and plenty of heavy breathing." Both men, exhausted

but grinning from ear to ear, were happy to come away with a 0–0 tie and a clunky gold-painted medal. See Cathy Henkel, "Was This Really a Great Notion," *Eugene (OR) Register-Guard*, April 27, 1982.

8. Ibid.

9. Ken Kesey, "Ken Kesey in Adelaide 1988, pt. 2," *The Archive: A History of Over 30 Years of UK Festivals*, www.ukrockfestivals.com/keseyinterview2.html.

10. As reported by Ken Kesey, tape recording #23, 1963, Kesey Papers.

11. Ward Winslow, *Palo Alto: A Centennial History* (Palo Alto, CA: Palo Alto Historical Society, 1993), 8.

12. George Buddy, "Ken Kesey: Ten Years After," *Oregon Daily Emerald*, January 24, 1973.

13. Kesey, tape recording #23.

14. U.S. Social Security Administration, "National Average Wage Indexing Series, 1951–2011," http://www.ssa.gov/oact/cola/AWI.html.

15. Todd Bauer, "A Delicate Balance of Forces: The Stanford Creative Writing Program, 1958–1963" (master's thesis, Northwestern University, 1996), 12. Many of the details regarding the Stanford Creative Writing Program contained in this chapter are drawn from Bauer's thesis and the interviews contained therein.

16. Wendell Berry, "Wallace Stegner and the Great Community," in *What Are People For? Essays by Wendell Berry* (San Francisco: North Point Press, 1990), 51.

17. Wallace Stegner, *On Teaching Creative Writing* (Hanover, NH: University Press of New England, 1980), 11.

18. Quoted in Bauer, "A Delicate Balance of Forces, 15.

19. Quoted in Jackson J. Benson, *Wallace Stegner: His Life and Work* (New York: Viking, 1996), 254, 251.

20. Bauer, "A Delicate Balance of Forces, 19.

21. Ken Kesey, "On Why Am I Not Writing My Last Term Paper," 1959, Kesey Papers.

22. Benson, *Wallace Stegner*, 254.

23. Richard W. Etulain, *Stegner: Conversations on History and Literature* (Reno: University of Nevada Press, 1996), 138–39.

24. Quoted in Martin Lasden, "Wallace Stegner on His Own Terms," *Stanford*, Spring 1989, 28.

25. Lish, "Ken Kesey," 25.

26. Metro Desk, "Speaking Up," *Los Angeles Times*, September 17, 1993.

27. Ken Babbs, letter to Mitch, May 30, 1962, Kesey Papers.

28. Nick Hasted, "How We Met: Ken Kesey and Ken Babbs," *The Independent*, August 8, 1999.

29. Ken Babbs, undated letter fragment, begins "fancies to be that way," 1963, Kesey Papers.

30. Steven Hager, "The High Times Interview: Ken Babbs," *High Times*, April 1991, 91.

31. Quoted in Bauer, "A Delicate Balance of Forces," 14.

32. As reported by Kesey, tape recording #23.

33. Jonathan Root, "Last Rites for a Rustic Bohemia," *Palo Alto Times*, July 21, 1963.

34. Veblen's time at Stanford is described in a book by one of his students and a fellow resident of Cedro Cottage, Robert L. Dufus, in *The Innocents at Cedro: A Memoir of Thorstein Veblen and Some Others* (New York: Macmillan, 1944).

35. Hughes Rudd, *My Escape from the CIA and Other Improbable Events* (New York: E. P. Dutton, 1966), 51. Vic Lovell recalls that the goat belonged to his friend Robb Crist, a graduate student in philosophy at Stanford.

36. Fred Nelson and Ed McClanahan, *One Lord, One Faith, One Cornbread* (Garden City, NY: Anchor Press, 1973), 22.

37. Vic Lovell, interview by author, tape, Menlo Park, CA, December 19, 2001.

38. Jim Wolpman, interview by author, tape, Walnut Creek, CA, December 20, 2001.

39. Blair Tindall, "Psychedelic Palo Alto," *Palo Alto Weekly*, March 8, 2000, 23.

40. Chloe Scott, interview by author, tape, Menlo Park, CA, December 28, 2001.

41. Vic Lovell, "The Perry Lane Papers: Prologue," in *One Lord, One Faith, One Cornbread*, ed. Fred Nelson and Ed McClanahan (Garden City, NY: Anchor Press, 1973), 23.

42. Kesey, interview by author.

43. Bill Kreutzmann, interviewed for *A Look Back*, a documentary included with the bonus material for the 2004 DVD release of the *Grateful Dead Movie*, dir. Jerry Garcia (Electrascope, 1977).

44. Robert Greenfield, *Dark Star: An Oral Biography of Jerry Garcia* (New York: W. Morrow, 1996), 20.

45. Dennis McNally, *A Long Strange Trip: The Inside History of the Grateful Dead* (New York: Broadway Books, 2002), 43.

46. Vic Lovell, "The Perry Lane Papers: Wayward Girls," in *One Lord, One Faith, One Cornbread*, ed. Fred Nelson and Ed McClanahan (Garden City, NY: Anchor Press, 1973), 113.

47. Ibid.

48. Ibid.

49. Kesey, tape recording #23.

50. Wolpman, interview by author.

51. Ann Lambrecht, interview by author, tape, Menlo Park, CA, December 2002.

52. Wolpman, interview by author.

53. Ken Kesey, tape recording #3, 1963, Kesey Papers.

54. Wolpman, interview by author.

55. Jeff Barnard, "Novelist Ken Kesey, 66, Dies," *Los Angeles Times*, November 12, 2001.

56. Scott, interview by author.

57. Norman Malnick, "Ken 'Cuckoo Nest' Kesey: One Who Wigged Out," *Village Voice*, May 12, 1966, 6.

58. Balliett, "Ken Kesey Goes Further," 25.

59. Gordon Lish, "What the Hell You Looking in Here For, Daisy Mae? An Interview with Ken Kesey," *Genesis West* 2, no. 5 (1963): 26.

60. Kesey, tape recording #23.

61. Paul Perry and Ken Babbs, *On the Bus: The Complete Guide to the Legendary Trip of Ken Kesey and the Merry Pranksters and the Birth of the Counterculture* (New York: Thunder's Mouth Press, 1990), 25.

62. Quoted in Bauer, "A Delicate Balance of Forces," 39.

63. Melinda Sacks, "Hometown Hippies," *Palo Alto Weekly*, July 3, 1991, 23.

64. Bauer, "A Delicate Balance of Forces," 39.

65. This account of a party at Perry Lane is drawn from various interviews, printed sources, and Kesey Journal.

66. Rudd, "Mavis at the Beach," 54.

67. Carolyn Snyder, "A New Breed Comes to Perry Lane," *Palo Alto Times*, March 4, 1967, 7.

68. Quoted in Bauer, "A Delicate Balance of Forces," 33.

69. Scott, interview by author.

70. Paul De Carli, interview by author, tape, Menlo Park, CA, June 6, 2002.

71. Ken Kesey, letter #1, August 3, 1959, Kesey Papers.

72. Lovell, "The Perry Lane Papers: Wayward Girls," 129.

73. Sacks, "Hometown Hippies."

74. Wolpman, interview by author.

75. Ken Kesey, undated letter #30, early 1963 (according to Faye Kesey), Kesey Papers.

76. Balliett, "Ken Kesey Goes Further," 21.

77. Ken Kesey, tape recording #16, 1963, Kesey Papers.

78. Lovell, "The Perry Lane Papers: Prologue," 22.

CHAPTER 4. A ROYAL ROAD TO INSIGHT

1. Ken Kesey, letter #2, September 18, 1959, Kesey Papers.

2. Keefer and Palmer, "Oregon Loses a Legend."

3. Kesey, letter #2.

4. Ibid.

5. Peter O. Whitmer and Bruce VanWyngarden, *Aquarius Revisited: Seven Who Created the Sixties Counterculture That Changed America* (New York: Citadel Press, 1991), 201.

6. Ibid., 201.

7. Charles Hayes, *Tripping: An Anthology of True-Life Psychedelic Adventures* (New York: Penguin Compass, 2000), 4.

8. Leo E. Hollister, *Chemical Psychoses: LSD and Related Drugs* (Springfield, IL: Charles C. Thomas, 1968), 16.

9. Martin A. Lee and Bruce Shlain, *Acid Dreams: The Complete Social History of LSD* (New York: Grove Press, 1992), 65–67.

10. See, e.g., R. Gordon Wasson, *Soma: Divine Mushroom of Immortality*, Ethno-Mycological Studies 1 (New York: Harcourt Brace Jovanovich, 1968), *The Wondrous Mushroom: Mycolatry in Mesoamerica* (New York: McGraw-Hill, 1980), and Wasson et al., *The Road to Eleusis: Unveiling the Secret of the Mysteries*, rev. ed. (Los Angeles: William Dailey Rare Books, 1998). The first scientific account of the mind-altering properties of plants is generally thought to be Ernst Von Bibra's *Die narkotischen Genussmittel und der Mensch* (1855).

11. R. Gordon Wasson, "Seeking the Magic Mushrooms," *Life*, May 13, 1957, 101, 120. In *The Search for the "Manchurian Candidate": The CIA and Mind Control* (New York: McGraw-Hill, 1979), John Marks succinctly discusses the role that this article played in promoting interest in the type of chemically induced transcendental state that Wasson described.

12. Jay Stevens, *Storming Heaven: LSD and the American Dream* (New York: Grove Press, 1988), 77.

13. Timothy Leary, *Flashbacks: An Autobiography* (Los Angeles: J. P. Tarcher, Inc., 1983), 33.

14. Ibid., 45.

15. For Hollingshead's account of this event, see Michael Hollingshead, *The Man Who Turned on the World* (London: Blond and Briggs, 1973).

16. Ken Kesey, "Ken Kesey Flashes Back to Leary," *Time*, April 29, 1996.

17. Ken Kesey, undated letter #26, January 1963 (according to Faye Kesey), Kesey Papers.

18. Lee and Shlain, *Acid Dreams*, xxiv.

19. Quoted in Robert Palmer, *Rock and Roll: An Unruly History* (New York: Harmony Books, 1998), 158.

20. U.S. Senate Select Committee on Intelligence and Committee on Human Resources, "Project MK Ultra, the CIA'S Program of Research in Behavioral Modification" (Washington, DC, 1977).

21. Ibid., sec. 92.

22. Ibid.

23. In January 1973, presumably cleaning house before he stood down, Helms ordered CIA personnel to destroy all records directly pertaining to MK-ULTRA. Helms's actions denied us a significant amount of information about this program's history, but John Marks's FOIA request fortunately turned up seven boxes of files that had escaped destruction only because, contrary to standard practice for highly sensitive materials of this type, someone had sent them to the CIA's Retired Records Center outside of Washington, DC. The U.S. government declassified these documents shortly after the 1977 Senate hearings.

24. U.S. Senate Select Committee, "Project MK Ultra," sec. 10.

25. Ibid., secs. 12, 10.

26. Hofmann would also be the first to identify the active ingredients in the "magic mushrooms" that Gordon Wasson had encountered. In 1958 Hofmann synthesized two new substances—psilocybin and psilocin—with properties similar to, though less potent than, LSD.

27. Midwives since at least the Middle Ages had used ergot in its natural form for similar purposes.

28. Albert Hofmann, *LSD: My Problem Child* (New York: McGraw-Hill, 1980), 14–15.

29. Ibid., 17.

30. Hollister, *Chemical Psychoses*, 68–69.

31. Quoted in ibid., 50.

32. Humphrey Osmond first coined the word "psychedelic," in his correspondence with Aldous Huxley in the mid-1950s. Osmond thought that the then current collective names for these particular types of drugs—"psychomimetic" or "hallucinogenic"— were both inaccurate and pejorative, and so he proposed to Huxley the word "psychedelic" (meaning "mind-manifesting," loosely translated from Greek). Osmond introduced the term to the psychiatric community at a meeting of the New York Academy of Sciences in 1957.

33. Lee and Shlain, *Acid Dreams*, 25, 27.

34. U.S. Senate Select Committee, "Project MK Ultra," sec. 16.

35. Hollister went on to enjoy a distinguished career in medicine and psychiatry, acclaimed at his peak as the world's leading psychopharmacologist. He worked for most of his professional life at the Stanford University School of Medicine, later spending time as a professor at the University of Texas, Houston. He was active on many government commissions and served as president of the American Society for Clinical Pharmacology and Therapeutics, the American College of Neuropsychopharmacology, and the International College of Neuropsychopharmacology. He was an outspoken critic of U.S. government policies regarding the classification and criminalization of certain drugs. He published a number of scientific articles exploring the medicinal value of cannabis and arguing for its relative safety.

36. Marks, *The Search for the "Manchurian Candidate,"* 120.

37. Hollister, *Chemical Psychoses*, 123.

38. Hollister subsequently published a number of articles using data drawn from these experiments, including Leo E. Hollister, J. J. Prusmack, and N. Rosenquist, "Comparison of Three Psychotropic Drugs (Psilocybin, Jb-329, and It-290) in Volunteer Subjects," *Journal of Nervous Mental Disease*, no. 131 (1960): 428–34; Leo E. Hollister, "Clinical, Biochemical and Psychological Effects of Psilocybin," *Archives Internationales de Pharmacodynamie et de Therapie Pharmacodyn* 130 (1961): 42–52; Leo E. Hollister, "Drug Induced Psychoses and Schizophrenic Reactions: A Critical Comparison," *Annals of the New York Academy of Science*, no. 96 (1962): 80–88; Leo E. Hollister and A. M. Hartmann, "Mescaline, Lysergic Acid Dietylamide and Psilocybin: Comparison of Clinical Syndromes, Effects on Color Perception and Biochemical Measures," *Comprehensive Psychiatry* 3 (1962): 235–41.

39. Lee and Shlain, *Acid Dreams*, 23.

40. Hollister, Prusmack, and Rosenquist, "Comparison of Three Psychotropic Drugs," 428.

41. Hollister and Hartman, "Mescaline, Lysergic Acid Dietylamide and Psilocybin," found that "heightened and unusual perception of colors following psychotomimetics may result from the action of normally inadequate stimuli" (238).

42. Ibid., 236.

43. Tindall, "Psychedelic Palo Alto," 23.

44. Tom Wolfe, "The Chief and His Merry Pranksters Take a Trip with Electric Kool-Aid," *New York: The World Tribute Magazine*, January 29, 1967, 18.

45. Hollister, *Chemical Psychoses*, 55.

46. "Ken Kesey," Digital Interviews, September 2000, http://www.digitalinterviews .com/digitalinterviews/views/kesey.shtml.

47. Ibid.

48. T. Wolfe, "The Chief and His Merry Pranksters," 17.

49. Ken Kesey, Ken Babbs, and Paul Foster, *Kesey's Garage Sale* (New York: Viking Press, 1973), 7.

50. Quoted in "Ken Kesey's First Trip," an audio recording in the special features section of Gibney and Ellwood, *Magic Trip*.

51. Ibid.

52. Kesey's participation in this particular study cannot be proven, but it seems likely since this appears to be the only study that Hollister ran using Ditran, and Kesey is on record discussing his encounters with that particular drug during the trials.

53. Hollister, "Comparison of Three Psychotropic Drugs," 428. Faye Kesey recalls that one reason that Kesey was accepted for the tests was because Hollister was looking for test subjects with a literary bent, hoping that they might be better able to describe their experiences (Faye Kesey, interview by author, tape, Pleasant Hill, OR, November 2003).

54. T. Wolfe, "The Chief and His Merry Pranksters," 18.

55. Hollister, "Comparison of Three Psychotropic Drugs," 431, 433.

56. T. Wolfe, "The Chief and His Merry Pranksters," 17.

57. "Ken Kesey," Digital Interviews.

58. Kesey, "Ken Kesey in Adelaide 1988, pt. 2."

59. Barbara Cloud, "Author Ken Kesey Gets Background for Novel by Working as Aide in Hospital Mental Ward," Fall 1961, clipping from Geneva Kesey collection.

60. Lish, "Ken Kesey," 23.

CHAPTER 5. BETTER LIVING THROUGH CHEMISTRY

1. Fahey, "Comes Spake the Cuckoo."

2. Balliett, "Ken Kesey Goes Further," 23.

3. John Babbs, *Prankster Memoirs* (Eugene, OR: Angle Productions, 2003), 61.

4. Quoted in *The Merry Pranksters*, video (Eugene, OR: Key-Z Productions, 1999).

5. Carol Brightman, *Sweet Chaos: The Grateful Dead's American Adventure* (New York: Simon and Schuster, 1998), 21.

6. McNally, *A Long Strange Trip*, 43.

7. Fred Goodman, "The Rolling Stone Interview: Jerry Garcia," *Rolling Stone*, November 30, 1989, 73.

8. Ibid.

9. Faggen, "Ken Kesey," 72.

10. Quoted in Allen Geller and Maxwell Boas, *The Drug Beat* (New York: McGraw-Hill, 1969), 220.

11. Quoted in Whitmer and VanWyngarden, *Aquarius Revisited*, 92.

12. Martin Torgoff, *Can't Find My Way Home: America in the Great Stoned Age, 1945–2000* (New York: Simon and Schuster, 2004), 46.

13. Whitmer and VanWyngarden, *Aquarius Revisited*, 201–2.

14. Ken Kesey, undated letter #16, before April 1961 (according to Faye Kesey), Kesey Papers.

15. Quoted in Parke Puterbaugh, "The Beats and the Birth of the Counterculture," in *The Rolling Stone Book of the Beats: The Beat Generation and American Culture*, ed. Holly George-Warren (New York: Hyperion, 1999), 360.

16. Ron Bevirt, interview by author, tape, Eugene, OR, July 5, 2002.

17. Ken Kesey, "The Day after Superman Died: A Fictional Memoir," *Esquire*, October 1979, 54.

18. Quoted in "Ken Kesey," Digital Interviews.

19. Ken Kesey, "The Citadel of Culture Besieged by a Barbarian," *Oregon Daily Emerald*, January 3, 1957.

20. Jack Kerouac, "Letter to Tom Guinzburg," October 19, 1961, in *Jack Kerouac: Selected Letters, 1957–1969*, ed. Ann Charters (New York: Penguin, 2000), 353. Kerouac mistakenly thought that *Cuckoo's Nest* was as autobiographical as much of his own work: "Tom, this guy is no doubt the Columbia George Indian himself, apparently 'Kesey' is his wife's name, Tee Ah Millatoona's probably his real name . . . I understand he's ashamed of being identified with the 'deafmute' hero himself" (353).

21. Kesey, undated letter #16.

22. "Ken Kesey," Digital Interviews.

23. Ken Kesey, "Zoo," unpublished manuscript, Kesey Papers.

24. Malcom Cook, "Ken Kesey Culture Hero," *High Times*, October 1979, 90.

25. As reported by Kesey, tape recording #23.

26. Kesey and Krassner, *The Last Supplement to the Whole Earth Catalog*, 83.

27. Quoted in Whitmer and VanWyngarden, *Aquarius Revisited*, 60.

28. Ken Kesey, undated letter #7, April 1960 (according to Faye Kesey), Kesey Papers.

29. De Carli, interview by author.

30. Ken Kesey, undated letter #7.

31. Ken Babbs, letter to Whoosh, November 1, 1962, Kesey Papers.

32. Erich Goode, *The Marijuana Smokers* (New York: Basic Books, 1970), 23.

33. Greenfield, *Dark Star*, 51.

34. Kesey, interview by Kun.

35. Sandy Troy, *Captain Trips: A Biography of Jerry Garcia* (New York: Thunder's Mouth Press, 1994), 106.

36. Burton H. Wolfe, *The Hippies* (New York: Signet Books, 1968), 38.

37. De Carli, interview by author.

38. Ken Kesey, letter #12, November 10, 1960, Kesey Papers.

39. Ken Babbs, letter to Keezers, June 1, 1963, Kesey Papers.

40. Ken Babbs, letter to Keezers, April 3 or 4, 1962, Kesey Papers.

41. Tim Appelo, "Shameless Shaman," *Seattle Weekly*, January 21–27, 2004.

42. Kesey, *Sometimes a Great Notion*, 57. Other passages in the book make mention of Lee's recreational use of pot and peyote buttons obtained from Laredo, Texas: "Eat eight, mate, and you got an Electra-Jet to Heaven" (274).

43. Sacks, "Hometown Hippies," 23.

44. Hollister, *Chemical Psychoses*, 7.

45. Ken Kesey, undated letter #13, December/January 1960/61 (according to Faye Kesey), Kesey Papers.

46. Ken Kesey, "Letter to Ken Babbs: People on the Ward," reprinted in Ken Kesey, *One Flew Over the Cuckoo's Nest: Text and Criticism*, ed. John C. Pratt (New York: Viking Press, 1973), 340.

47. Cloud, "Author Ken Kesey Gets Background for Novel."

48. Kesey, interview by Kun.

49. Kesey, Babbs, and Foster, *Kesey's Garage Sale*, 7.

50. Don Bishoff, "Lane Author Pens Novel in Hospital," *Eugene (OR) Register-Guard*, January 9, 1962.

51. Laura Linden, "Late Idol Tripped out in La Honda," *San Mateo County Times Online*, November 21, 2001.

52. Jeff Barnard, "'Cuckoo': From Psych Ward to Broadway," *Seattle Times*, April 27, 2001.

53. Faggen, "Ken Kesey," 77.

54. Whitmer and VanWyngarden, *Aquarius Revisited*, 201–2.

55. Bishoff, "Lane Author Pens Novel in Hospital."

56. Cloud, "Author Ken Kesey Gets Background for Novel."

57. Malnick, "Ken 'Cuckoo Nest' Kesey," 6.

58. Kesey, undated letter #13.

59. "Ken Kesey," Digital Interviews."

60. Wolpman, interview by author.

61. Kesey, "Letter to Ken Babbs," 336–37.

62. Ibid., 338.

63. B. Wolfe, *The Hippies*, 199.

64. Ken Kesey, undated letter #42, December 1963 (according to Faye Kesey), Kesey Papers.

65. B. Wolfe, *The Hippies*, 31

66. For Cowley's account of this event, see "Ken Kesey at Stanford," in *The Portable Malcolm Cowley*, ed. Donald W. Faulkner (New York: Viking, 1990), 324–27.

67. Clark and Berrigan, "A Little Bit of Magic," 44.

68. Letter excerpted in Cowley, *The Portable Malcolm Cowley*, 468.

69. Letter from Malcom Cowley to Pascal Covici, winter 1961, reprinted in full in ibid., 508.

70. Whitmer and VanWyngarden, *Aquarius Revisited*, 203.

71. "On the Bus with Ken Kesey," *Firezine* 1, no. 5 (1999), http://www.firezine.net/issue5/fz5_14.htm. Neither of these drugs were any laughing matter. MP-14 was originally approved by the FDA in 1959 to treat psychotic disorders and schizophrenia. It was marketed under the trade name Thioridazine or Mellaril by Sandoz pharmaceuticals. Thioridazine/Mellaril has also been used to treat anxiety associated with major depression, dementia in the elderly, posttraumatic stress disorder, and severe behavioral problems in children. Because of the risk of dangerous cardiovascular side effects, this drug is usually prescribed only when other similar antipsychotic drugs have proved ineffective. IT-290 or AMT (a-methyltryptamine) is a synthetic drug of the tryptamine family. It was first developed as an antidepressant and used commercially for this purpose in the Soviet Union during the 1960s. At sufficient doses, IT-290 produces psychedelic effects, which can last for up to eighteen hours. It also possesses a similar chemical structure to amphetamine (speed), and so it acts as a stimulant. IT-290 was classified as a Schedule I controlled substance in the United States in April 2004.

72. Balliett, "Ken Kesey Goes Further," 22.

73. Kesey, undated letter #17.

74. Clark and Berrigan, "A Little Bit of Magic," 46.

75. Ken Kesey, undated letter #20, October 1961 (according to Faye Kesey), Kesey Papers.

76. Ken Kesey, undated letter #18, September/October 1961 (according to Faye Kesey), Kesey Papers.

77. "On the Bus with Ken Kesey."

78. Kesey, "Letter to Ken Babbs," 339.

79. Timothy Leary et al., "The Politics of the Nervous System," *Bulletin of the Atomic Scientists*, no. 5 (1962): 27.

80. Leary, *Flashbacks*, 175.

81. Kesey and Krassner, *The Last Supplement to the Whole Earth Catalog*, 4.

82. David Jay Brown, Rebecca McClen Novick, and Jerry Garcia, *Voices from the Edge: Conversations with Jerry Garcia, Ram Dass, Annie Sprinkle, Matthew Fox, Jaron Lanier, and Others* (Freedom, CA: Crossing Press, 1995), 369.

83. Faggen, "Ken Kesey," 71.

84. Hayes, *Tripping*, 212, 213.

85. A. J. S. Rayl, "The Merry Pranksters Cyberjam: Ken Kesey and Ken Babbs Do the Future of Rebellion," *Omni Magazine*, October 27, 1996, available at http://www.apogeebooks.com/omnimag/archives/chats/in102796.html.

86. Rob Elder, "Down on the Peacock Farm," Salon.com, November 16, 2001, http://www.salon.com/2001/11/16/kesey99/.

87. Rayl, "The Merry Pranksters Cyberjam."

88. Kesey, "Ken Kesey in Adelaide 1988, pt. 2."

89. Palmer, *Rock and Roll*, 166.

CHAPTER 6. SOMETIMES A GREAT NOTION

1. Ken Babbs, letter to Crappatitus, November 5, 1961, Kesey Papers.

2. Ken Babbs, letter to Keezers, December 4, 1962, Kesey Papers.

3. Ken Babbs, letter to Westcoasters, April 3 or 4, 1961, Kesey Papers.

4. J. Babbs, *Prankster Memoirs*, 2.

5. Ken Babbs, undated letter to Kesey, begins "Hey! Hot shit," Kesey Papers.

6. Kesey claimed in one interview that he first met Cassady in 1960, but it may have been later, after he and Faye returned to the Lane early in 1962.

7. Quoted in Faggen, "Ken Kesey," 64.

8. Ken Babbs, letter to Jon the Younger, February 18, 1962, Kesey Papers.

9. "Life in a Loony Bin," *Time*, February 16, 1962.

10. Ken Kesey, *One Flew Over the Cuckoo's Nest*, 1st ed. (New York: Viking Press, 1962), 35, 85.

11. Gwen Davis was actually an author in her own right. In 1962 she published *Someone's in the Kitchen with Dinah*, a titillating pulp comic novel about modern manners and morals. Somewhat ironically, many of the characters in this book appear to be based on people from the Perry Lane scene. "Take one innocent, happily married couple" read the blurb on the back cover, "set them down in a suburban housing development complete with shrubbery and barbecue pits. Mix well with uninhibited neighbors engaged in a sizzling game of wife-swapping. Add a crop of marijuana, planted on a golf course at midnight." In later years, Davis got a taste of her own litigious medicine. Her 1971 novel, *Touching*, contained a scene in which a writer visits a nude therapy session run by a domineering "quack" therapist called Simon Herford. In 1969 Davis herself had actually attended just such a therapy session run by Paul Bindrim, one of the pioneers of nude therapy. Bindrim sued Davis for libel, arguing that her portrayal of Herford defamed his own reputation. "I was known all over the world as the man who started nude psychotherapy," Bindrim claimed. "If you write about an elephant who flies by his ears, you can call him Herman but everyone knows he's Dumbo." To make matters worse, Davis had signed a confidentiality agreement at the time of her treatment that stipulated that none of the participants would write about their experiences in Bindrim's therapy group. The court found against Davis and Doubleday, her publisher, eventually awarding Bindrim twenty-five thousand dollars. Doubleday then turned around and sued Davis for their costs. The case created quite a furor in the literary community, few of whom seemed to be aware of Davis's lawsuit against Kesey almost a decade earlier.

12. Dale Wasserman, *The Impossible Musical* (New York: Applause Theatre and Cinema Books, 2003), 67–68.

13. Ken Kesey, undated letter #23, January 1962 (according to Faye Kesey), Kesey Papers.

14. Barnard, "'Cuckoo.'"

15. K. Babbs, letter to Jon the Younger.

16. Lovell, "The Perry Lane Papers: Wayward Girls," 114.

17. Gretchen Douglas, interview by author, tape, Portland, OR, July 2, 2002.

18. K. Babbs, letter to Jon the Younger.

19. Lovell, "The Perry Lane Papers: Wayward Girls," 117.

20. Timothy Leary, "Deal for Real," in *Underground Press Anthology*, ed. Thomas King Forcade (New York: Ace Books, 1968), 13.

21. David Gans, *Playing in the Band: An Oral and Visual Portrait of the Grateful Dead*, 1st ed. (New York: St. Martin's Press, 1985), 42.

22. Robert Greenfield, *Bill Graham Presents: My Life Inside Rock and Out* (New York: Doubleday, 1992), 148.

23. Joe Smith, *Off the Record*, ed. Mitchell Fink (New York: Warner Books, 1988), 230–31.

24. McClanahan had first met Vic Lovell by chance back in 1955, when the two had roomed together at a three-week writing conference in Colorado. At Lovell's urging, McClanahan dropped his plans to study English at Columbia University in New York and instead enrolled in the creative writing program at Stanford. A sociology major as an undergraduate, the young and inexperienced McClanahan quickly found himself out of his depth in the program, and after only two quarters he dropped out and headed back to Kentucky. There, he enrolled briefly in the English literature graduate program at the University of Kentucky—which is where he first met Berry, Hall, and Norman—before heading off to Oregon State College to take up a job as an instructor of English. Sometime in 1961, while McClanahan was in the process of re-applying to Stanford, his friend Jim Hall wrote to him about Kesey, describing him as a "gregarious young genius." Intrigued, McClanahan drove down to Springfield and spent a happy couple of hours drinking in a loggers bar called the Spar and laying the foundations for a long friendship. Upon his friend's death, McClanahan edited a collection of anecdotes and stories about Kesey, titled *Spit in the Ocean 7: All About Kesey* (New York: Penguin, 2003).

25. Perry and Babbs, *On the Bus*, 26.

26. Bauer, "A Delicate Balance of Forces," 45.

27. Perry and Babbs, *On the Bus*, 26, 15.

28. Ibid., 31, 26.

29. Ibid., 31.

30. Lish, "Ken Kesey," 22.

31. Quoted in Ralph Gleason, "Sometimes a Great Notion Is More Demanding Than a Cuckoo's Nest," *San Francisco Sunday Chronicle*, July 26, 1964.

32. Larry McMurtry, "On the Road," *New York Review of Books*, December 5, 2002, 46.

33. Ibid.

34. Robert Stone, "American Dreamers: Melville and Kerouac," *New York Times*, December 7, 1997.

35. Perry and Babbs, *On the Bus*, 18.

36. Bauer, "A Delicate Balance of Forces," 46.

37. Perry and Babbs, *On the Bus*, 28.

38. Robert Stone, "The Prince of Possibility," *New Yorker*, June 14 and 21, 2004, 74, 72, 87.

39. Late in 1963 Norman moved back to Kentucky and started working for a newspaper called the *Hazard Herald*. Four years later, he returned to California, where he hooked up with a man called Stewart Brand, a veteran of the Acid Tests and soon to be publisher of the *Whole Earth Catalog* (a hippie version of the famous Sears Roebuck catalog). When Brand decided to publish a large compendium edition of the *Whole Earth Catalog*, Norman suggested that they include a novel about the counterculture within its four hundred pages. Brand agreed to the idea as long as Norman would write it. Thus was born Norman's best-known full-length work, *Divine Right's Trip*. It was eventually published as a book in its own right in 1972, and it is still considered one of the best works of fiction about the counterculture.

40. Bevirt, interview by author.

41. Hager, "The High Times Interview," 14–15.

42. Ibid., 15

43. Ken Babbs, "Viet-Nam," *Marine Corps Gazette*, July 1963, 5.

44. Ibid., 10.

45. Hager, "The High Times Interview," 15.

46. Ken Babbs, letter to Keezers, May 1963, Kesey Papers.

47. "Kesey's 'Cuckoo' Broadway Bound," *Eugene (OR) Register-Guard*, October 6, 1963.

48. "West Menlo's 'Bohemia,' to Close," *Palo Alto Times*, July 25, 1963.

49. Ibid.

50. Perry and Babbs, *On the Bus*, 29.

51. Root, "Last Rites for a Rustic Bohemia."

52. Ken Kesey, tape recording #5, Kesey Papers.

53. Vic Lovell, "The Perry Lane Papers: A Prologue," *The Free You*, October 1968, 23.

Chapter 7. A New Prometheus

1. Tom Stockley, "La Honda: The Peninsula's Maverick Community," *San Mateo Advance-Star and Green Sheet*, June 19, 1966.

2. Stone, "The Prince of Possibility," 70.

3. I am indebted to Terry Adams and Eva Knodt, the current co-owners of Kesey's house, for providing me an essay that Terry has written about the house and its restoration titled "Picking Up the Pieces—Rebuilding Ken Kesey's House in La Honda." Kesey had been forced to sell the property in 1997, primarily to pay a local police officer who had sued and won a settlement from Kesey after the officer fell off the bridge while responding to a call about the house. In February 1998 a torrential

downpour virtually washed away the property when the La Honda Creek overflowed its banks. Two walls at the back of the house were practically destroyed and the front wall was left listing badly. At tremendous expense, the new owners have restored the house to its former glory, albeit with new concrete pile foundations that leave it standing six feet higher than in earlier times.

4. Lish, "Ken Kesey," 19.

5. Ken Kesey, letter #32, June 12, 1963, Kesey Papers.

6. Lish, "Ken Kesey," 24. A copy of one of these charts can be found in Ken Kesey and Michael Strelow, *Kesey*, 2nd ed. (Eugene, OR: Northwest Review Books, 1977). This book also includes some of Kesey's outline notes for *Sometimes a Great Notion*. The notes make fascinating reading because they allow us to see Kesey developing the narrative and distinctive style of the book.

7. Kesey, undated letter #26.

8. Ibid.

9. Quoted in J. Babbs, *Prankster Memoirs*, 74.

10. Ken Kesey, undated letter #34, summer 1963 (according to Faye Kesey), Kesey Papers.

11. Ken Kesey, undated letter #37, fall 1963 (according to Faye Kesey), Kesey Papers.

12. Ken Kesey quoted in Charles Kiselyak, dir., *Completely Cuckoo: A Film* (Pioneer Entertainment, 1997).

13. Barnard, "'Cuckoo.'"

14. Walter Kerr, "Kerr at Cort: 'One Flew Over the Cuckoo's Nest,'" *New York Herald Tribune*, November 14, 1963.

15. John McCarten, "Psychiatry, Anyone?," *New Yorker*, November 23, 1963, 143.

16. Wasserman, *The Impossible Musical.*

17. Quoted in Dan Wyant, "New York Writer Admits: Critics Do 'Kill' Plays," *Eugene (OR) Register-Guard*, July 22, 1965.

18. Kirk Douglas, *The Ragman's Son: An Autobiography* (New York: Simon and Schuster, 1988), 341.

19. Kesey, undated letter #42.

20. George Walker, speech at Kesey memorial, Koret Auditorium, San Francisco Library, San Francisco, December 5 2001.

21. Douglas Martin, "Sandy Lehmann-Haupt, One of Ken Kesey's Busmates, Dead at 59," *New York Times*, November 3, 2001. Sandy's eldest brother was Christopher Lehmann-Haupt, now an established critic at the *New York Times*. It fell to Christopher to write Kesey's obituary in the *New York Times*.

22. Carl Lehmann-Haupt, "Ken Kesey," *My Generation*, March–April 2002, 87.

23. Ken Kesey, "The Loss of Innocence," *Newsweek*, November 28, 1983, 78.

24. Ken Kesey, undated letter #41, after November 23, possibly December 1963 (according to Faye Kesey), Kesey Papers.

25. Kesey, "The Loss of Innocence."

26. Ibid.

27. G. Walker, speech at Kesey Memorial.

28. Kesey, "The Loss of Innocence," 78.

29. Gus Blaisdell, "Shazam and the Neon Rennaissance," *Author and Journalist,* June 1963, 7.

30. Lish, "Ken Kesey," 3.

31. Kesey, "Letter to Ken Babbs," 337–38.

32. Ken Kesey, "One Lane," unfinished manuscript, Kesey Papers.

33. Quoted in Perry and Babbs, *On the Bus,* 35.

34. Blaisdell, "Shazam and the Neon Renaissance," 7.

35. Lish, "Ken Kesey," 21.

36. Ibid.

37. Blaisdell, "Shazam and the Neon Renaissance," 8.

Bibliography

Anderson, Terry H. *The Movement and the Sixties*. New York: Oxford University Press, 1996.

Anderson, Walter Truett. *The Upstart Spring: Esalen and the American Awakening*. Reading, MA: Addison-Weasly, 1983.

Anthony, Gene. *The Summer of Love: Haight Ashbury at Its Highest*. San Francisco: Last Gasp, 1980.

Appelo, Tim. "Shameless Shaman." *Seattle Weekly*, January 21–27, 2004. http:// www.seattleweekly.com/2004-01-21/arts/shameless-shaman.

Asher, Levi. The John Cassady Interview. 1995. http://www.litkicks.com/JCI/JCI -Two.html.

Babbs, John. *Prankster Memoirs*. Eugene, OR: Angle Productions, 2003.

Babbs, Ken. Interview by author. Tape. Dexter, OR, July 3, 2002.

———. Interview by Jake Langmuir. E-mail. February 7, 2003. http://www.skypi lotclub.com/oldpages7.html.

———. "Viet-Nam." *Marine Corps Gazette*, July 1963, 5.

Baker, Jeff. "All Times a Great Artist, Ken Kesey Is Dead at Age 66." *Oregonian*, November 11, 2001.

Balliett, Allan. "Ken Kesey Goes Further." *Beat Scene* 32, January 1999, 16–27.

Barlow, John Perry. "Cassidy's Tale." 1994. http://www.litkicks.com/Topics/Barlow OnNeal.html.

Barnard, Jeff. "'Cuckoo': From Psych Ward to Broadway." *Seattle Times*, April 27, 2001.

———. "Novelist Ken Kesey, 66, Dies." *Los Angeles Times*, November 12, 2001.

Bauer, Todd. "A Delicate Balance of Forces: The Stanford Creative Writing Program, 1958–1963." Master's thesis, Northwestern University, 1996.

Benson, Jackson J. *Wallace Stegner: His Life and Work*. New York: Viking, 1996.

Berriault, Gina. "Neal's Ashes." *Rolling Stone*, October 12, 1972, 32, 34, 36.

Berry, Wendell. "Wallace Stegner and the Great Community." In *What Are People For? Essays by Wendell Berry*, 48–57. San Francisco: North Point Press, 1990.

Bevirt, Ron. Interview by author. Tape. Eugene, OR, July 5, 2002.

Bishoff, Don. "Lane Author Pens Novel in Hospital." *Eugene (OR) Register-Guard*, January 9, 1962.

Blaisdell, Gus. "Shazam and the Neon Renaissance." *Author and Journalist*, June 1963, 7–8.

Brightman, Carol. *Sweet Chaos: The Grateful Dead's American Adventure*. New York: Simon and Schuster, 1998.

Brown, Chip. "Ken Kesey Kisses No Ass." *Esquire*, September 1992, 208.

Brown, David Jay, Rebecca McClen Novick, and Jerry Garcia. *Voices from the Edge: Conversations with Jerry Garcia, Ram Dass, Annie Sprinkle, Matthew Fox, Jaron Lanier, and Others*. Freedom, CA: Crossing Press, 1995.

Buddy, George. "Ken Kesey: Ten Years After." *Oregon Daily Emerald*, January 24, 1973.

Burton, Jane. "Lazy Isn't Simply Not Working. Lazy Is *Acting* Like You're Working and Not Working." *Spit in the Ocean*, no. 6 (1981): 27–31.

Calvert, Len. "Krempel's Directing Debut 'Impressive.'" *Oregon Daily Emerald*, February 1, 1954.

Cassady, Carolyn. *Off the Road: My Years with Cassady, Kerouac and Ginsberg*. New York: William Morrow, 1990.

Cassady, Neal, and Ken Babbs. *The Cassady Issue*. Spit in the Ocean 6. Pleasant Hill, OR: Sito, 1981.

Cawthorne, Nigel. *Sex Lives of the Hollywood Goddesses*. London: Prion, 1997.

CBS. *CBS Sunday Morning*. November 18, 1990.

Christensen, Mark. *Acid Christ: Ken Kesey, LSD and the Politics of Ecstasy*. Tucson: Schaffner Press, 2010.

Clark, Robert. Interview by author. Tape. Eugene, OR, November 18, 2003.

Clark, Tom, and Ted Berrigan. "A Little Bit of Magic: Ken Kesey on Writing." *Beat Scene* 46, Autumn 2004, 43–48.

Cloud, Barbara. "Author Ken Kesey Gets Background for Novel by Working as Aide in Hospital Mental Ward." Fall 1961. Clipping from Geneva Kesey collection.

Cohen, Allen. "Ken Kesey and the Great Pumpkin." *San Francisco Oracle*, November 1966, 3–4.

Cook, Malcom. "Ken Kesey Culture Hero." *High Times*, October 1979, 88–92.

"Country Senses." In *Kesey's Garage Sale*, by Ken Kesey, Ken Babbs, and Paul Foster, 203–7. New York: Viking, 1970.

Cowley, Malcom. *The Portable Malcolm Cowley*. Edited by Donald W. Faulkner. New York: Viking, 1990.

De Carli, Paul. Interview by author. Tape. Menlo Park, CA, June 6, 2002.

Desjardins, Mary. "Systematizing Scandal: Confidential Magazine, Stardom, and the State of California." In *Headline Hollywood: A Century of Film Scandals*, ed. Adrienne L. McLean and David A. Cook, 206–31. New Brunswick, NJ: Rutgers University Press, 2001.

Douglas, Gretchen. Interview by author. Tape. Portland, OR, July 2, 2002.

Douglas, Kirk. *The Ragman's Son: An Autobiography*. New York: Simon and Schuster, 1988.

Dufus, Robert L. *The Innocents at Cedro: A Memoir of Thorstein Veblen and Some Others*. New York: Macmillan, 1944.

Elder, Rob. "Down on the Peacock Farm." Salon.com. November 16, 2001. http://www.salon.com/2001/11/16/kesey99/.

Editorial. "The Prankster's Death." *New York Times*, November 13, 2001.

Etulain, Richard W. *Stegner: Conversations on History and Literature*. Reno: University of Nevada Press, 1996.

Faggen, Robert. "Ken Kesey: The Art of Fiction CXXVI." *Paris Review* 35, no. 130 (1994): 58–94.

Fahey, Todd Brendan. "Comes Spake the Cuckoo. Ken Kesey: The *Far Gone* Interview." September 13, 1992. http://www.fargonebooks.com/kesey.html.

Farber, David. *The Age of Great Dreams: America in the 1960s*. New York: Hill and Wang, 1994.

Farrell, Barry, Albert Rosenfield, and Larry Schiller. "The Spread and Perils of L.S.D." *Life*, March 25, 1966, 28–33.

Flora, Joseph. "Westering and Women: A Thematic Study of Kesey's *One Flew Over the Cuckoo's Nest* and Fisher's *Mountain Man*." *Heritage of Kansas* 10 (1977): 3–14.

Flowers, Jeffrey Jane, ed. *Pioneers, Scholars and Rogues: A Spirited History of the University of Oregon*. Eugene: University of Oregon Press, 2002.

"Football Spirit Proves Good Enough for Basketball Season." December 10, 1952. Clipping from Geneva Kesey collection.

Frank, Thomas. *The Conquest of Cool: Business Culture, Counterculture, and the Rise of Hip Consumerism*. Chicago: University of Chicago Press, 1998.

Gaik, Dick. "Inching Back into Action." *Good Times*, February 5, 1970, 6–7.

Gans, David. *Conversations with the Dead: The Grateful Dead Interview Book*. Cambridge, MA: Da Capo Press, 2002.

———. *Playing in the Band: An Oral and Visual Portrait of the Grateful Dead*. New York: St. Martin's Press, 1985.

Geller, Allen, and Maxwell Boas. *The Drug Beat*. New York: McGraw-Hill, 1969.

George-Warren, Holly, ed. *Garcia*. New York: Little Brown, 1995.

———, ed. *The Rolling Stone Book of the Beats: The Beat Generation and American Culture*. New York: Hyperion, 1999.

Gibney, Alex, and Alison Ellwood, dirs. *Magic Trip*. DVD. New York: Jigsaw Productions, 2011.

Gilmore, Mikal. "Ken Kesey's Great American Trip." *Rolling Stone*, December 27, 2001, 58–60, 61–62, 64, 142–44.

Ginsberg, Allen. *Deliberate Prose: Selected Essays, 1952–1995*. Edited by Bill Morgan. New York: Harper Collins, 2000.

Gitlin, Todd. *The Sixties: Years of Hope, Days of Rage*. Toronto: Bantam Books, 1987.

Gleason, Ralph. "Sometimes a Great Notion Is More Demanding Than a Cuckoo's Nest." *Sunday San Francisco Chronicle*, July 26, 1964.

Goode, Erich. *The Marijuana Smokers*. New York: Basic Books, 1970.

Goodman, Fred. "The Rolling Stone Interview: Jerry Garcia." *Rolling Stone*, November 30, 1989, 66–68, 73–74, 118.

Greenfield, Robert. *Bill Graham Presents: My Life Inside Rock and Out*. New York: Doubleday, 1992.

———. *Dark Star: An Oral Biography of Jerry Garcia*. New York: W. Morrow, 1996.

Hager, Steven. "The High Times Interview: Ken Babbs." *High Times*, April 1991, 12–16.

Hajdu, David. "How the Dead Came to Life." *Rolling Stone*, September 8, 2005, 82–85, 88, 90, 127.

Harrison, Hank. *The Dead Book: A Social History of the Grateful Dead*. New York: Links, 1973.

Hasted, Nick. "How We Met: Ken Kesey and Ken Babbs." *The Independent*, August 8, 1999.

Hayes, Charles. *Tripping: An Anthology of True-Life Psychedelic Adventures*. New York: Penguin Compass, 2000.

Heatherington, Madelon. "Romance without Women: The Sterile Fiction of the American West." *Georgia Review* 33, no. 3 (1979): 643–56.

Hemingway, Ernest. *The Complete Short Stories of Ernest Hemingway*. Edited by Finca Vigía. New York: Scribner's, 1987.

Hendra, Tony. *Going Too Far*. New York: Doubleday, 1987.

Henkel, Cathy. "He's Wrestled with Life All Along." *Eugene (OR) Register-Guard*, April 28, 1982.

———. "Was This Really a Great Notion." *Eugene (OR) Register-Guard*, April 27, 1982.

Hofler, Robert. *The Man Who Invented Rock Hudson: The Pretty Boys and Dirty Deals of Henry Willson*. New York: Carroll and Graf, 2005.

Hofmann, Albert. *LSD: My Problem Child*. New York: McGraw-Hill, 1980.

Hollingshead, Michael. *The Man Who Turned on the World*. London: Blond and Briggs, 1973.

Hollister, Leo E. *Chemical Psychoses: LSD and Related Drugs*. Springfield, IL: Charles C. Thomas, 1968.

———. "Clinical, Biochemical and Psychological Effects of Psilocybin." *Archives Internationales de Pharmacodynamie et de Therapie Pharmacodyn* 130 (1961): 42–52.

———. "Drug Induced Psychoses and Schizophrenic Reactions: A Critical Comparison." *Annals of the New York Academy of Science*, no. 96 (1962): 80–88.

Hollister, Leo E., and A. M. Hartman. "Mescaline, Lysergic Acid Dietylamide and Psilocybin: Comparison of Clinical Syndromes, Effects on Color Perception and Biochemical Measures." *Comprehensive Psychiatry* 3 (1962): 235–41.

Hollister, Leo E., J. J. Prusmack, and N. Rosenquist. "Comparison of Three Psychotropic Drugs (Psilocybin, Jb-329, and It-290) in Volunteer Subjects." *Journal of Nervous Mental Disease*, no. 131 (1960): 428–34.

Horst, Leslie. "Bitches, Twitches, and Eunuchs: Sex-Role Failure and Caricature." *Lex et Scientia: The International Journal of Law and Science* 13, no. 1–2 (1977): 14–17.

Howser, Tom. "Wrestlers Encounter Agricultural Group." *Oregon Daily Emerald*, February 8, 1957.

Huffman, Bennett, Jeff Forrestor, Jim Finley, and Lynn Jeffress. "Coach Kesey." *Oregon Quarterly*, Spring 2002, 14–19.

Jackson, Blair. *Garcia: An American Life*. New York: Penguin, 1999.

———. *Goin' Down the Road: A Grateful Dead Traveling Companion*. New York: Harmony Books, 1992.

Jones, Robert. "The Hippies: Philosophy of a Sub-Culture." *Time*, July 7, 1967, 12–20.

Karl, Frederick R., ed. *The Naked I: Fiction for the Seventies*. Greenwich, CT: Fawcett, 1971.

Kashner, Sam, and Jennifer MacNair. *The Bad and the Beautiful: Hollywood in the Fifties*. New York: W. W. Norton, 2002.

Keefer, Bob, and Susan Palmer. "Oregon Loses a Legend." *Eugene (OR) Register-Guard*, November 11, 2011.

"Ken Kesey." Digital Interviews, September 2000. http://www.digitalinterviews.com/digitalinterviews/views/kesey.shtml.

"Ken Kesey Is Still His Mom's Boy." *Eugene (OR) Register-Guard*, November 6, 2011.

Kerouac, Jack. "Letter to Tom Guinzburg." October 19, 1961. In *Jack Kerouac: Selected Letters, 1957–1969*, ed. Ann Charters, 353–54. New York: Penguin, 2000.

———. *On the Road*. New York: Viking, 1957.

Kerr, Walter. "Kerr at Cort: 'One Flew Over the Cuckoo's Nest.'" *New York Herald Tribune*, November 14, 1963.

Kesey, Faye. Interview by author. Tape. Pleasant Hill, OR, November 2003.

Kesey, Ken. "The Citadel of Culture Besieged by a Barbarian." *Oregon Daily Emerald*, January 3, 1957.

———. "The Day after Superman Died: A Fictional Memoir." *Esquire*, October 1979, 42–44, 46–50, 53–54, 59–60, 62–64.

———. *Demon Box*. New York: Viking, 1986.

———. "The Earth Is Your Canvas and You Are the Artist." 1950s. Ken Kesey Papers, 1960–1973, Special Collections, University of Oregon, Eugene, box #23, folder #5.

———. "Earthshoes and Other Remarks." *The CoEvolution Quarterly*, Fall 1976, 109–14.

———. "Eugene Businessman Lauds Campus Action." *Oregon Daily Emerald*, January 31, 1956.

———. *The Further Inquiry*. New York: Viking, 1990.

——. "I Have My Fling at the Sport of Kings." *Oregon Daily Emerald*, January 17, 1956.

——. Interview by author. Tape. Pleasant Hill, OR, July 2001.

——. Interview by Bob Costas. *Later . . . with Bob Costas*. NBC, April 18, 1992.

——. Interview by Kun. *Sputnik*, n.d. http://www.sputnik.ac/interview%20page/trip.html. Accessed March 26, 2003.

——. "Ken Kesey Flashes Back to Leary." *Time*, April 29, 1996, 59.

——. "Ken Kesey in Adelaide 1988, pt. 2." *The Archive: A History of Over 30 Years of UK Festivals*. http://www.ukrockfestivals.com/keseyinterview2.html.

——. "Ken Kesey: The *Far Gone* Interview." Interview by Todd Brendan Fahey. Telephone. September 13, 1992.

——. *Kesey's Jail Journal: Cut the Motherfuckers Loose*. New York: Viking, 2003.

——. "Killer." *Playboy*, January 1986, 112–14, 202, 204–6, 208, 210–12.

——. "Letters from Mexico." Reprinted in *The Naked I: Fiction for the Seventies*, ed. Frederick R. Karl, 352–61. Greenwich, CT: Fawcett, 1971.

——. "Letter to Ken Babbs: 'People on the Ward.'" Reprinted in Ken Kesey, *One Flew Over the Cuckoo's Nest: Text and Criticism*, ed. John C. Pratt, 339–51. New York: Viking Press, 1973.

——. "Letter to Ken Babbs: 'Peyote and Point of View.'" Reprinted in Ken Kesey, *One Flew Over the Cuckoo's Nest: Text and Criticism*, ed. John C. Pratt, 335–38. New York: Viking Press, 1973.

——. "The Loss of Innocence." *Newsweek*, November 28, 1983, 78.

——. "My Oregon Trail." *Vis a Vis*, March 1989, 66, 68, 70.

——. "Oil and Water and Blood." Early 1950s. Ken Kesey Papers, 1960–1973, Special Collections, University of Oregon, Eugene, box #23, folder #5.

——. "On Why Am I Not Writing My Last Term Paper." 1959. Ken Kesey Papers, 1960–1973, Special Collections, University of Oregon, Eugene, box #13, folder #21.

——. *One Flew Over the Cuckoo's Nest*. First ed. New York: Viking Press, 1962.

——. *One Flew Over the Cuckoo's Nest: Text and Criticism*. Edited by John C. Pratt. New York: Viking Press, 1973.

——. "Portland High Principals Refuse Opportunity for Review of Show." *Oregon Daily Emerald*, February 7, 1956.

——. "The Real War." *Rolling Stone*, October 25, 2001, 90–91.

——. "Senate Action Lauded by City Influential." *Oregon Daily Emerald*, October 23, 1956, 2.

——. *Sometimes a Great Notion*. New York: Bantam Books, 1965.

——. "Southerners Oppose New Cottonpicker." *Oregon Daily Emerald*, February 14, 1956, 2.

——. "Sunset at Celilo." 1956. Ken Kesey Papers, 1960–1973, Special Collections, University of Oregon, Eugene, box #15, folder #4.

——. "Tranny Man." *Spit in the Ocean*, no. 1 (1974): 37–54.

——. "Was He after Her Bod, or What?" *Spit in the Ocean*, no. 6 (1981): 46–49.

———. "Zoo." 1960. Ken Kesey Papers, 1960–1973, Special Collections, University of Oregon, Eugene, box #11, 12, folder #4–5, 1–3.

Kesey, Ken, and Ken Babbs. *Intrepid Traveler and His Merry Band of Pranksters Look for a Kool Place: Episode One: A Journey to the East.* DVD. Edited by Ken Kesey. Eugene, OR: Key-Z Productions, 2001.

———. *Intrepid Traveler and His Merry Band of Pranksters Look for a Kool Place: Episode Two: North to Madhattan!* DVD. Edited by Ken Kesey. DVD. Eugene, OR: Key-Z Productions, 2001.

Kesey, Ken, Ken Babbs, and Paul Foster. *Kesey's Garage Sale.* New York: Viking Press, 1973.

Kesey, Ken, and Paul Krassner. *The Last Supplement to the Whole Earth Catalog.* Menlo Park, CA: Portola Institute, 1971.

Kesey, Ken, and Michael Strelow. *Kesey.* 2nd ed. Eugene, OR: Northwest Review Books, 1977.

"Kesey's 'Cuckoo' Broadway Bound." *Eugene (OR) Register-Guard*, October 6, 1963.

Kiselyak, Charles, dir. *Completely Cuckoo: A Film.* Pioneer Entertainment, 1997.

Krassner, Paul. "An Impolite Interview with Ken Kesey." *The Realist*, 1971.

———. "The Love Song of Timothy Leary." *Tikkun*, November 1999.

———. *Murder at the Conspiracy Convention.* Fort Lee, NJ: Barricade Books, 2002.

Lambrecht, Ann. Interview by author. Tape. Menlo Park, CA, December 2002.

Lasden, Martin. "Wallace Stegner on His Own Terms." *Stanford*, Spring 1989, 24–31.

Law, Lisa. *Flashing on the Sixties.* San Francisco: Chronicle Books, 1987.

Leary, Timothy. "Deal for Real." In *Underground Press Anthology*, ed. Thomas King Forcade, 13–14. New York: Ace Books, 1968.

———. *Flashbacks: An Autobiography.* Los Angeles: J. P. Tarcher, Inc., 1983.

Leary, Timothy, George Litwin, Michael Hollingshead, Gunther Weil, and Richard Alpert. "The Politics of the Nervous System." *Bulletin of the Atomic Scientists*, no. 5 (1962): 26–27.

Lee, Martin A., and Bruce Shlain. *Acid Dreams: The Complete Social History of LSD.* New York: Grove Press, 1992.

Leeds, Barry H. *Ken Kesey.* Modern Literature Series. New York: F. Ungar Pub. Co., 1981.

Lehmann-Haupt, Carl. "Ken Kesey." *My Generation*, March–April 2002, 82–84, 87.

Lehner, Donna Maulding. "Touch of Venus, Said, Mediocre." *Oregon Daily Emerald*, April 30, 1954, 6.

Lesh, Phil. *Searching for the Sound: My Life with the Grateful Dead.* New York: Little Brown, 2005.

"Life in a Loony Bin." *Time*, February 16, 1962, 96.

Linden, Laura. "Late Idol Tripped out in La Honda." *San Mateo County Times Online*, November 21, 2001.

Lish, Gordon. "Ken Kesey: A Celebration of Excellence." *Genesis West* 2, no. 5 (1963): 3–16.

————. "What the Hell You Looking in Here For, Daisy Mae? An Interview with Ken Kesey." *Genesis West* 2, no. 5 (1963): 17–29.

Loiederman, Roberto. "Prankster's Memorable Gift." *Los Angeles Times*, November 15, 2001.

Lovell, Vic. Interview by author. Tape. Menlo Park, CA, December 19, 2001.

————. "The Perry Lane Papers: A Prologue." *The Free You*, October 1968, 20.

————. "The Perry Lane Papers: Prologue." In *One Lord, One Faith, One Cornbread*, ed. Fred Nelson and Ed McClanahan, 21–23. Garden City, NY: Anchor Press, 1973.

————. "The Perry Lane Papers: Wayward Girls." In *One Lord, One Faith, One Cornbread*, ed. Fred Nelson and Ed McClanahan, 113–33. Garden City, NY: Anchor Press, 1973.

Lydon, Michael. "Dead Zone." *Rolling Stone*, August 23, 1969.

Malnick, Norman. "Ken 'Cuckoo Nest' Kesey: One Who Wigged Out." *Village Voice*, May 12, 1966, 6, 15.

Marks, John. *The Search for the "Manchurian Candidate": The CIA and Mind Control*. New York: McGraw-Hill, 1979.

Martin, Douglas. "Sandy Lehmann-Haupt, One of Ken Kesey's Busmates, Dead at 59." *New York Times*, November 3, 2001.

McCarten, John. "Psychiatry, Anyone?" *New Yorker*, November 23, 1963, 143.

McKenna, Kristine. "Visionary at Work." *My Generation*, September–October 2001.

McMurtry, Larry. "Letter to Ken Babbs." *Spit in the Ocean*, no. 6 (1981): 43–44.

————. "On the Road." *New York Review of Books*, December 5, 2002, 46–48.

McNally, Dennis. *A Long Strange Trip: The Inside History of the Grateful Dead*. New York: Broadway Books, 2002.

The Merry Pranksters. Video. Eugene, OR: Key-Z Productions, 1999.

Metro Desk. "Speaking Up." *Los Angeles Times*, September 17, 1993.

"Miller Students Display Talent in Assembly." April 27, 1951.

Moore, Barbara, Marvin R. Bensman, and Jim Van Dyke. *Prime-time Television: A Concise History*. New York: Praeger, 2006.

Murphy, Anne. "Meat and Metaphysics." *Spit in the Ocean*, no. 6 (1981).

Nelson, Fred, and Ed McClanahan. *One Lord, One Faith, One Cornbread*. Garden City, NY: Anchor Press, 1973.

"On the Bus with Ken Kesey." *Firezine* 1, no. 5 (1999). http://www.firezine.net/issue5/fz5_14.htm.

Oregona. Eugene: Student Publication Board, University of Oregon, 1956.

"Over 1200 High School Seniors Sign for Duck Preview Weekend." *Oregon Daily Emerald*, April 25, 1955.

Ozonewood, Glen. "Interview with Ken Kesey." *Oregon Daily Emerald*, March 12, 1979.

Palmer, Robert. *Rock and Roll: An Unruly History*. New York: Harmony Books, 1998.

Perry, Charles. *The Haight-Ashbury: A History*. New York: Vintage Books, 1985.

Perry, Paul, and Ken Babbs. *On the Bus: The Complete Guide to the Legendary Trip of Ken Kesey and the Merry Pranksters and the Birth of the Counterculture.* New York: Thunder's Mouth Press, 1990.

Pintarich, Paul. "Still Kesey after All These Years." *The Oregonian,* August 24, 1986.

Porter, M. Gilbert. *One Flew Over the Cuckoo's Nest: Rising to Heroism.* Boston: Twayne Publishers, 1989.

Rayl, A. J. S. "The Merry Pranksters Cyberjam: Ken Kesey and Ken Babbs Do the Future of Rebellion." *Omni Magazine,* October 27, 1996. http://www.apogee books.com/omnimag/archives/chats/in102796.html.

Reich, Charles, and Jann Wenner. *Garcia: The Rolling Stone Interview.* San Francisco: Straight Arrow Books, 1972.

Root, Jonathan. "Dope Raid Author's Story." *San Francisco Chronicle,* April 27, 1965, 10–11.

———. "Last Rites for a Rustic Bohemia." *Palo Alto Times,* July 21, 1963.

Rorabaugh, William. *Berkeley at War, the 1960s.* New York: Oxford University Press, 1989.

Ruas, Charles. "A Talk with Robert Stone." *New York Times,* October 18, 1981.

Rudd, Hughes. *My Escape from the CIA and Other Improbable Events.* New York: E. P. Dutton, 1966.

Sacks, Melinda. "Hometown Hippies." *Palo Alto Weekly,* July 3, 1991, 23.

Scott, Chloe. Interview by author. Tape. Menlo Park, CA, December 28, 2001.

Sebern, Roy. Interview by author. Tape. La Honda, CA, June 25, 2002.

Selvin, Joel. *Summer of Love: The Inside Story of LSD, Rock and Roll, Free Love, and High Times in the Wild West.* New York: Dutton, 1994.

Sinisi, J. Sebastian. "You Don't Need to Dial 911 If You Want the PC Police." *Denver Post,* July 24, 1994.

Sipchen, Bob. "Kesey and Co." *Los Angeles Times,* February 11, 1990, 5.

Smith, Joe. *Off the Record.* Edited by Mitchell Fink. New York: Warner Books, 1988.

Snyder, Carolyn. "A New Breed Comes to Perry Lane." *Palo Alto Times,* March 4, 1967, 7.

Sorenson, Keith C. "Memorandum in Opposition to Defendants' Motion to Set Aside Indictments." July 23, 1965, San Mateo Courthouse, San Mateo, CA.

Stanley, Owsley "Bear." Interview by author. E-mail correspondence. January 2003.

Stegner, Wallace. *On Teaching Creative Writing.* Hanover, NH: University Press of New England, 1980.

Stevens, Jay. *Storming Heaven: LSD and the American Dream.* New York: Grove Press, 1988.

Stockley, Tom. "La Honda: The Peninsula's Maverick Community." *San Mateo Advance-Star and Green Sheet,* June 19, 1966.

Stone, Robert. "American Dreamers: Melville and Kerouac." *New York Times,* December 7, 1997.

———. "The Man Who Turned on the Here." In *One Lord, One Faith, One Cornbread,* ed. Fred Nelson and Ed McClanahan, 54–69. Garden City, NY: Anchor Press, 1973.

——. "The Prince of Possibility." *New Yorker*, June 14 and 21, 2004, 70–91.

Sutherland, Janet R. "A Defense of Ken Kesey's *One Flew Over the Cuckoo's Nest.*" *English Journal* 61, no. 1 (1972): 28–31.

Syrett, Nicholas L. *The Company He Keeps: A History of White College Fraternities.* Chapel Hill: University of North Carolina Press, 2009.

Tanner, Stephen L. *Ken Kesey.* Boston: Twayne Publishers, 1983.

Thompson, Hunter S. "Ken Kesey: Walking with the King." In *Songs of the Doomed: More Notes on the Death of the American Dream*, 112–13. New York: Pocket Books, 1991.

——. "Lsd-25: Res Ipsa Loquitor." In *Songs of the Doomed: More Notes on the Death of the American Dream*, 113–14. New York: Pocket Books, 1991.

——. *Proud Highway: The Fear and Loathing Letters.* Volume 1, 1955–1967. New York: Bloomsbury, 1997.

Tindall, Blair. "Psychedelic Palo Alto." *Palo Alto Weekly*, March 8, 2000.

Torgoff, Martin. *Can't Find My Way Home: America in the Great Stoned Age, 1945–2000.* New York: Simon and Schuster, 2004.

Troy, Sandy. *Captain Trips: A Biography of Jerry Garcia.* New York: Thunder's Mouth Press, 1994.

"Truth Must Motivate Writer, Says Faulkner." *Oregon Daily Emerald*, April 15, 1955.

U.S. Senate Select Committee on Intelligence and Committee on Human Resources. "Project MK Ultra, the CIA'S Program of Research in Behavioral Modification." Washington, DC, 1977.

Walker, George. Speech at Kesey memorial. Koret Auditorium, San Francisco Library, San Francisco, December 5, 2001.

Walker, Lola. Interview by author. Tape. Menlo Park, CA, June 28, 2002.

Wasserman, Dale. *The Impossible Musical.* New York: Applause Theatre and Cinema Books, 2003.

Wasson, R. Gordon. "Seeking the Magic Mushrooms." *Life*, May 13, 1957, 100–107, 120.

"West Menlo's 'Bohemia,' to Close." *Palo Alto Times*, July 25, 1963.

Whitmer, Peter O., and Bruce VanWyngarden. *Aquarius Revisited: Seven Who Created the Sixties Counterculture That Changed America.* New York: Citadel Press, 1991.

Wilson, Jack. "Ken Kesey Can Turn to Other Endeavors." *Eugene (OR) Register-Guard*, February 27, 1957.

Winslow, Ward. *Palo Alto: A Centennial History.* Palo Alto, CA: Palo Alto Historical Society, 1993.

Wolfe, Burton H. *The Hippies.* New York: Signet Books, 1968.

Wolfe, Tom. "The Chief and His Merry Pranksters Take a Trip with Electric Kool-Aid." *New York: The World Tribune Magazine*, January 29, 1967, 4, 6–7, 14–15, 17–19, 21, 23, 27–28.

——. *The Electric Kool-Aid Acid Test.* New York: Bantam Books, 1969.

Wolpman, Jim. Interview by author. Tape. Walnut Creek, CA, December 20, 2001.

Wyant, Dan. "New York Writer Admits: Critics Do 'Kill' Plays." *Eugene (OR) Register-Guard*, July 22, 1965.

Index

Acid Tests, xiii, 7, 86, 97, 101, 122, 162, 164

Alpert, Dick (later Ram Dass), xxvi, 103, 105–8, 145

American dream, 12, 15, 23

American values, 11, 12, 23

Anderson, Lee, xxvii, 85, 172, 174

Angelino Heights, 47

"Anonymous," xiii, xviii

Arbuckle, Fatty, 49

Arnold, Newt, 59, 60, 61

Atkinson, Anne, 84, 143

Babbs, Anita (née Esberg), xxviii, 92, 153–54, 156

Babbs, John (*Sometimes Missing*), xxiii, 123, 160

Babbs, Ken: brother and, 123, 160; Cassady and, 155–56; Dodgson and, xii–xvi, xx; drugs and, 130, 133, 135, 144, 154; family and, 77–78, 160; individualism and, 23–24; Kesey and, 73–75, 77, 92, 100, 138, 178–79; military and, 14, 93, 101, 153, 159–61, 169–72; Perry Lane and, 87, 92–94, 155–56; pranks and, 79, 153; at Stanford, 78–79; writing and, 74–75, 139

Baez, Joan, 72, 86

Barlow, Perry, 145–46

Beatles, The, 131

Berkeley, xix, xxi, 162, 163

Berry, Wendell, xxvii, 163

Beta Theta Pi, 24, 27, 31–36, 42, 53, 55–56

Bevirt, Ronald (*Hassler*), xxvii; drugs and, 123; Hip Pocket Bookstore, 86; *On the Road* as influence on, 123; Perry Lane and, 169; in U.S. Army, 168–69

Billington, Barry, 68

Bloch, Felix, 81

Boise, Ron, xxviii, 152, 177

Bolin, Dick, 84, 91, 93, 128–29

Bondoc, Gigi, xxvii, 155–56

Bondoc, Ron, xxvii, 84, 155

Booth, Brian, 27

Brand, Stewart, xvii, xxviii, 208n39

Brando, Marlon, 43, 45, 46–47, 91, 126, 149, 194n2

Brown vs. Board of Education, 11

Browning, Page (*Des Prado, ZeaLot*), xxviii, 85, 162

Bruce, Lenny, 168, 189

Burroughs, William, 11, 99, 104, 125, 156

Burton, Jane (*Generally Famished*), xxviii, 84–86, 88, 91–95, 108, 167, 172, 174